HONEST MEDICINE

HONEST

*Shattering the Myths About
Aging and Health Care*

MEDICINE

DONALD J. MURPHY, M.D.

THE ATLANTIC MONTHLY PRESS
NEW YORK

Published simultaneously in Canada
Printed in the United States of America

FIRST EDITION

Library of Congress Cataloging-in-Publication Data

Murphy, Donald J.
    Honest medicine: shattering the myths about aging and health care / Donald J. Murphy.—1st ed.
    Includes bibliographical references and index.
    ISBN 0-87113-587-6
    1. Aged—Medical care.   2. Aged—Health and hygiene.   I. Title.
RA777.6.M86   1995   362.1'9897—dc20   94-27801

DESIGN BY LAURA HAMMOND HOUGH

The Atlantic Monthly Press
841 Broadway
New York, NY 10003

10 9 8 7 6 5 4 3 2 1

TO MY PARENTS, DR. JOSEPH AND RITA MURPHY

Contents

Introduction

The goal of *Honest Medicine* is to help you better understand the benefits and burdens of everyday health care by exploring and explaining common medical practices. As a geriatrician, I focus on how these practices affect seniors. The principles, however, apply to people of all ages.

Have you ever wondered how valuable it is to lower your blood pressure, especially if you are over sixty-five years old? Whether a low cholesterol diet is a good idea? If women should take calcium after menopause? If yearly mammograms are worth it? Whether you should continue to take the medicines your doctor prescribes if they don't make you feel better?

I realize many seniors want to believe that their doctors will do the best job of answering these and many other questions for them. We frequently hear "Whatever you say, Doctor" or "Do what *you* think is best."

Times are changing. I believe that most seniors want to better understand health care before considering their doctor's recommendations. Without this understanding, seniors are likely to overestimate the value of health care, and it is precisely this overestimation, this uncritical faith in medicine, that underlies much of the anxiety I sense in my patients.

For example, ten years ago an eighty-five-year-old wouldn't think twice about her cholesterol level. Now many eighty-five-year-olds worry unduly about their cholesterol levels. Is this progress in health care? Has the medical profession served the public well by getting people so concerned about cholesterol? Would my patients worry as much if they understood the true value of cholesterol reduction? Some would; many would not. But by learning the true value of reducing their cholesterol levels, and the value of many other health care measures, they can improve their health *and* reduce their anxiety.

I believe we have begun to replace old myths about aging with new myths. For example, an old myth was that people naturally get senile as they grow older. Today we know that, although many seniors do suffer from dementia, it is not an inevitable part of aging. An emerging new myth is that if people do all the right things, they can live forever, or at least until they are 120 years old. The fatalistic attitude we had about aging forty years ago is giving way to an unbridled optimism as we approach the new millennium. Is that so bad? No, but let's not go overboard.

This book started one day when one of my patients, an eighty-five-year-old gentleman, asked me what I thought were important health habits. Tongue in cheek, I told him I have four consistent health habits. First, I jog regularly. Every summer my wife, kids, and I visit my extended family in Wyoming. I don the jogging gear—tennis shorts and old tennis shoes—and jog around Sunrise shopping center. It's about a mile. I repeat this ritual every year and feel satisfied that I, too, am a jogger.

Second, I never smoke. Third, I always wear seat belts. And fourth, I never salt my food with the salt shaker.

"Yeah, that's the one I wonder about," he replied. After telling me he didn't enjoy his food without salting it, he handed me an article from the *Washingtonian Magazine* (August 1990) titled "Overkill." Thomas Moore, a journalist, wrote an exposé on the salt craze. His message was straightforward and simple: we had been duped. Not intentionally, of course, but we had been misled nonetheless. It turns out that societies where people consume a lot of salt do have increased incidences of high blood pressure and all of the evils associated with it. However, it is not clear at all that members of those societies who avoid salt shakers end up any different than their neighbors who succumb to Big Mac attacks.

Imagine how I felt when I learned that one of my health habits—avoiding the salt shaker—probably wasn't adding to my life expectancy. I didn't know what to make of this heretic's report. Would he next tell me that I should unbuckle my kids in the car, let them devour all the candy or tobacco they want, and discourage them from jogging?

I had to pause. Although his message was discomfiting, I recognized that Moore's question—Is it worth it?—was the same one I frequently have when I prescribe medicine or order tests for my senior patients. My patients can't know if these medical practices are valuable because they don't know the actual risks and rewards involved. Many doctors, unless they look behind the headlines, probably don't either. I know I didn't until I decided to look deeper.

I was reluctant to question current dogma about the value of preventive medicine. For the previous two years I *had* questioned dogma about intensive care, particularly cardiopulmonary resuscitation for chronically ill seniors. I had concluded that in this instance the medical profession had taken a wrong turn and had yet to get back on the right path. But I found comfort in knowing that many other areas of medicine (for example, preventive care) were following the straight and narrow path, never deviating from the public's best interest. I wouldn't let my faith in preventive medicine falter.

It was my patients, not a journalist or medical investigator, who forced me to reconsider my position and the myths I had learned. My patients taught me that there are no pat answers. An individual's decisions about health care depend on so many factors. When doctors try to account for many of these factors, we are practicing the art of medicine, not simply applying the science of medicine.

I wondered, What would my patients think if they truly understood the benefits and burdens of the usual health care recommendations? Would a better understanding puzzle them? Relieve them? Frighten them? I didn't know, but I thought I owed it to my patients to find out.

This book has many stories about my senior patients and some of my colleagues (their real names are not used). I will begin with four seniors who led me to the conclusion that is the foundation of this book: Individuals weigh benefits and burdens differently. Therefore, doctors need to be honest with patients so that patients can decide what's best for them. Seniors should understand that some of our medical dogma is based on myths and misconceptions.

Although it may be obvious to you that different people think differently about health care, doctors frequently overlook this truism when we order tests, prescribe medicines, and counsel patients about health care. We frequently make recommendations without knowing how a patient perceives benefits (reducing risk, relieving symptoms) and burdens (cost, inconvenience, side effects). The following senior opened my eyes.

Mrs. Ware is a sixty-nine-year-old with high cholesterol. She took a medicine to lower her cholesterol that a cardiologist had prescribed about five years ago. She had taken it every day since then.

The first time I saw her, she proudly stated that she followed her doctor's instructions to the letter. After reviewing her medical history, I asked her if the medicine helped lower her cholesterol.

Mrs. Ware said that it did, but then asked if there was another medicine that would work just as well but not cost as much. She told me that the expense of her medicine was stretching her limited income.

This was an interesting development, I thought. Patients don't usually mention their concerns about cost; the cost of her medicine must really be a burden for her. I told her we could try something else that wouldn't cost as much but would probably still do the job.

After I prescribed a new medicine, she dutifully followed my recommendations, taking it twice a day for the next three months.

During that time, I first read some of the medical articles I will refer to later in this book. Several of the articles informed me that a cholesterol-lowering strategy that had been promoted as offering a 25 percent reduction in risk might actually only offer a 2 percent reduction in risk (see chapter 2).

Would she want to take her cholesterol-lowering medicine for the rest of her life if she knew that it would reduce her risk of a heart attack by only 2 percent? I decided to ask her.

When she returned for her next visit, I explained risk reduction—I told her what I will outline for you in chapter 2. Mrs. Ware was surprised and exclaimed, "Do you mean I've been paying all this money and it might not do anything for me?"

I explained that there's a chance it might help her but that the chance of it helping was not nearly as high as she or I had thought. I estimated that the medicine would reduce her risk of a heart attack by about 2 percent (I didn't tell her that it could also increase her chance of developing other serious problems by 2 percent).

She stopped taking the medicine and has felt content with that decision. She has also saved some money.

I wondered how many other seniors would feel like her if they understood the benefits of various treatments. How many seniors believe the myth that their doctors always prescribe what's right for them? I designed a series of charts to illustrate risk reduction to my patients.

One day I used these pie charts to explain risk reduction to one of my patients, Mrs. Franklin, an eighty-five-year-old with high cholesterol and no other health problems. I wanted to see if she thought the benefit of her medicine was worth the burden of it.

After our conversation, I tried to summarize her decision. "Okay, let me make sure I understand you. If your chance of a heart attack is two percent without medicine and one percent with medicine, you would want the medicine. Correct?"

"That's correct," Mrs. Franklin affirmed.

"Now this means there's a ninety-nine percent chance the medicine wouldn't help you and only a one percent chance that it would help you. You would want the medicine, right?"

"That's right."

"But you also told me that you would want the medicine even if we thought there was a one percent chance of a heart attack while taking the medicine and a one percent chance of a heart attack off the medicine. I'm not sure I understand why you would want the medicine if it has no benefit."

"I know that doesn't make sense, Doctor, but here's how I see it. I think you'd probably be wrong if you thought there was no benefit. There's got to be some benefit. If you told me all the researchers found no benefit, I'd say they were probably wrong. I don't want to chance it if they are wrong. That's why I want to take the medicine. And even if I'm wrong, I feel safer taking the medicine."

"Does the cost of the medicine bother you?"

"Well, it does add up. But that's okay. I think it's very important to take the medicine. I can't think of a better way to spend my money right now."

These two women I treat weigh benefits and burdens very differently. One wants to know if the benefit of cholesterol reduction for seniors is a myth or not. The other doesn't care if it is a myth; she still wants to lower her cholesterol. The following two seniors also have different perceptions about health care.

Mr. Byron is a seventy-two-year-old with asthma. He seldom sees a doctor. During my first visit with him, we talked about his asthma medicines. Realizing that he would not return to see me for another year or more, I asked him to consider several health maintenance issues.

He didn't want a complete physical exam. I suggested a prostate exam and that we talk about screening for high cholesterol, colon cancer, and prostate cancer. I thought he should know the options.

Before I got very far, Mr. Byron interrupted me.

"You know, Doctor, I don't think we need to worry about all that stuff. I feel fine now and I'd rather not spend my time looking for trouble. I know the reason for doing those tests. You want to find something early, right? Well, I'd rather not bother with it."

That was that. We didn't bother with those tests.

Six months later Mr. Byron returned because his asthma was worse. We changed his medications. The next scheduled patient had canceled his appointment, so I had some extra time with Mr. Byron. I decided to discuss advance directives (for example, a living will and durable power of attorney for health care) with him.

I usually open such discussions with a questionnaire because several colleagues and I are studying seniors' perceptions of advance directives and life-sustaining care. I expected Mr. Byron to have certain preferences. He had told me on the first visit that he "didn't want to look for trouble." I knew he wanted little to do with the health care system. I assumed that he would not want certain life-sustaining care (for example, cardiopulmonary resuscitation) if the chance of recovery was remote.

His responses caught me by surprise. Not only would he want cardiopulmonary resuscitation even if his chance of recovery was only 1 percent, he would also want to be on a breathing machine or a feeding tube for a long time if they were necessary to keep him alive.

Not many seniors share his preferences. I was puzzled. Why would he want these aggressive treatments if he didn't want to bother with some simple screening tests?

Mr. Byron explained. "It's like this, Doctor. I want every chance to live when something happens. But I don't want to look for trouble before anything happens. If my heart stops beating or I have an accident, I want the best medical care possible. I want every chance to live, even if I end up with a lot of problems. But if nothing has happened, I don't want to spend my time looking for trouble. Does that make sense?"

Yes, it did make sense. I didn't expect these preferences and values, but it did make sense.

The other senior, Mrs. Sutton, is a seventy-nine-year-old

with anxiety. Her greatest fear is cancer. She wants me to do everything possible to detect an early cancer. For example, she has yearly Pap smears and mammograms even though Medicare doesn't pay for either of these on a yearly basis.

Her second greatest fear is anything else that might impair her health. Death frightens Mrs. Sutton.

Before I discussed advance directives with her, I thought I could predict her responses. She, like Mr. Byron, would want every aggressive measure to save her life. It follows, doesn't it?

Not at all. Mrs. Sutton almost scolded me for mentioning cardiopulmonary resuscitation. She made it clear that she wouldn't want this even if she had a 100 percent chance of surviving to leave the hospital. "When my time comes, it comes. Please don't interfere, Doctor."

These two seniors weigh benefits and burdens differently. Everyone does. And it is up to the patient, not me or another doctor, to weigh health care's benefits and burdens. But first they have to understand them. The best way for them to understand is for doctors to be honest about what health care can and cannot do for them.

I wrote this book to help you better understand your health care. In part I (chapters 1–4), I ask you to look at health care with a more critical eye. If we don't, new myths will readily replace old ones, no matter how sophisticated medical science becomes.

In part II (chapters 5–7), we begin our journey into the doctor's office. I will focus on health maintenance and help you decide if you need a physical exam and routine or complex tests if you have no new symptoms.

Part III (chapters 8–14) focuses on risk reduction. I will discuss the use of medicines and diet to control problems that usually don't involve symptoms (for example, high blood pressure or high cholesterol).* These problems can contribute to symptoms and, worse yet, death. Doctors usually prescribe medicines or dietary changes for these problems to prevent such bad outcomes. The medicines, however, do not typically control symptoms, at least not in the early stages of the disorder.

Part IV (chapters 15–20) focuses on symptom relief. I will discuss the use of medicines for diseases that involve symptoms. Although these medicines may help prevent other symptoms or premature death, their immediate value is that they control your symptoms. I have chosen the most common symptoms for seniors, those associated with diseases of the heart, lung, joints, stomach, bladder, and brain.

In part V (chapters 21 and 22), I focus on what I think matters most in health care. The first goal is to take care of yourself outside the doctor's office. In chapter 21, I will assume you have no new health problems and want to do whatever you can to remain healthy. I will discuss the role of nutrition and the other dimensions (physical, social, sexual, spiritual, intellectual, etc.) of a healthy life, which probably affect your health more than anything that happens inside the doctor's office. The second goal is to have a trusting relationship with your doctor. I suggest ways for you and him† to be honest with each other. Your doctor can help teach you the real value of health care, while only you can teach your doctor what really matters most to you.

---

*I hesitate to label high cholesterol, or other problems that don't directly cause symptoms, a "disease."

†In this book, I will refer to your doctor as "he" (or "him" or "his"). Why do I stick with this tradition when the number of female doctors is almost equal to the number of male doctors? I have only one reason. One of the reviewers of this book (a senior) was distracted when I referred to a doctor as "him or her."

An honest appraisal of health care will help you and your doctor tailor a plan that fits your personal needs. Perhaps you and your doctor want to continue to live with the myths and misconceptions surrounding health care. Many people do, and some feel healthier because of it. Perhaps you want to break through the myths and misconceptions. Many people do, and some feel healthier because they understand what health care can (and cannot) do for them.

Part I

AN HONEST VIEW OF MEDICINE

1

Healthy Skepticism

The history of medicine is full of wonder and folly. Some of today's wisdom will seem like folly decades from now. Therefore, you should maintain a healthy skepticism about medical "discoveries."

Think back to 1984. You had just opened the morning paper. Your cup of coffee was still hot when you read the headline at the bottom of page 1, "Coffee May Cause Pancreatic Cancer." You already knew that the cream you put in your coffee was bad for you. But plain old black coffee? Pancreatic cancer? Your morning cup of coffee just wasn't the same after you read what the experts had to say.

How should you respond to these headlines, to all the dos and don'ts you hear in the doctor's office or from your son-in-law? Guilt, fear, and anxiety are common responses. They usually don't make you feel any better and may be harmful. Healthy skepticism is more appropriate.

If you have healthy skepticism, this is what you might think when reading the newspaper headline: "This is interesting. It might apply to me. But if this is true, why haven't researchers discovered this before? The association between coffee and pancreatic cancer can't be that great. If it is, other studies should find it. After all, one study does not prove anything. I think I'll enjoy my coffee for now and not worry about this until other studies show the same connection. Even then I might not worry because the connection is probably very small."

With healthy skepticism, you take the latest medical news with a grain of salt. You are unlikely to accept the doctor's advice with blind faith. Instead, you ask how that advice affects you as an individual.

Blind faith in the medical profession may be necessary and healthy at times. For example, once you've decided to have an operation, you should trust that your surgeon and anesthesiologist will do their best to take care of you. Second-guessing them until the moment they put you to sleep is usually not a healthy way to prepare for surgery. In most instances, however, it is healthy skepticism, not blind faith, that has helped modern medicine evolve as one of the marvels of the twentieth century.

The world of medicine is constantly changing. The scientific truth for one generation may be an old wives' tale to the next. One hundred years from now people will read about medicine in the twentieth century. They will be as amazed at us as we are about our ancestors.

In their book *Follies and Fallacies in Medicine,* Drs. Petr Skrabanek and James McCormick tell several of these extraordinary stories. We don't have to look back to the eighteenth century to see how medical wisdom can change dramatically. Consider the treatment of heart attacks in the last few decades.

The authors state, "Only a few years ago patients who had myo-cardial infarcts [heart attacks] were ordered six weeks absolute bed rest. This was the time adjudged necessary in order to allow the damaged myocardium [heart] to heal. Few doctors even al-lowed the patients to use the commode rather than the bedpan. Those doctors who did so were both eccentric and brave. Now early mobilization, even within twenty-four hours, is the rule, and those patients who were kept in bed for a long time and as a result developed clots in their legs could conceivably sue their doctors for malpractice."[1]

In 1992, Drs. Paul Stolley and Tamar Lasky wrote an essay about Dr. Johannes Fibiger, the 1926 recipient of the Nobel Prize in medicine.[2] Dr. Fibiger "discovered" that a certain worm caused stomach cancer. In 1926, the Nobel Prize committee considered his work to be "a beacon of light in the effort of sci-ence to seek truth." We now know that worms do not cause stomach cancer. The authors conclude, "Today, his story serves to remind us of the many blind alleys down which science must wander in the search for truth. It also illustrates the ease with which intelligent and educated scientists can mistake illusion for truth. With hindsight, we can spot the blind alleys of yesteryear, but who can say which are the blind alleys of today?"

You might think that we are much more knowledgeable and sophisticated than our predecessors from the 1920s. Perhaps we are, but that doesn't keep us from mistaking illusion for truth. Let's consider medical practice in 1995. Lynn Payer, a journalist who has studied health care practices in different countries, em-phasizes the effect of culture on health care.[3] Doctors in France, Great Britain, Germany, and the United States view medical problems through different cultural perspectives.

Imagine that you just don't feel well. You can't quite put

your finger on the problem; you just know that things aren't right. Assume your doctor does some tests that don't reveal a specific diagnosis. If you're in France, your doctor is likely to attribute your problem to your liver. If you're in Great Britain, your doctor may think you have a problem with your bowels. If you're in Germany, your doctor would likely give you medicine for your heart or arteries. And in the United States, your doctor would likely blame a virus.

There is much room for folly and fallacy in our world of medical science. Occasionally skeptics speak out, and medicine moves forward. You can do your part by viewing new medical "discoveries" with healthy skepticism.

Before you can view medical science with a critical eye, you need a simplified view of what health care is all about.

Let's split the whole topic of health care into two general areas. The first is disease prevention. For example, Miss Smith feels fine during an annual checkup, but her doctor finds that her cholesterol level is elevated. He advises her to change her diet to decrease her risk of developing heart disease. Miss Smith has no symptoms. In this case, the doctor cannot lessen symptoms (since there aren't any), but he can suggest measures that might help her live longer or prevent symptoms from developing later in her life. These measures include a change in lifestyle, medicines, or, in other cases, even surgery. The doctor might recommend that Miss Smith eat only one hamburger a week instead of five. He might recommend that she takes a medicine to lower her cholesterol level.

The second area of health care is treatment of symptoms. For example, Mr. Jones has chest pain and goes to his doctor for tests. His doctor makes a diagnosis of coronary artery disease (blockage of the arteries supplying the heart) and begins appropriate treatment. Mr. Jones does have symptoms. In this case, the doctor can recommend treatment that makes him feel better. The treatment could also improve his chance of living longer. Treatments include a change in lifestyle, medicines, or surgery. The doctor might recommend that Mr. Jones ask his wife to shovel the snow and that he take one or more medicines to help control the chest pain. If the tests reveal that Mr. Jones's disease is severe enough, the doctor may recommend surgery or some other procedure to improve the blood flow to Mr. Jones's heart.

Both general areas—preventing disease and treating symptoms—involve diagnostic tests, changes in lifestyle, medicines, and surgical procedures.

Summary

Health care wisdom is constantly changing. Some of today's wisdom will seem like folly decades from now. You should view the latest medical discoveries with healthy skepticism.

The media present many stories about health care. Don't accept everything you hear or read as truth. You can question the value of the news stories using a simplified view of health care and by understanding two fundamental concepts about statistics (chapter 2).

2

Numbers Behind
the Medical "Facts"

Your decisions about your health care depend on medical science, on the statistics that support the science, and on your values. All science, including medical science, generates facts. If scientific experiments discover something, laypersons tend to think it must be true. All of us, laypersons and scientists, want to believe that the laws that govern the human body are as quantifiable and lasting as the laws of physics. We like to think that it's just a matter of discovering these laws through medical research.

Statistics are the tools we use to determine if the facts discovered by scientists mean anything or if they are just a matter of chance. Statistics are the numbers behind the facts.

Understanding two statistical concepts will help put the television news flash, the front page headline, or your doctor's advice in perspective. It will soften the fear engendered by many stories in the media. Most important, a basic understanding of statistics will allow you to understand how new medical studies—or accepted medical wisdom—affects you as an individual.

When medical journals and the media report important medical findings, they refer to statistical significance. Statistics are based on probabilities, not on absolutes. Therefore, the results of medical studies leave much room for interpretation. A study that is statistically significant may not be clinically significant for you.

Medical journals and the media report *relative risk reductions*. The relative risk reduction tells you very little about the value of the finding for you. You need to know your *individual risk reduction*. Only then can you weigh the benefits and burdens of a health care measure.

Let's begin by learning the basics of statistics and risk reduction. I know what you're thinking. Statistics? Learn about it now? Give me a break. I know the feeling. Medical school was full of intimidating situations. But nothing made me as squeamish as statistics.

Don't panic. The statistics lesson in this chapter is easy. You need to learn only two concepts: statistical significance and risk reduction.

If a medical study reports that a finding is statistically significant, it means that the finding is probably real and not just a matter of chance. Researchers determine statistical significance by a mathematical formula.

The message about statistical significance is simple but perhaps difficult to accept. Statistics are based on probabilities. In other words, science does not consist just of black and white facts. It is full of gray areas and can be very subjective.

How do scientists determine that a finding is statistically significant? And how does this matter to you?

Consider the following example. Imagine a study to determine if aspirin prevents heart attacks. Researchers recruit volunteers from ten medical centers around the country. Two thousand volunteers agree to take one pill a day for the next five years. The pill could be an aspirin or a placebo, a pill that looks like an aspirin pill but has no active medicine in it. The volunteers don't know what pill the researchers give them. At the end of five years, the researchers compare the number of volunteers who had heart attacks while taking aspirin with the number who had heart attacks while taking the placebo.

Of the one thousand volunteers taking aspirin, ten had heart attacks. Of the one thousand volunteers taking placebo, twenty had heart attacks. The researchers use a formula to determine if this difference—1 percent versus 2 percent—is statistically significant. If it is, you can bet that the manufacturers of aspirin are going to advertise this important finding. If it isn't, the researchers may conclude that the difference in the number of heart attacks in this study just happened by chance.

The answer that comes out of the statistical formula depends on two factors. One is the number of volunteers who participated in the study. The other is the difference between the response to aspirin and the response to the placebo.

If the number of participants is large (say, one thousand in each group, as in this example), then a small difference, such as 1 percent, might be statistically significant. It's unlikely that the difference, even though it's a small one, is due to chance because the study is so large. If there's a real difference between aspirin and placebo, the large study is likely to find it.

On the other hand, if the number of participants is small (say, ten in each group), then a large difference, such as 50 percent, might not be statistically significant. The difference, even though it is a large one, may be the result of chance, because the study is too small to detect a real difference between aspirin and placebo.

When the researchers report that there is a statistically significant difference between aspirin and placebo, what they are really claiming is that if they repeated the study in different groups of patients, aspirin would do better than placebo in 95 percent of the studies.

When doctors read about a statistically significant difference, lights go on. Some doctors change the way they treat a disorder because they feel they have enough proof with only one study. Other doctors wait to see the difference confirmed in other studies before they change the way they practice.

You can see that a lot depends on this statistical formula. Recall that the answer to the formula depends on the size of the study and the difference the scientists find between responses. If the answer to the formula falls above a certain threshold (it happens to be 5 percent), scientists consider the difference statistically significant. If the answer falls below the threshold, scientists consider the difference statistically insignificant.

Who determined the threshold? A renowned statistician in the 1930s arbitrarily chose 5 percent as the threshold. There is nothing magic about it. This arbitrary figure has served the medical profession well. However, the practice of medicine might look a lot different today if the statistician had chosen a different threshold in the 1930s.

When you understand that medical science is based on an arbitrarily chosen threshold of significance, you realize that the facts may not be so factual after all. You realize that there is a lot of room for interpretation of research findings—that health care is not black and white.

The gray areas are bad news for people who like to see the

world, particularly the medical world, in absolute terms. They want to know that aspirin is definitely better than placebo, that vitamins are definitely good for them, that they should definitely have a mammogram once a year. Uncertainty makes them uncomfortable.

Mike Moore, editor of the book *Health Risks and the Press,* offers this explanation for the discomfort with uncertainty: "To non-scientists and sometimes to reporters, the fact that such well-credentialed, thoughtful, and professionally careful people as scientists should disagree over the meaning of the same evidence suggests a metaphor of hopelessness for mankind. If scientists can't agree on anything, who can?"[1]

The gray areas are good news—or at least the expected news—for people who have a healthy skepticism about media stories or the advice their doctor offers with a preacher's zeal. Your health—including your physical, psychological, spiritual, and financial health—is likely to be better if you learn to live with the gray areas in health care. Looking for the black and white answers may in itself be unhealthy.

Your health is likely to be better if you think about the *clinical* significance—not the *statistical* significance—of new findings or of your doctor's advice. The clinical significance is the importance of the finding for you or any other individual. When the newspaper headline reports that there is a significant difference between aspirin and placebo, it refers to the *statistical* significance of that difference. Many research findings are statistically significant. The key question is, Is this clinically significant. Does this new information really make a difference to you?

To decide if something is clinically significant, you need to understand the second statistical concept—risk reduction.

Risk reduction is the measure of how much something

reduces your chance of a bad outcome. For example, avoiding a high fat diet reduces your chance of a heart attack.

Let's consider the aspirin example again. In our hypothetical study, the researchers found that ten of one thousand volunteers who took one aspirin a day had a heart attack during the five years of the study. They found that twenty of the one thousand volunteers who took the placebo had a heart attack.

How will the medical journals and the media report this difference? How will the scientist and the media emphasize the importance of this finding? They will most likely report the *relative* risk reduction. In this example, the relative risk reduction is an impressive 50 percent: going from twenty to ten is a 50 percent change. You get the impression that you can cut your risk of a heart attack in half by taking aspirin. Who wouldn't want to take aspirin, especially if its cost was modest and it didn't cause any side effects?

Take a closer look at these numbers. Only 10 out of the 1,000 volunteers taking aspirin benefit from this drug. The study shows that 980 of the volunteers taking aspirin wouldn't have a heart attack anyway because 980 of the volunteers taking the placebo didn't have a heart attack. Ten of the volunteers would have had a heart attack whether they took aspirin or not. The other 10 volunteers are the only ones who prevented a heart attack.

In this example, the *absolute* risk reduction is 1 percent.* Going from 2 percent (20 ÷ 1,000) to 1 percent (10 ÷ 1,000) is a 1 percent change. The likelihood that you would prevent a heart attack if you took aspirin is 1 percent. I will refer to the

---

*I have made up the numbers in this chapter to illustrate the concepts. In chapter 9, I will outline your real risk reduction with aspirin.

absolute risk reduction as your *individual risk reduction* throughout this book. Table 1 shows you how to calculate your individual risk reduction for yourself.

The tabloid headline that reads "Cut your risk of a heart attack by 1 percent" doesn't have the punch of the headline "ASPIRIN CUTS RISK OF HEART ATTACK BY 50 PERCENT!" If you don't think reducing your risk of a heart attack by 1 percent is worth the cost and inconvenience of taking aspirin, maybe you shouldn't rush to the drugstore to buy it. If a 1 percent risk reduction is worth the burdens of aspirin, then you may choose to take one every day.

Screening for colon cancer provides another example of these statistical concepts at work. A study published in 1993 indicated that annual testing of the stool for blood reduced the long-term mortality rate from colon cancer by 33 percent.[2] This was a very large study (46,551 participants), so the medical profession considered the results very important. In the group that received annual screening for blood in the stool, 2.6 percent died of colon cancer. In the group that did not receive annual screening for blood in the stool, 3.4 percent died of colon cancer. The differ-

Table 1

ence between 2.6 percent and 3.4 percent turns out to be statistically significant because the study is so large. Is this difference *clinically* significant for you? To determine this, you can calculate your individual risk reduction. The difference between 2.6 percent and 3.4 percent is 0.8 percent. Therefore, the chance that annual screening for blood in the stool will prevent you from dying of colon cancer is less than 1 percent.

Again, ask yourself which newspaper headline is likely to get more attention: "YEARLY STOOL TEST REDUCES COLON CANCER DEATHS BY 33 PERCENT" or "YEARLY STOOL TEST REDUCES YOUR CHANCE OF COLON CANCER DEATH BY LESS THAN 1 PERCENT." It is not surprising that the medical profession and the media advertise relative risk reduction and not individual risk reduction.

Most doctors are familiar with relative risk reduction. However, it is your individual risk reduction that matters to you. It is the missing piece in most day-to-day visits with doctors.

If the benefits of aspirin or screening for blood in the stool are small, why would the media tout them as such important steps in maintaining health? And why would your doctor advise them with such enthusiasm? There are several reasons the medical profession and the media might be more excited about these health care measures than you would be after you understand the statistics behind them. I will discuss these reasons in the next chapter. It is your understanding of these reasons that will help you maintain a healthy skepticism toward what you learn from the media and from your doctor.

Summary

Medical science is very subjective. It is based on statistics, which do not provide clear-cut, black-and-white answers. Statistics are based on probabilities and on an arbitrary threshold.

Statistically significant medical findings may or may not be clinically significant for you. Medical journals and the media typically report a study's statistical significance, not its clinical significance. You need to decide the clinical significance for yourself.

Similarly, medical journals and the media typically report relative risk reduction, not your individual risk reduction. To weigh the benefits and burdens of health care, you need to know your individual risk reduction. If the news report doesn't provide enough information to calculate your individual risk reduction, ask your doctor for the information.

3

Medicine
and the Media

How do you get answers to your questions about health care? How do you learn about advances in health care so that you feel confident that your answers are the most current? Doctors and nurses provide information when they have the time, but often they are too busy to explain everything you want to know. The greatest source of information—besides the beauty parlor and the barber shop—is the media. Newspapers and the nightly news report the latest medical news before doctors learn about it in the medical journals.

The pace of medical progress is astounding. Each week you learn of some new treatment. Doctors use the 1990 *Physicians' Desk Reference* as a bookend in 1995. Five short years have made it obsolete.

Most of you will never develop problems that require the

latest medical technology. Instead of worrying about what these technologies mean in your own life, you can marvel at the benefit these advances provide for others. But your interest in new treatments, already high because of our society's attraction to advanced technology, becomes much more intense when the news is about a disease you have.

Stories about prevention may pique your interest because the message applies to you no matter how old you are. The exceptions, of course, are gender-related diseases, such as breast or prostate cancer. Still, a story about breast cancer might catch a man's eye because of his concern for his spouse or female children. Although stories about prevention do not typically have the high-tech mystique that stories about new treatments have, they do hit home. Does coffee cause pancreatic cancer? Will dietary bran help prevent colon cancer? How effective is sunscreen in preventing skin cancer? How much cholesterol do McFast burgers really have? Will easy exercises prevent falls for eighty-year-olds?

There is no high-tech wizardry here, but something about the stories makes you pause. The stories suggest you should make a change in *your* lifestyle.[1]

The media strongly influence how we think about health care. Three groups of people shape the news stories you and your doctor hear: researchers, medical journal editors, and the media.

Medical knowledge starts with researchers. Researchers report findings in the medical journals, where doctors gain most of their knowledge about new medical advances. The media select the most important stories to report to the public. You learn from your doctors and from the media.

In general, the people in the media who control the flow of medical knowledge have a public health perspective. They focus on a test to diagnose your illness only if the same test will diagnose the illness in many others; they focus on a particular re-sponse to therapy only if many others share the same response.

You, on the other hand, concentrate on your own health and how you value health care. You are probably less concerned about the public health perspective. Your doctors are usually in the middle. They are concerned about your health and the health of the public.

Medical journal editors and the media influence your doc-tor. The influence can be so strong that your doctor may over-look your perspective and approach your personal concerns from a public health perspective.

Consider this example. Assume you have a serious illness. It is the most important development in your life. Your view of this illness depends on how you weigh the benefits and burdens of the treatment for the illness. Different seniors will weigh the ben-efits and burdens differently.

One senior decides she doesn't want the tests the doctors recommend. Furthermore, she declines certain treatments that might prolong her life. She prefers to live her last years or months without the inconvenience, cost, and side effects of therapy. At the other end of the spectrum is a senior who wants her doctors to pursue all measures, no matter how painful or costly, to treat the serious illness. This senior wants to live as long as possible.

Most seniors' perspectives would fall somewhere between the two. Your doctor will know how you feel if he takes time to discuss your values, hopes, fears, and expectations. Only then can he help you weigh the benefits and burdens. If all your doctor has thought about is what the experts say—i.e., the public health perspective—he may advise a plan that doesn't fit your personal perspective. As a result, both you and your doctor will feel frus-trated.

As we have seen, the public health perspective is not the

absolute truth. While in some cases it is the best approximation we have, in others it is far off the target. How can this be?

As suggested earlier, scientific knowledge is full of gray areas. No matter how sophisticated the research project and statistics may be, interpretation of the data can vary. Fancier study designs and statistics cannot solve the inherent limitations of science.

Neither can researchers, editors, or journalists. All have their quirks and biases that add imperfections to the way medical science is reported. Understanding these biases will help you interpret news stories about health care.

Most people think that researchers are objective. It's true that good experiments increase objectivity (unbiased observation) and reduce subjectivity (being influenced by feelings, biases, and hopes). But scientists are not coldly rational machines. A scientist who has no *feeling* about his work probably doesn't belong in science.

All scientists have some expectation, some hope that the experiment will turn out a certain way. Academics may underlie the hope—the scientist believes one theory and not another. Professional pride may underlie the hope—certain results could lead to publication in a prestigious journal. Financial concerns may underlie the hope—a positive study could lead to a patent for a new drug. Compassion for a friend with a certain disease may underlie the hope—a discovery means a cure for the friend.

The same forces that motivate other people motivate scientists. These forces add to the imperfections in science as they do to the imperfections in all other human endeavors.

Medical journal editors have their own biases. For example, some editors may favor articles that report positive findings ("Aspirin prevents heart attacks"). Studies with negative findings ("Aspirin does not prevent heart attacks") are not as attractive to most editors.[2] Researchers may be as responsible as editors for the publication bias in the medical literature.[3] For example, researchers may pursue studies with expected positive findings with more enthusiasm than those with expected negative findings.

Editors also look for variety. If an editor has already published three articles on aspirin during one year, he may not publish the fourth, which may be the most conclusive study.

The media have the last chance to shape a medical story before it reaches you. What are the biases of the media?

First, journalists simplify complex topics. Victor Cohn, a medical science reporter for the *Washington Post*, stated, "So we reporters over-simplify. Some years ago I decided, tongue only partly in cheek, that there were only two kinds of medical stories: 'New Hope' and 'No Hope.' The same is true of stories about environmental or chemical risks. The in-betweens get buried or lost."[4] The media are unlikely to focus on the many gray areas of health care.

Second, the media often alarm the public. Cohn explained, "Alarms make news . . . Let us admit that we are influenced in our decisions by the intense and growing competition to tell the story first and to tell it most dramatically."[4] Does this surprise anyone who watches the nightly news or scans the tabloids while waiting to pay for groceries?

Third, the media, like the public, are enamored with high technology. Gary Schwitzer, former medical news producer-correspondent for Cable News Network, wrote an essay, "The Magical Medical Media Tour," for the *Journal of the American Medical Association*. He noted, "A 1989 survey of health news reporters showed that stories on new drugs and new treatments are favorites of television medical reporters—second on a list of 25 health care topics. At the bottom of the list were some topics that might be described as 'old, dull, nonvisual stories': ethical issues in health care, Medicare and Medicaid issues, mental illness, health care policy, and health care for the homeless." Schwitzer continued, "When stories on the latest laparoscope, laser, or lithotriptor outnumber stories on issues concerning health policy, access to care, and quality of care, something is out of balance."[5]

Fourth, many medical news reporters are inexperienced. They may not have the time, money, or inclination to carefully investigate a story before reporting it.[5]

Finally, industries that produce health care products may influence reporters. Schwitzer claimed, "Too many of today's broadcast medical reporters are puppets—marionettes whose strings are yanked daily by self-promoting physicians or their paid public relations appointees or by fiercely competitive hard sellers or by pharmaceutical flacks."[5]

Schwitzer provided a good example. "While local television news has shown less maturity in this area of reporting, network television news has had its own embarrassing moments, as in the coverage of the prescription drug tretinoin (Retin-A), the acne cream being converted into an 'antiaging' cream. One network, after touting that the product 'can make fine lines and surface wrinkles disappear,' concluded, 'After today's report on wrinkles, people with acne better hope there's some left.' Another network spouted that the dream of 'a cream that will reduce the wrinkles of age and make skin young again . . . now . . . could be a reality.' That report's summary comment stated that, 'Physicians across the country expect to be flooded with requests for the drug.' Were those lines written by journalists or by drug advertisers?"[5]

I don't know, but Mr. Schwitzer's question sure makes me wonder. And it should make you wonder, too.

Summary

You should accept medical discoveries (and the prevailing medical wisdom) with caution.

Researchers, journal editors, and the media all shape a medical news story. Most of them focus on the public health perspective, not on your individual perspective. Although your doctor focuses on your health, he also shares the public health perspective. Sometimes he may lose sight of your perspective because the public health perspective is so strong.

All people who shape a medical news story have biases that can distort medical science. They are all human.

Ask how the medical news story affects you. Your perspective may be much different than your neighbor's. For example, you might think that a 1 percent individual risk reduction is worth the expense and possible side effects of a medicine. Your neighbor might think that the individual risk reduction has to be at least 10 percent to justify the burdens. It's up to you to let your doctor know your perspective.

4

The Biases of
Doctors and Patients

Unless you diagnose and treat yourself, you probably seek your doctor's advice about most health care matters. Doctors try to sort through the mounds of information and filter out all the biases that can distort medical science. Some succeed. Some do not. Some doctors are so good at caring that it doesn't matter that they don't have command of all the facts. Others may be so distant that all the factual knowledge in the world won't make them good doctors in the eyes of their patients.

Interpretation of the medical literature is only one factor that may influence the advice a doctor gives you. Three other factors are also worth considering.

First, doctors tend to advise familiar plans. Assume that I have regularly prescribed a particular water pill (diuretic) for the last ten years. I feel comfortable using this medicine. What happens when a drug manufacturer introduces a new water pill, one that is perhaps better than the one I use? No matter what the drug company representatives tell me, it will take a while before I become comfortable prescribing the new pill. Consider a different example. Assume one of my patients has an illness that I can treat with either medicines or surgery. Furthermore, assume that the advantage of surgery over medicine is only slight. If I have a lot of experience with medicines for that illness, I am likely to suggest medicines as the first approach. If I happen to be a surgeon, I may be more likely to recommend surgery.

Second, doctors practice "defensive medicine." They do not like malpractice lawsuits and practice medicine cautiously. Over the last five years I have informally surveyed colleagues. I ask, "What percentage of the things you do, including careful documentation, ordering tests, and referring patients to specialists, is done mainly to prevent a lawsuit?" The responses vary from 20 to 40 percent.

Think about it. Almost one-quarter to nearly one-half of the typical doctor's energy is spent preventing a lawsuit. This may be an exaggeration, but I don't think it's too far off the mark. You might ask, Why don't doctors just practice good medicine and not worry about malpractice? There are several reasons. One is that many doctors who get sued believe that they *were* practicing good medicine. Another is that doctors want to avoid the emotional trauma involved with a malpractice lawsuit.

Doctors have been told that the best way to prevent a malpractice lawsuit is to have good relationships with their patients. Unfortunately, this may not be true. A recent study suggests that good rapport with patients doesn't prevent lawsuits as much as we thought it did.[1]

Since doctors cannot feel safe from malpractice—even when they think they're doing the best job they can—they tend to do whatever they can to minimize the risk. I believe this is the major reason that doctors order so many tests that are unlikely to help the patient (other than offer reassurance).

Third, doctors like to get paid for their services. I am not suggesting that doctors are greedy (sure, there are bad apples in the medical profession as there are in any profession). I am simply stating the obvious; doctors are like anyone else providing services.

There is a difference between health care and many other professional services. That difference is third party payers. Insurance covers most medical bills. You and your doctor don't feel the burden of the cost of your decisions as much as you and your lawyer or your accountant might.

Consider the following scenario. The year is 1995. You have Medicare and supplemental insurance. Your doctor has a choice between test A and test B to determine the cause of your symptoms. Test A might provide the answer more quickly than test B, but it costs a lot more. You may not know the cost of either test because your insurance covers both. Your doctor will get paid $350 for doing test A and $35 for doing test B. What test is your doctor likely to choose in a fee-for-service arrangement?

Now let's travel ahead to the year 2005. You're in a health maintenance organization (HMO) where the cost of your medical care is capitated. That means that your doctor receives a flat fee (say, $500) for taking care of you during a one-year period. If you're sick and require a lot of tests and hospitalizations that year, your doctor gets $500. If you're healthy and require no tests or hospitalizations that year, your doctor still gets $500. Now, assume that your doctor has a choice between test A ($350) and test B ($35). In this setting, your doctor doesn't get paid any more for doing test A. In fact, ordering test A will cost your doctor (or your doctor's health maintenance organization) more than ordering test B, and he won't have as much of your $500 left. What test is your doctor likely to order in a capitated health care system?

As you can see, a number of factors—including many I haven't discussed—influence your doctor's decisions about your health care. The same is true for patients. Many factors besides patients' interpretations of medical science influence their health care decisions.

We are all patients at some point in our lives. Most of us share one bias: we want to believe in medical science and its power to heal. When we hear the latest medical discovery, we want to believe. When our doctor advises us, we want to follow. Our belief may be so strong that we, like the researchers, editors, media, and our doctors, can distort medical science.

Placebos illustrate this point. Imagine that you have pain in your back and someone gives you a placebo. They say, "You've got to try this. It's the best pain reliever I've ever had. I've had absolutely no pain since I started taking this." There's roughly a 30 percent chance that the placebo will relieve your back pain. Several studies comparing placebos with medicines have shown that many people respond to placebos.[2]

It's no wonder; humans may be programmed for the placebo effect. Recent studies show that human brains have receptors for morphine-like chemicals. Receptors are chemicals that attach to other chemicals to send a message. If the receptor is there, then the chemical it attaches to must also be there. Thus, humans have morphine-like chemicals in their bodies without taking morphine. The expectation that something (a placebo) will relieve pain may actually cause release of these morphine-like chemicals, which in fact act like morphine to relieve pain.

Placebos can be very helpful, especially when the doctor and patient believe in them. Drs. Petr Skrabanek and James McCormick noted, "The physician's belief in the treatment and the patient's faith in the physician exert a mutually reinforcing effect; the result is a powerful remedy that is almost guaranteed to produce an improvement and sometimes a cure."[2]

Another factor that influences patients' decisions is the likelihood that something will help them. For the last three years my colleagues and I have studied seniors' preferences based on the likelihood that something would help them. We found that the likelihood that cardiopulmonary resuscitation (CPR) would work strongly influences their preferences for CPR.[3] For example, some seniors would want CPR even if there was only a 1 percent chance of them surviving to leave the hospital after CPR. Other seniors said they wouldn't want CPR even if there was a 100 percent chance of surviving. Most seniors had thresholds somewhere between these extremes.

We also studied seniors' preferences for cancer screening tests.[4] Some seniors just don't want to bother with cancer screening. They would not want a test—either a simple blood test or something more complex—even if there was an excellent chance (say, one in two) of it detecting an early cancer. On the other hand, some seniors would want any possible test regardless of the chance of the test helping them. They would want a complex test and would be willing to pay for the test even if the chance of it detecting an early cancer was very small (say, 1 in 10,000). Again, most seniors respond somewhere between these extremes.

We see the same variety of preferences when seniors consider medicines to prevent heart attacks, strokes, or hip fractures.[4] Some don't want to take a medicine even if the chance of it preventing a heart attack is very good. On the other hand, some want to take a medicine even if the chance of it preventing a heart attack is extremely small.

The likelihood of benefit is information doctors don't always share with their patients. Yet we know that it may strongly influence patients' decisions about their health care.

Summary

The decisions that you and your doctor make about your health care are influenced by many factors. Three factors that influence doctors are their comfort level with certain treatments, their fear of malpractice (causing them to practice defensive medicine), and the way they are paid for their services.

Similarly, many factors affect patients. One is the placebo effect. Another factor is the likelihood that something will benefit you. You may have very different thoughts about a plan once you know the likelihood that the plan will help you.

It's important to recognize that many factors influence the way you and your doctor view medical care. Medicine is not a science with black and white answers; rather, it is an art that has many shades of gray.

Part II

ROUTINE VISITS WITH YOUR DOCTOR

5

The Annual Checkup

U p to this point, we have concentrated on the world of health care outside your doctor's office. Now let's go into that office. Assume you are visiting your doctor for the annual checkup. Also, assume that you have no new symptoms.

The routine checkup is most valuable because it gives you and your doctor a chance to know each other. If you need reassurance that everything is okay, the annual checkup is a good way to get it.

Do you need an annual checkup? Yes and no.

Yes, you should have an annual checkup for two reasons. First, you can detect some problems early, which may prevent problems later. Second, annual checkups help you feel that you've done all you can to take care of yourself. Patients who don't see a doctor for years and then develop cancer often feel guilty that their cancer is the result of negligence. Although annual checkups may have made no difference, patients feel guilty nonetheless.

Annual checkups provide reassurance. The trip to your doctor's office may be worth the peace of mind you have knowing that everything is okay. These psychological benefits are important for many people.

The reason you *don't* need an annual checkup every year is because the likelihood of detecting something that requires new therapy is so small. For example, the likelihood that your doctor will detect an early cancer is very low if you have no new symptoms.

Much of the annual checkup is a ritual, as you will see in this chapter. Although we may not *need* these rituals, we can benefit from them. For example, a doctor may have no suspicion of lung disease but will listen to his patient's lungs anyway. Why? The doctor knows that the patient expects it and wants reassurance. Most important, patients want to be touched.[1]

Mrs. Mullen illustrates this point. She is an eighty-two-year-old with several medical problems. None are serious. I spent a lot of time talking with her during our first visit. The medical resident working with me examined her and also spent time discussing her concerns. Two months later Mrs. Mullen returned. This time the medical resident *and* a geriatric nurse practitioner examined her. I then discussed our findings and spent another forty-five minutes discussing other concerns. I thought we had given her the best care possible. What more could we do?

Mrs. Mullen returned to our office three weeks later. I was out, and one of my colleagues, Dr. Carr, saw her. Her problem was straightforward. He briefly examined her ears and throat and gave her a prescription. That was the extent of their visit.

One month later Mrs. Mullen returned to talk with me. She

anxiously stated, "I appreciate all you've done for me, Doctor, but I was wondering if I could see Dr. Carr from now on."

I like Dr. Carr too, but I didn't understand her dissatisfaction with my care. She enlightened me. "I thought the medical resident and nurse practitioner were both very good. But you see, Doctor, the problem is that you never examined me. Dr. Carr did."

From a strictly medical point of view, Mrs. Mullen did not need another exam during the first two visits. From a psychological point of view, she needed an exam—from her doctor—more than she needed anything else. Rituals can be very important.

What if you don't worry about cancer and you don't need reassurance that everything is okay? What if you don't need the ritual of the doctor laying his hands on you? Is there any reason for you to see your doctor once a year or more?

Two reasons stand out. First, you need to trust your doctor. Although you may have no medical problems now, at some point you will need the doctor's help. He may take care of the problem himself or refer you to another doctor. Either way, you need to trust his judgment, and that trust needs nurturing. It doesn't happen after one visit. You should know your doctor's values. He should know your values. Your doctor can take better care of you when you are sick if he knows you as a person, not as a collection of organs. Like any relationship, the doctor-patient relationship takes time to develop.

Second, you may have many questions that your doctor can help answer. Should I check my cholesterol level? Does the smoke from my husband's cigarettes affect my health? Do I really need to wear seat belts? What do I do to fill out a living will or durable power of attorney for health care? My mother needs a nursing home—what do you know about Shady Grove Care Center? My son needs a psychiatrist—can you help me?

You may have questions about what to expect as you grow older. Almost every part of your body undergoes some change as you age. Some of these changes lead to subtle symptoms, sometimes so subtle that you're not sure anything is wrong. You just feel a little different than you did five years ago. Discussing these changes with your doctor can help you decide whether you should have more tests, see a specialist, or simply wait and see what happens.

At the turn of the century doctors spent all of their time taking care of sick people. They did not examine healthy people. In 1900, at the annual meeting of the American Medical Association (AMA), Dr. George M. Gould exhorted his colleagues to carry the banner of prevention. "Absence of symptoms is no evidence whatever of absence of disease," Gould told the AMA. "How is disease in the making ever to be discovered except by examinations, continuous observation, of the living supposably-well organism?" At that time the notion of examining patients without symptoms was a radical idea.

By 1922 Gould's idea took hold, and the AMA issued forms for routine checkups. *Washington Post* writer Don Colburn outlined the emergence of the routine physical exam in his critique "The Annual Physical: Who Needs It?"[2] According to Colburn, "The AMA in 1947 recommended that every healthy individual over age 35 have an annual medical check-up, and for millions of Americans in the post–World War II era, the annual physical became a ritual."

Let's take a close look at the elements that make up the now-traditional yearly checkup. I will start with the vital signs (for example, blood pressure and pulse) and end up with the neurological exam (for example, test of reflexes). I will follow the sequence that your doctor uses to record your physical exam.

Blood Pressure

Most people with high blood pressure (hypertension) have no symptoms. Yet hypertension can damage the heart, brain, kidneys, eyes, and blood vessels.

You must know that you have high blood pressure before you can take measures to lower it. If you don't have your blood pressure measured at a store or health fair, the routine checkup may be the only way to detect hypertension. (In chapter 11 I will discuss the value of treating hypertension.)

How often should you check your blood pressure? It depends on many factors, including other medical problems you might have and the medicines you are taking; whether or not you've had high blood pressure in the past; your level of comfort with uncertainty; and your view of the value of risk reduction (see chapter 11).

You need a few definitions before proceeding. We use two numbers to measure blood pressure. The top number is the systolic pressure; the bottom number is the diastolic pressure. If your systolic blood pressure is above 160 (for example, 180/80), you have high blood pressure. If your diastolic blood pressure is above 90 (for example, 150/98), you have high blood pressure. One high blood pressure reading doesn't mean much. Repeatedly high readings mean that you have hypertension.

Blood pressure gradually rises with age. Therefore, mild hypertension in a thirty-year-old is not necessarily the same as mild hypertension in an eighty-year-old. The following guidelines apply to seniors.

Mild hypertension implies that the systolic (top) blood pressure is between 140 and 159 *or* the diastolic (bottom) blood pressure is between 90 and 99.[3] Moderate hypertension implies that the systolic blood pressure is between 160 and 179 *or* the diastolic blood pressure is between 100 and 109. Severe hypertension implies that the systolic blood pressure is between 180 and 209 *or* the diastolic blood pressure is between 110 and 119. Malignant hypertension implies there are symptoms caused by high blood pressure. For example, people may be short of breath, nauseous, swollen in their legs, or confused.

Mr. Young, a seventy-five-year-old man, had seen doctors monthly for two consecutive years. The nurses dutifully checked his blood pressure at every visit. He showed me his records of his blood pressure measurements. The top number, the systolic pressure, was never over 130. The bottom number, the diastolic pressure, was never over 90.

After the third visit to our office—a lengthy visit where we discussed many issues—Mr. Young was disgruntled. I asked him why. He told me that no one had checked his blood pressure. Never mind that we had addressed several more pressing matters. In his mind Mr. Young had not really seen the doctor until the doctor checked his blood pressure. Measuring the blood pressure had become a ritual. It had very little to do with maintaining his health.

Other patients with blood pressures as high as 230/120 leave the office knowing that they won't return anytime soon. It may be another three months before they return to check their blood pressure. Despite the many warnings others and I offer, these seniors don't think it's important to visit the doctor just for a blood pressure check. They share the attitude of patients in 1900—you go to the doctor when you feel sick.

Keep in mind that a routine checkup offers only a snapshot in time, a momentary glimpse of your body. Your body is dynamic, changing from hour to hour. Blood pressure is a good example. It varies throughout the day.[4] One high blood pressure reading may not be a good indication of your average blood pressure.

Assume your doctor measures a high blood pressure of 160/96. It could be that this was the highest blood pressure you had all day. Perhaps your average blood pressure that day was 140/84. The same is true for a lower blood pressure. Your average may be higher than the one value measured by your doctor. Try not to get too worried (or too complacent) about any one reading unless your blood pressure is very high.

You should have your blood pressure checked at least once a year.

Pulse Rate

Doctors determine the rate and rhythm of your heart by checking your pulse. You should have symptoms if your heart is unusually slow, unusually fast, or very irregular. There is one exception that is common in seniors.

Atrial fibrillation, one of the irregular heart rhythms that occasionally causes a fast beat, might not cause symptoms. Checking the pulse can detect this rhythm abnormality. Does it matter if your doctor detects atrial fibrillation when you have no symptoms? Again, it depends on how you value risk reduction (see chapter 13).

As with blood pressure, the pulse is dynamic. Seniors can change from a normal heart rhythm to atrial fibrillation and back again without having palpitations. Checking the pulse more than once a year is probably unnecessary for seniors without symptoms.

Respiratory Rate

The respiratory rate is rarely a helpful indicator of health in seniors who have no symptoms such as shortness of breath.

Temperature

Measuring the temperature is another common ritual in outpatient care. The chance of finding a very low temperature (hypothermia) or a fever in an apparently healthy senior is remote. The thermometer has little if any value in the routine exam of seniors without symptoms.

Weight

Knowing your usual weight is helpful, because it can alert you if you start losing weight. The amount of weight loss is important information for planning the timing and extent of the medical evaluation. Measuring weight has also become a ritual for many doctors and nurses, but you do not need to measure your weight at every office visit.

Skin

Most seniors know when they have a rash or bump on their skin. However, some of the skin changes that lead to skin cancer are barely noticeable. If you detect and remove them early enough, there is no risk of skin cancer arising from them.

Actinic keratoses (sun spots) are common in seniors. They occur most often in people with light skin who have had a lot of sun exposure. Removing them early (usually with liquid nitrogen) may prevent skin cancer.

Melanoma is the most serious skin cancer. Almost one-third of newly diagnosed melanomas occur on areas of the skin that people may not routinely see, such as the back and buttocks. This figure alone might justify a routine examination of the skin. However, there is no study showing that early detection of melanomas in these areas makes a difference in the outcome for patients.

In their analysis of the annual physical exam, Drs. Sylvia Oboler and Marc LaForce from Denver suggest that routine examination of the skin is not justified. They stated, "The absence of any data showing that screening for melanoma is effective, together with the low prevalence of the disease, leads us to recommend that examination of the skin of the fully disrobed patient not be included in the routine physical examination."[5]

Doctors should make exceptions for seniors with many moles. Many people lose freckles and gain moles as they age. The most common mole in seniors is the seborrheic keratosis, the "patched-on mole." Seniors might worry that these are cancerous because they are often irregularly shaped. While these moles are not cancerous, people with many moles do have a higher risk of melanoma. These seniors should have routine skin exams.

Lymph Nodes

Doctors detect most enlarged lymph nodes in the neck. An acute infection, usually in the upper respiratory tract, is the most common cause of the swollen node. Frequently we don't know the cause, and the lymph node returns to its normal size.

Cancer also causes enlarged lymph nodes. The cancer may have spread from a nearby organ (for example, the breast or lung) or it may be a lymphoma. Either kind of cancer is very unlikely if you have no other symptoms. Therefore, a routine checkup of lymph glands (neck, armpits, groin) is unnecessary.

Eyes

Seniors can have impaired vision without recognizing the problem.[6] Although impaired visual acuity may not affect your quality of life, it may predispose you to traffic accidents. For this reason, Drs. Oboler and LaForce recommended routine checkups for visual acuity.[5]

The value of screening for glaucoma is questionable.[5,7] Few internists or family practitioners can accurately determine the presence of glaucoma. An ophthalmologist can perform the exam more accurately. Since glaucoma does not usually arise in old age, yearly exams to check for glaucoma late in life are unnecessary.

Have you ever wondered why your doctor looks in the back of your eyes with a small beam of light? I have wondered, too.

A master clinician and professor of medicine used to tell my colleagues and me that the eye exam is invaluable. "It is the only way to see a blood vessel," he proclaimed. "You can actually see the disease with your fundoscope." Yes, your doctor may find an abnormal blood vessel, especially if you have diabetes or hypertension. Unless you have diabetes, however, it is rare that something he sees in your eyes will change your medical management or your outcome. If you need routine eye exams because you have diabetes, see your ophthalmologist.

Routine exams for cataracts are unnecessary if you have no visual problems. Even if your cataracts are dense, your ophthalmologist will not remove them until you have visual problems. You can wait for the cataracts to mature.

Ears

Hearing loss is very common in seniors. Since the onset is insidious, you may not recognize it as a new symptom until the loss is significant. Hearing aids can markedly improve the quality of life of seniors with hearing loss.[8] This may be true even for seniors who don't complain of hearing loss but have abnormal audiology tests. Therefore, a routine exam of hearing is prudent.

Nose

Doctors learn little by examining the nose of someone without symptoms.

Mouth and Throat

Periodontal disease and dental caries are preventable at all ages. Regular plaque removal is the most important part of this prevention. Ideally, patients would see their dentists yearly. Unfortunately, many cannot afford these routine checkups.

Oral cancer responds well to treatment if detected early. Seniors who smoke and drink heavily can justify yearly mouth exams, for they are at higher risk of oral cancer. Yearly exams are unnecessary for other seniors because the prevalence of oral cancer in the general population is so low.

Seniors without symptoms are very unlikely to have abnormalities of the throat. Yearly throat exams are unnecessary.

Neck

Doctors look for three things in the neck: bumps (lymph nodes—see above), carotid bruits (a swishing sound from a blood vessel we hear with a stethoscope), and abnormal thyroid glands.

About 8 percent of seniors over age seventy-five have carotid bruits.[9] A bruit signals obstruction of blood flow. If you have some obstruction, your risk of a stroke or transient ischemic attack (TIA) increases about 2 to 3 percent compared to people who have no obstruction.[10] The question is, Can anything be done to decrease this risk? In other words, is it worth knowing that you have some obstruction to blood flow in your neck?

Currently there is no evidence that either surgery[11–13] or medicines decrease the risk of stroke in patients with carotid bruits and no symptoms. But let's assume that new studies will show a benefit from surgery. Would you want a major operation if your risk reduction from surgery was only 2 or 3 percent?

Dr. Martin Samuels, a neurologist from Boston, tells medical audiences that doctors should use the stethoscope for the heart and lungs, not for the neck. Listening for carotid bruits in seniors without symptoms may do nothing more than add a new symptom—anxiety.

Doctors can detect thyroid cancer and thyroid nodules on physical exam. Thyroid cancer is rare, and early detection has not been shown to change the course of this disease. Routine screening for thyroid cancer is unnecessary unless the patient had irradiation to the head, neck, or upper chest during childhood.[5] Although 7 percent of adults may have thyroid nodules, the vast majority of the nodules are benign.[14] There is no evidence that early detection of thyroid nodules leads to better outcomes.

Lungs

Doctors rarely suspect lung cancer by findings from a routine physical exam. Even large tumors, which would likely cause symptoms, are difficult to detect on physical exam.

The lung exam is helpful to detect congestive heart failure and chronic lung disease. Seniors with mild congestive heart failure or chronic lung disease might not have symptoms, such as shortness of breath, if they do not exert themselves. Detecting these problems early may prevent symptoms later. Seniors who exert themselves and are not short of breath do not need a yearly lung exam.

Heart

"How's my heart?" is a frequent question doctors hear after a physical exam. Many patients expect doctors to know the condition of their heart from a physical exam of the heart. Doctors actually learn more about your heart by listening to your lungs.

We cannot reliably diagnose coronary artery disease, the most common type of heart disease, by listening to the heart.

This diagnosis depends on the patient's history and certain tests. Detecting a murmur is usually not helpful because as many as 40 percent of seniors will have murmurs anyway (typically from age-related changes in the aortic valve). Therefore, a yearly heart exam is not very helpful for a senior who has no new symptoms.

Abdomen

Doctors focus on three parts of the abdomen in a routine exam: the liver, spleen, and aorta.

Alcoholism is the most common cause of an enlarged liver. Seniors who are alcoholic may have enlarged livers and have no symptoms. Detection of the enlarged liver may lead to effective treatment for alcoholism. Other causes of an enlarged liver usually cause symptoms (for example, nausea or fatigue) or are not amenable to therapy.[5] The same is true for an enlarged spleen.

An aneurysm is an abnormally wide part of a blood vessel. Aneurysms of the abdominal aorta, the large vessel that carries blood to the lower half of the body, are common in seniors. If we detect an aneurysm early enough, we can remove it surgically. If the aneurysm goes undetected, it can rupture. People usually die when this happens.

When doctors press deep into your abdomen, they are trying to feel the pulsation from the aorta. If the aorta feels like it's four centimeters or wider, doctors wonder about an aneurysm and consider ordering an ultrasound to confirm this suspicion. Often the aorta feels enlarged but the ultrasound does not confirm an aneurysm. Alternatively, the aorta may feel normal on exam, but an ultrasound reveals an aneurysm. Frequently the aorta is difficult to feel because of obesity and other problems. The physical exam is not always accurate. Usually, however, we can detect large aneurysms, which do need attention. An annual exam to detect an aneurysm is reasonable.

Breast

Several panels of experts recommend annual breast exams for women over fifty.[15,16] The recommendation is that women have both a physical exam and a mammogram (I will address the value of mammography in chapter 7).

A physical exam can detect some breast cancers missed by mammography. Conversely, mammograms detect some cancers that we miss on physical exam. Although many doctors encourage women to check their own breasts monthly, there is little evidence that this practice is effective in detecting early cancers.[17]

Prostate

Checking the prostate gland is one of the goals of the rectal exam in men. Without the routine use of this exam, seniors with prostate cancer would be more likely to have advanced cancers at the time of diagnosis.[18] However, 40 to 50 percent of prostate cancers are located beyond the reach of the doctor's finger (we can feel only parts of the prostate). Therefore, seniors with prostate cancer can have normal prostate exams.

Recent critiques of the yearly prostate exam are mixed. Drs. Oboler and LaForce believe "the data to recommend screening asymptomatic men for prostate cancer are insufficient."[5] The U.S. Preventive Services Task Force agreed.[7] The Canadian Task Force on the Periodic Health Examination concluded, "Since there is no alternative technology that performs better than digital rectal exam in detecting early-stage prostate cancer and since the burden of illness is potentially heavy, digital rectal exam should not be excluded from the periodic health examination of asymptomatic men over 40 years of age."[19]

Seniors who are very old ought to keep the following in mind. Prostate cancer is typically very slow growing. You could rightfully ask your doctor, So what if you detect an early cancer? What would you do about it anyway? For many very old seniors, the answer would be, "Probably nothing."

Rectum

Doctors look for two other problems with the rectal exam: tumors in the rectum and blood in the stool. A doctor's finger can detect only about 10 percent of colon (rectal) cancers. Most cancers are higher up in the colon. Many of the cancers that are higher up ooze blood. We suspect these cancers when we detect blood in the stool.

The value of testing for blood in the stool (fecal occult blood testing, or Hemoccult testing) is controversial for two reasons. First, the false-positive and false-negative rates for Hemoccults are high.[20,21] A false-positive test is a positive test that should be negative because there is no disease. A false-negative test is a negative test that should be positive because there is disease (I will discuss this problem with tests more fully in chapter 6). Imagine that your doctor tests your stool and the Hemoccult card is positive. You'll worry that you have colon cancer. Your worry is unhealthy if this is a false-positive test.

Imagine that your doctor reassures you there's no blood in your stool because the Hemoccult card is negative. You'll think you don't have colon cancer. Your reassurance is unhealthy if this is a false-negative test.

If you have no symptoms and have blood detected in your stool, you have a one in ten chance of having colon cancer.[22] Under the same circumstances, you have a one in three chance of having either cancer *or* polyps (which can grow into cancers).[22]

If you have a negative Hemoccult test, you have a 0.2 percent chance of having a colon cancer diagnosed within two years of testing and a 0.7 percent chance of having a polyp.[22]

The second reason Hemoccult tests are controversial is that there is little evidence they save lives.[23] In 1990, the U.S. Preventive Services Task Force concluded, "There is insufficient evidence to recommend for or against fecal occult blood testing as an effective screening test for colorectal cancer in asymptomatic persons. There are also inadequate grounds for discontinuing this form of screening where it is currently practiced or for withholding it from persons who request it."[7]

However, a study published in 1993 may change these recommendations. This study suggests that you would reduce your individual risk of dying from colon cancer over thirteen years by 0.6 percent if you had Hemoccult testing annually.[24] Keep in mind that 0.6 percent is your individual risk reduction; the relative risk reduction is 33 percent.[24] It may be that the reduction in mortality seen in this study is due to chance, not to Hemoccult testing.[25]

Based on the inaccuracy of Hemoccult testing, some seniors may want to forget this part of the exam and save themselves the worry of a false-positive test. On the other hand, seniors with risk factors for colon cancer should have this exam yearly. The risk factors include first-degree relatives with colon cancer; personal history of breast, ovary, or uterus cancer; and personal history of inflammatory bowel disease, colon polyps, or colon cancer.

Pelvic Exam and Pap Smears

Mrs. Peterson returned to my office earlier than I had expected. At our first visit I had written "Return to clinic in six months." Mrs. Peterson returned in four months. She had hypertension and arthritis. Both were under control. She did not need to see a doctor more frequently than every six months unless she had a new symptom.

I asked how she was feeling, expecting her to tell me about her new symptom.

"Fine, thanks, but I need that test," Mrs. Peterson responded. She must have detected a puzzled look because she continued, "I haven't had my Pap test this year. My gynecologist used to do the tests each year, but he retired. I thought I could get them done here."

Most seniors aren't quite as conscientious about routine Pap smears as this woman. She wouldn't be so conscientious if she understood the value of routine Pap smears for seniors.

Doctors used to recommend yearly Pap smears for young and middle-aged women. However, studies revealed that screening for cervical cancer (the cancer the Pap smear is designed to detect) every three years was more cost-effective. Screening every three years was much less expensive than screening every year and it was almost as effective in detecting early cervical cancer.[26] Therefore, experts changed the recommendation of screening every year to screening every three years. Apparently my patient's gynecologist didn't agree with that change.

Is there an age above which screening is unnecessary? Imagine that you go to your doctor on your seventieth birthday expecting a Pap smear. Assume you haven't had this in three years. Your doctor says, "Happy birthday! You no longer need Pap smears because an expert panel decided that they are unnecessary after age seventy." You probably wouldn't be too disappointed.

It's not quite as simple as the imaginary birthday greeting, but it's close. Many seniors do not need routine Pap smears.

A panel of experts from Canada recently suggested that women over age sixty-nine who have had at least two normal Pap smears in the last nine years—and have never had cervical cancer—don't need Pap smears.[27] If you have your first Pap smear at age sixty-seven, get another Pap smear six months later. If both Pap smears are normal, you do not need any more Pap smears.[27]

A recent study from England suggests that women over age fifty don't need Pap smears if they had negative Pap smears before age fifty.[28] In this study, no new cases of cervical cancer were found in women over fifty who had undergone screening every three years.

Keep in mind that doctors in Canada and England may practice differently than doctors in the United States. Since cervical cancer may still occur in women over the age of sixty who have had negative Pap smears (albeit rarely), many U.S. doctors believe there should be no upper age limit to screening for cervical cancer.

Consider a sixty-five-year-old woman who has had negative Pap smears every three years (for example, at ages fifty-three, fifty-six, fifty-nine, and sixty-two). Dr. David Eddy from Duke University concluded that this woman would decrease the chance of death from cervical cancer by about 18 in 10,000 by continuing Pap smears every three years.[26] She would increase her life expectancy by about three days.

The effect on life expectancy is about a third of that for a seventy-four-year-old under the same circumstances.[26] The increase in her life expectancy would be about one day.

These are not impressive benefits for an exam that can be difficult for many senior women. Are routine Pap smears worth it? You can decide. You know the benefits. Now consider the costs.

Medicare covers Pap smears done every three years. You must pay for yearly Pap smears. Pap smears cost about twenty dollars.

The other reason to have a pelvic exam is to detect ovarian cancer. Drs. Oboler and LaForce concluded, "No evidence shows that routine pelvic examination increases the detection of early ovarian cancer or improves survival rates. Therefore, routine palpation of ovaries cannot be recommended as a screening procedure."[5]

Ovaries in older women tend to be very small and difficult to feel on exam. Most internists and family practitioners have little experience feeling ovaries in older women. If you worry about ovarian cancer, I suggest you have a gynecologist do the exam.

Hernias
If your hernia is so small that you don't know about it, then it's not worth knowing about.

Joints
If you have no joint pain, don't look for trouble.

Pulses
The physical exam is unreliable for detecting peripheral vascular disease, the gradual clogging of arteries in the legs. Even if you do have peripheral vascular disease, you wouldn't have surgery or take new medicine until you developed symptoms.

Neurologic Exam
When your doctor makes you feel like a three-year-old by asking you to roll your eyes, stick out your tongue and smile, he is performing part of the neurologic exam. Doctors use it to test strength, sensation, balance, reflexes, and other functions controlled by the nervous system.

The neurological exam is unlikely to lead to a new diagnosis or new therapy in seniors without symptoms. Observation of someone walking is usually the most revealing part of the exam. Your doctor can do this when greeting you or saying good-bye. This will tell him more about your neurological function than multiple thumps with a reflex hammer. An annual neurological exam is unnecessary.

Brain

I recall a very healthy-looking and pleasant eighty-four-year-old who came to the office at the request of her daughter. She said she felt fine. Having never seen her before, I assumed she was there for a routine checkup. The medical intern did the history and physical and reported that she was in perfect health. Furthermore, the intern said she was the funniest eighty-four-year-old he had ever met.

Indeed, she was entertaining. But every time I asked something that taxed her memory, she pulled out another joke or witticism. Finally, I coaxed her into a structured mental status exam. I soon realized that we were not on the same page. She thought it was 1984 (not 1991), that we were in Ohio (not Colorado), and that Nixon was president.

The brain is of course part of the nervous system, and the neurologic exam tests some of the functions of the brain. However, the neurologic exam mentioned above does not test the functions of the brain that make us human. Doctors test the brain's higher functions—attention, memory, language, spatial orientation, judgment, etc.—with a mental status exam.

As you get older, doctors are more likely to ask you questions that seem silly, such as: Where are you? What year is this? and Who is the president? You should not feel offended if your doctor asks you these questions as part of a mental status exam. Many doctors have missed the diagnosis of a memory problem (such as early Alzheimer's disease) because they did not ask these questions.

Many seniors worry that they may be getting Alzheimer's disease because their memory is not as sharp as it was ten years earlier. For example, they may not recall names of acquaintances or objects as readily. Most of these seniors have benign senescent

forgetfulness (BSF). The temporary lapse in memory is benign—
it does not progress to a dementia like Alzheimer's disease. It
occurs as a natural part of aging.

The mental status exam may be important for diagnosing
early memory problems and providing reassurance. Many seniors
do not need the mental status exam because it is clear they have
no memory problem.

Summary

The routine checkup gives you and your doctor a chance to know
each other better. An annual checkup is a good way to give you
reassurance that everything is okay. However, the annual exam is
not absolutely necessary because the likelihood that it will find
something is so small.

The most important parts of the physical exam are blood
pressure measurement, skin exam, lung exam, abdominal exam,
breast exam for women, and prostate exam for men. If you see
your doctor several times a year, he may do parts of the physical
exam during different visits.

Discussion of your concerns is probably more valuable than
the exam itself. It is certainly more valuable than many routine
laboratory tests, the focus of the next chapter.

6

Routine Tests

Assume you have completed the annual physical exam, and assume your doctor tells you that everything looks all right. Your physical exam is normal, and you have no new symptoms. You chat for a little while, and your doctor answers your questions.

Should you have routine laboratory tests done before leaving your doctor's office?

This chapter will focus on the tests that are routinely done in your doctor's office. The next chapter will focus on more complex tests—outpatient tests that require appointments or trips to labs or other offices.

Seniors without symptoms should consider having only a few routine tests. These include a cholesterol test for seniors with high risk of heart disease; a baseline electrocardiogram for seniors with high risk of heart disease; urinalysis; and thyroid function tests. The prostate specific antigen (PSA) test may be a good screening test for prostate cancer—not enough research has been done to know its value.

As you will see, routine tests rarely uncover problems if you have no new symptoms. The most likely benefit is reassurance that you are healthy. On the other hand, routine tests can be misleading. There's a trade-off. You will have to decide what is most important for you.

Doctors order tests for many reasons that have little to do with clinical judgment. If your doctor orders tests every time you see him, ask him if the tests are necessary.

False-Positive and False-Negative Tests
If your doctor orders a lot of tests, there is a reasonable chance that at least one of the tests will be abnormal even if you have no disease. In other words, the test result will fall out of the normal range. It will be a false-positive test because you don't have a new disease.

An understanding of the normal range is necessary to appreciate one reason a healthy person might have an abnormal test. Consider the measurement of the calcium concentration in blood.

If I measure the blood calcium levels in one hundred healthy seniors, I will get a distribution of values that resembles a bell-shaped curve.

One or two values will be very high. A few others will be not quite so high, but higher than the rest. One or two will be very low. A few others will be not quite so low, but lower than the rest. Most of the values will cluster in the middle of the curve.

The normal range includes most, but not all, of the calcium values for these one hundred healthy individuals. In medical statistics, the normal range includes the middle 95 percent of the values. The lowest 2.5 percent and the highest 2.5 percent fall outside the normal range. Although the people with these outlying calcium values have no disease, they would have abnormal calcium values on a routine blood test.

Even if we erase all human error, there is a 5 percent chance that you will have an "abnormal" test result for any test your doctor orders. Your chance of having at least one abnormal test result increases with the more tests your doctor orders.

Let's assume you have an abnormally high calcium level. What is the likelihood that this is a false-positive test and that you have no new disease? What is the likelihood that this represents a new disease?

It depends on the prevalence of diseases associated with high calcium and on the accuracy of the test.

First assume that the test is very accurate. If these diseases are rare for people like you, it's very likely that your high calcium level is a false-positive test.

For example, metastatic cancer, tuberculosis, and sarcoidosis are diseases that cause high calcium levels in the blood. Imagine a stadium full of healthy seniors. The prevalence of these diseases would be very small in that stadium. A high calcium level would likely be a false-positive test.

If, on the other hand, these diseases are common for people like you, it's likely that your high calcium is a true positive test and you have a disease. Imagine you are no longer healthy. Imagine a stadium full of seniors who have had night sweats, fatigue, cough, and weight loss for the last six months. The prevalence of these diseases would be much higher in that stadium. A high calcium level would likely be a true positive test.

Now assume that the test is not very accurate. All bets are off. The test result is almost meaningless.

Without any suspicion of disease (that is, symptoms), doctors have little justification for ordering routine tests except to reassure you with normal results. There are exceptions, but the following review of tests shows that very few people derive medical benefit from routine tests.

Preoperative Laboratory Screening

Much of the information about routine tests comes from studies of tests done before surgery or on admission to the hospital. If you've had any surgery, you've had a complete set of blood tests done before the surgery.

Mrs. Green is an eighty-eight-year-old who had just returned from Syracuse, New York, where she swam in the Senior Olympics. Although she performed admirably, she felt frustrated with her deteriorating vision. She vowed to have cataract surgery when she returned home.

Mrs. Green is a healthy woman. The chance of finding a true positive test result (that is an abnormal result that indicates disease) is remote. The chance of finding a false-positive test is higher. In this situation, the false-positive rate may be as high as 70 percent.[1]

I told the ophthalmologist that Mrs. Green didn't need the routine preoperative blood tests. He replied, "I agree, but try telling the anesthesiologist that. He won't start until he's seen that all the tests are normal."

Because of the defensive medicine we practice in our society, practically everyone gets routine tests before surgery.

Do these tests help? Consider the following studies. Dr. Bradly Narr and colleagues from the Mayo Clinic reviewed the results of preoperative screening laboratory tests in healthy patients who underwent elective surgical procedures at the Mayo Clinic in 1988. They discovered that only 1 of 3,782 healthy patients had a disease that required a new medicine.[2]

In a study of patients admitted to the internal medicine

wards, only 0.5 percent of routine admission laboratory tests led to change in the treatment of patients.[3]

Do these studies apply to seniors, a group of patients likely to have more undetected disease? Dr. Katherine Domoto and colleagues from Boston studied seniors in a chronic care facility, the group of patients most likely to have undetected disease. Only 0.1 percent of all routine tests led to changes in patient management. None of the changes benefited the patient in an important way.[4] Many experts agree that testing should be more judicious.[5]

It is likely that the value of routine testing in your doctor's office is about the same as routine testing prior to surgery. In either case, your doctor orders tests without suspicion of disease.

You might ask, What about the value of individual tests? What if I'm worried about my blood count or blood sugar? The following summary of individual tests leads to the same conclusion. Routine tests rarely help and may mislead you and your doctor.

Complete Blood Count

The complete blood count measures three kinds of blood cells: red blood cells, white blood cells, and platelets. Red blood cells carry oxygen to all parts of the body. White blood cells fight infections. Platelets form clots when there is damage to blood vessels.

People with low red blood cell counts have anemia. Anemia is the most common disorder of blood cells, and it has many causes. Red blood cell counts can be high in people who smoke or who have chronic lung disease. White blood cells are rarely low in people who are not on chemotherapy. They are elevated in people with infections or with leukemia. Platelets are rarely low or high without other major problems.

The U.S. Preventive Services Task Force (USPSTF) does not recommend routine testing for anemia for seniors without symptoms.[6]

In one study, the few abnormal complete blood cell counts found in 595 young patients rarely mattered. False-positive tests led to unnecessary repeat visits. Doctors made a new diagnosis that changed their plans in only 3 (0.5 percent) of the 595 patients.[7]

The percentages may be higher in an older population. The general message, however, is the same. A routine complete blood cell count will rarely lead to a new therapy that will improve your health.

Blood Sugar

Many seniors have family members with diabetes and want to check their own blood sugar to make sure they don't have diabetes.

The USPSTF does not recommend routine screening for diabetes in adults without symptoms.[6] Many experts agree with the USPSTF; the benefits of screening for diabetes are too small.[8]

Detecting diabetes in its early stages usually will not change the course of the disease (see chapter 14). The exceptions are early detection in pregnancy and in obese adults, where weight reduction may correct the problem. If you are not overweight, however, early detection will do little more than label you a diabetic. This probably won't help you; it may just cause anxiety.

Electrolytes

Electrolytes are chemicals in the blood such as sodium, potassium, chloride, calcium, phosphorus, and magnesium. These chemicals are important for many different body functions. Doctors measure them with other chemicals, such as blood sugar and cholesterol, in biochemical profiles. The smaller profiles measure six or seven different chemicals. The larger profiles measure eighteen to twenty different chemicals.

Drs. Randall Cebul and Robert Beck reviewed the value of routine biochemical profiles for adults without symptoms and concluded that the benefits are not worth the burdens of cost, discomfort, and anxiety.[9] The chance of being misled is much greater than the chance of detecting early disease.

They emphasized that the likelihood of a false-positive test increases as doctors include more tests. Assume you are healthy. If your doctor measures only one chemical, there is a 95 percent chance that the test will be normal. If he measures six chemicals in a profile, there is a 74 percent chance that all tests will be normal. If he measures twelve chemicals in a profile, there is a 54 percent chance that all tests will be normal.[9]

In other words, there is roughly a one in two chance that one of the twelve chemicals your doctor measures will be abnormal. This may cause unnecessary anxiety.

If you are taking a diuretic (water pill) for hypertension or swelling in your legs, you should have your sodium and potassium checked every six to twelve months.

Kidney Function Tests

Many people think that doctors measure kidney function with a urine test. It is actually chemicals in the blood (creatinine and blood urea nitrogen) that are used to measure kidney function. Seniors without symptoms may have abnormal results on these tests. Early detection of these abnormalities, however, is very unlikely to lead to a new therapy that will improve your health. The exceptions are rare. The USPSTF has not even commented on screening for kidney disease in seniors.[6]

If you are taking a diuretic, you should have kidney function tests done when you have your sodium and potassium checked.

Liver Function Tests

Abnormalities of liver function tests are unusual in adults without symptoms. The USPSTF has not commented on screening for liver disease[6]—there is no good indication for it. If you drink too much alcohol, you may have abnormalities of your liver function tests without having any symptoms.

Thyroid Function Tests

Unlike the previous tests, thyroid function tests may be useful for seniors without symptoms. The reason is that a thyroid problem may not cause suspicious symptoms in seniors until the problem is advanced. Often, seniors may have the usual symptoms of low thyroid production (hypothyroidism) and have normal thyroid function tests. Conversely, seniors may deny all of the usual symptoms and have very low thyroid production. Therefore, a blood test is necessary to make the diagnosis.

The USPSTF concluded that routine thyroid function tests may be clinically prudent for seniors, especially women.[6] Once every two years is enough.

Cholesterol

Thirty years ago most seniors hadn't even heard of cholesterol. Today you dare not confess that you don't know your cholesterol level.

Two elderly sisters came to the office for a routine checkup. One worried about her cholesterol level, which was 230 when she had it checked at a health fair five months earlier. If she lived in Canada, her doctor would consider her level normal.[10] But in the United States, many doctors would consider her level abnormally high. And she worries.

I tried to allay her anxiety by explaining that this level may mean nothing for someone her age (eighty-eight years). She persisted. A repeat total cholesterol level wouldn't suffice. She wanted to fast and return to the office to have a complete cholesterol profile run. She would rest only after knowing if she had the "good kind and the bad kind of cholesterol."

On the way out of the office, her sister tapped me on the shoulder and whispered, "She's not that worried about her cholesterol." After a furtive glance at her sister, she continued, "She has a bridge party coming up."

A bridge party, I thought. Did she think she would have a massive heart attack while serving hors d'oeuvres?

Her sister continued, "Doctor, everyone knows at the bridge party. They all know their cholesterol levels." Why of course. She had talked enough about her grandchildren, politics, and gardening. The topic that carried the day was cholesterol. Why not—about 64 percent of seniors will have cholesterol levels over 200.[11]

Should seniors be screened for high cholesterol? Dr. John Eisenberg from Philadelphia suggested that cholesterol screening may be worthwhile for seniors, particularly for seniors with a high risk of heart disease or those who have preexisting heart disease.[12] Drs. Margo Denke and Scott Grundy from Dallas agreed that age alone should not be a reason to neglect cholesterol screening.[13]

But there are burdens. Drs. Alan Garber and Judith Wagner note that the experts in this field chose to ignore costs when developing guidelines for cholesterol screening. They stated, "The National Heart, Lung, and Blood Institute organized the National Cholesterol Education Program in 1985 with the goal of developing a national policy for cholesterol reduction in the United States. As part of that program, an Adult Treatment Panel (ATP) was appointed to develop recommendations for screening adults for elevated cholesterol levels and for preventive treatment when necessary. ATP membership consisted of specialists in [cholesterol] metabolism, cardiology, endocrinology, epidemiology, dietetics, and public health. ATP was directed not to consider costs in making its recommendations."[14]

Dr. Garber and colleagues took it upon themselves to estimate the costs and consequences of cholesterol screening for asymptomatic older Americans. They concluded, "If all Americans 65 years of age and older adhered to a cholesterol screening program similar to the one proposed by the National Cholesterol Education Program, minimum annual expenditures for screening and treatment would be between $1.6 billion and $16.8 billion, depending on the effectiveness of diet and the cost of the medications used to treat hypercholesterolemia. There is no direct evidence that this program would lessen overall morbidity or extend the lives of elderly Americans."[15]

Guess who would pay the taxes to support such a program.

It is too early to tell if this analysis is correct. If further research reveals that the costs are very high and the benefits very small, seniors may choose to advocate for more judicious use of limited health care resources. Until the answer becomes more clear, seniors should consider cholesterol screening optional.[16]

Here's another problem with routine cholesterol screening. You don't know what one measurement means.

Some believe that one measurement in a postmenopausal woman gives a good estimate of her long-term level.[17] However, others think that an individual's cholesterol varies too much for doctors to rely on one measurement.[18-20]

Health fairs thrive on cholesterol screening. Dr. Paul Fischer and colleagues from Augusta surveyed participants of a mall-based cholesterol screening program one year after their screening. They concluded, "Cholesterol screening programs of the type now commonly offered are unlikely to contribute greatly to the national efforts to further reduce coronary artery disease."[21] They also noted that those with high cholesterol levels reported high distress from screening.

Maybe the distress is worth it if the benefits are good. In chapter 12 I will discuss the benefits of lowering cholesterol. Here's a preview: the benefits are marginal.

Dr. Murray Krahn and colleagues from Toronto concluded that the aggressive U.S. policy for cholesterol screening and treatment provides no more benefit than the less aggressive Canadian policy. It does cause more burdens.[22]

Coagulation Tests

The prothrombin time (protime) and partial thromboplastin time are tests that measure how well your blood clots. If you do not have a history of bleeding or bruising easily, these should be normal. A positive test is very likely a false-positive test. There is no reason to regularly screen for blood-clotting abnormalities. However, if you take the blood thinner coumadin, you need to have your protime checked regularly.

Prostate Specific Antigen (PSA)

The PSA test is unique. It is the first widely used blood test that can detect early cancer.

Mr. Sanchez is a healthy seventy-seven-year-old who had not seen a doctor in two years. He came to the office and, after exchanging pleasantries, got right down to business. "I came here for only one reason, Doctor. I want you to check my PSA."

I followed his lead and bypassed a lot of the rituals of the physical exam. He did share some of his medical history.

After hearing that he had a history of polyps in the colon and that he felt more tired lately, I decided to check his complete blood count as well as his PSA. One could hardly call that extravagant.

Several days later I called to tell Mr. Sanchez that his PSA was normal. He was satisfied. Several weeks later he called to express his frustration that we had billed him for a complete blood count. As far as he was concerned, he didn't need this particular test and he didn't see the point of paying for it.

I explained that his history (colon polyps) and symptom (fatigue) made me suspicious of anemia. He understood but still didn't like paying for a test he had not requested. Fair enough.

Mr. Sanchez is suspicious of the medical profession. He wants little to do with tests and doctors. However, a message got through to him: Check your PSA, detect prostate cancer early, and save your life.

Is the message correct? We don't know yet.

Dr. William Catalona and colleagues from St. Louis reported results favoring PSA screening. In their study, one in five men with PSA levels from 4.0 to 9.9 (a PSA below 4.0 is considered normal) had cancer confirmed on prostate biopsy. Two of three men with PSA levels of 10.0 or higher had cancer confirmed on prostate biopsy.

The authors noted that rectal exam alone would have missed a third of the cancers. An ultrasound test would also have missed a third of the cancers. The PSA had the lowest error rate of all tests.[23]

This study prompted a number of commentaries in the *New England Journal of Medicine*. Dr. Robert Coney from Atlanta responded, "Prostate cancer is a particularly difficult cancer from a screening perspective. Many, perhaps the majority, of cases of prostate cancer never become clinically evident because of their indolent nature. Efforts to detect every prostate cancer are misguided since the detection of tumors that are not going to cause clinical disease results in [physician induced] harm and no benefit to the men identified."[24]

Other commentators noted that the false-positive rate for

PSA may be high. For example, benign prostatic hypertrophy (enlargement of the prostate), a very common problem in older men, can cause elevated PSA levels. Alternatively, the false-negative rate (a normal PSA level in someone with prostate cancer) may be higher than expected.

Doctors used to think that a rectal exam in someone without any prostate problem might elevate the PSA level. However, a recent study showed that a rectal exam doesn't affect the PSA results.[25]

One PSA level may not tell us much. Perhaps a series of PSA levels (for example, one test a year) will be the best way to detect early prostate cancer.[26] The rate of change of PSA levels distinguishes early prostate cancer from benign prostate enlargement.[27]

Here's the critical question: Does early detection of prostate cancer make a difference? Can you increase your life expectancy if you detect prostate cancer in its infancy?

A study reported in 1968 said yes.[28] More recent studies said no.[29] The definitive study hasn't been done.[30]

Again, it is too early to tell if the benefits of this test will outweigh the burdens.

Urinalysis

A urinalysis can determine if you are spilling glucose (an indication of diabetes), protein (kidney disease), red blood cells (infection or cancer), white blood cells (infection), or bacteria in your urine. The USPSTF concluded that yearly urine testing is prudent for seniors but they do not recommend urinalysis as a screening test to detect diabetes in adults without symptoms.[6]

Blood in the urine may be the first sign of bladder or kidney cancer. Doctors can cure these cancers if they detect them early enough.

Early detection of kidney disease by finding protein in the urine is unlikely to improve your health if you have no symptoms.

A senior with white blood cells and bacteria in her urine has a urinary tract infection, even though she may have no symptoms. Your doctor should treat these infections with antibiotics. Many seniors have bacteria in their urine but no white blood cells. We call this asymptomatic bacteriuria. There is no good reason to treat this unless white blood cells are also present.[31]

Urine Culture

The urine culture is the test that confirms a urinary tract infection. You should not expect this test routinely. Rather, it is appropriate only if symptoms or results of the urinalysis suggest a urinary tract infection.

Chest X-Ray

Hospitalized patients can count on several routines. The identification wrist band is one. The chest x-ray is another.

Doctors overuse chest x-rays as much as any other test. Routine chest x-rays result in more misleading results than helpful results.[32,33]

The question is not whether chest x-rays detect disease; the question is whether the detection makes a difference. In a study of 368 patients with no risk factors for an abnormal chest x-ray, only one patient had an abnormal preoperative chest x-ray.[34] It did not affect this patient's care.

If we could identify high-risk target groups, screening chest x-rays might be worthwhile.[35] (For example, heavy smokers might benefit from screening chest x-rays.) Currently, the USPSTF does not recommend screening seniors without symptoms for lung cancer using chest x-rays.[6]

Electrocardiogram

Miss Hathaway is a sixty-seven-year-old patient of mine who has atrial fibrillation, an irregular heart rhythm. She never had symptoms that showed her heart was going too fast or too slow. Her pulse was irregular. The electrocardiogram obtained on her first visit showed exactly what I expected—atrial fibrillation.

After her second visit, Miss Hathaway asked, "Why didn't you check an electrocardiogram this time? The cardiologist I used to see would check my electrocardiogram four times a year. He wanted to see how my heart rhythm was doing."

How could I convince her that electrocardiograms every three months—perhaps even every year—were unnecessary? I could not tell her what I was really thinking: that her cardiologist was abusing the system (more on this later).

Routine admission electrocardiograms infrequently add new information to the clinical evaluation but are useful when they do.[36] However, if you are not hospitalized and have no new symptoms, an annual electrocardiogram will rarely lead to changes that improve your health. The same is true of preoperative electrocardiograms for people having outpatient surgery.[37]

A baseline electrocardiogram may be helpful if you ever need evaluation for chest pain in an emergency room. In one study, six of forty-seven seniors benefited from treatment changes resulting from the electrocardiograms.[38]

In response to this study, Dr. Harold Sox from Dartmouth concluded, "The baseline [electrocardiogram] is most likely to be useful in patients with heart disease, the elderly, and asymptomatic persons with risk factors for [heart] disease. The baseline [electrocardiogram] is not likely to be useful in asymptomatic persons with no risk factors for [heart] disease."[39]

In summary, if you have no symptoms and no risk factors for

heart disease (hypertension, obesity, diabetes, tobacco use, or strong family history of heart disease), an electrocardiogram is unnecessary.

The Benefits of Testing

Tests benefit you in two ways. First, normal results reassure you. This is a common benefit. Second, you may discover a disease that your doctor can treat while it's in its early stages. This is an uncommon benefit if you have no new symptoms.

If you are a person who needs the reassurance of normal tests as well as the reassurance of your doctor, screening tests are right for you. If you don't need the reassurance, the benefits are not worth the burdens, such as false-positive test results.

The Burdens of Testing

Drs. Steven Woolf and Douglas Kamerow from the Office of Disease Prevention and Health Promotion in Washington, D.C., outlined the potential burdens of testing.[40]

First, the test procedure itself can cause physical harm, even though this is rarely a problem with the routine tests done in your doctor's office.

Second, although the routine test may cause no physical harm, a positive result may necessitate a bigger test that could cause harm.

Third, positive results can generate anxiety and fear. The unnecessary anxiety from a false-positive test may persist long after your doctor corrects the error.[40] Conversely, the false reassurance you get from false-negative tests may cause you to ignore symptoms.

Finally, the cost of the "little-ticket items" adds up.[41] You end up paying for them one way or another (for example, higher taxes, higher insurance copayments, etc.).

Why Do Doctors Order So Many Tests?

This chapter has focused on the relative value of routine tests. Understanding the motives for testing will also help you judge the need for both routine and complex tests.

The first reason your doctor may order a test is that you expect it.[42-44] Drs. Woolf and Kamerow noted, "Physicians who provide extensive screening or diagnostic testing are viewed by the public as being thorough, concerned, and well-trained. Patients who receive tests often feel greater satisfaction with their care and may even perceive psychologically mediated improvement in their symptoms. Those who have become accustomed to receiving certain tests might feel they were receiving less care if their physicians stopped ordering them. Even individuals who are philosophically opposed to excessive health care costs and medical technology may adopt different views as patients, desiring the full range of available diagnostic services."[40]

Patient education can alter patient expectations.[42] Perhaps the more patients know about the benefits and burdens of routine tests, the more credit they will give to doctors who do not test excessively.

The second reason for excessive testing is that doctors don't like to be left in the dark. Dr. Jerome Kassirer, editor of the *New England Journal of Medicine,* stated, "Despite the limitations of our diagnostic procedures, we continue to test excessively, partly because of our discomfort with uncertainty. We have assiduously woven the goal of minimizing uncertainty into the fabric of clinical practice and teaching."[45] In other words, medical schools train doctors to uncover everything.

Third, doctors may test excessively because of what Dr. Eugene Robin from Stanford calls the "lemming syndrome." He stated, "Once the leaders of a subspecialty endorse a given test procedure, followers flock to emulate the leadership."[46] Decades ago leaders advocated routine testing without good scientific reasons; lemmings have been following ever since.

Fourth, your doctor may have financial incentives for ordering tests. Doctors' incomes vary significantly depending on how many tests they do in their office[47] and how insurance companies pay them.

For example, recall the difference between a fee-for-service practice (the doctor gets paid for each service he provides) and a prepaid plan (the doctor gets a fixed amount per person no matter how many services he provides). The use of certain high-profit, high-cost tests (for example, electrocardiograms and chest x-rays) is higher (about 50 percent higher) in large fee-for-service groups than in large prepaid groups.[48]

In one study, doctors who get paid for doing their own x-rays ordered x-rays four times more often than doctors who referred their patients to radiologists for x-rays. These doctors also charged more than the radiologists for similar x-rays.[49]

Congress has moved to regulate self-referral practices and physicians' ownership of clinical laboratories. As of 1992, doctors can no longer refer their Medicare patients to laboratories in which they have a financial interest.[50]

Fifth, organizational factors influence your doctor's practice.[51] Some clinics encourage testing because tests generate more revenue.[52] Other kinds of organizations, such as health maintenance organizations (HMOs) or other prepaid plans, discourage extensive testing.[53]

Sixth, practices vary from one part of the country (or state) to another.[54] Doctors in one town may be more likely to order certain tests than their counterparts in a neighboring town. We don't fully understand why doctors practice differently in different communities, but they do.

Finally, your doctor may order tests to help protect himself from a lawsuit.[55] The defensive medicine that all doctors practice encourages extensive testing. Drs. Woolf and Kamerow noted that some state and local legislation requires tests that are very unlikely to help you.[40]

Summary

Seniors without symptoms should consider only a few routine tests. These include: cholesterol tests for seniors with a high risk of heart disease; baseline electrocardiogram for seniors with a high risk of heart disease; urinalysis; and thyroid function tests. Even these routine tests are of questionable value. The PSA may be a good screening test for prostate cancer, but it's too early to know how valuable this test is.

Other routine tests are more likely to be misleading than helpful.

Doctors order tests for many reasons that have little to do with clinical judgment. If your doctor orders tests every time you see him, ask him if the tests are really necessary.

7

Complex Tests

$\mathbf{A}$s we saw in chapter 6, routine tests aren't very helpful if you have no new symptoms. What about more complex tests that require an extra appointment?

The complex tests your doctor has in mind detect early disease or help determine your risk of developing disease later. There's a good chance your doctor will recommend one of these tests during your annual checkup.

The take-home message for this chapter is the same as the message for the last chapter. These tests rarely help you if you have no symptoms. Perhaps you want to know the likelihood that one of these tests will help you before you agree to have the test.

A brief description of each test is necessary. I'll divide these tests into two categories. The first group includes screening tests to detect early cancer. These tests are:

1. *Mammogram.* This is a special x-ray of the breast. It detects small cancers.
2. *Flexible sigmoidoscopy.* This is an examination of the last two feet of the colon. It involves a flexible scope with a light on the end. A doctor can use this test to biopsy anything that might look like a cancer.
3. *Colonoscopy.* This is similar to flexible sigmoidoscopy. The difference is that colonoscopy allows the doctor to examine the entire colon (all the way to the small intestine).
4. *Barium enema.* This is an x-ray of the colon. First an enema is given to distribute barium throughout the colon. Then x-rays of the barium-filled colon are taken to outline anything that looks suspicious for cancer.
5. *Ultrasound of the prostate.* This detects prostate cancer. A small probe in the rectum sends sound waves toward the prostate. Certain patterns signal prostate cancer.
6. *Ultrasound of the ovaries.* This detects ovarian cancer. A small probe in the vagina or on the abdomen sends sound waves toward the ovaries. Certain patterns signal ovarian cancer.

The second group of tests gives you an idea of how various other organs are functioning. Most doctors do not routinely order these last four tests. However, your doctor may order one or more of them. These tests are:

1. *Exercise treadmill test.* This tests the condition of the heart. Patients exercise while monitored by an electrocardiogram.
2. *Pulmonary function tests.* These tests measure the condition of the lungs. Patients take in a deep breath and blow it out as fast as they can through a mouthpiece.

3. *Abdominal ultrasound.* This detects aneurysms in the abdomen. A device on the abdomen sends sound waves toward the aorta. Certain patterns signal an aneurysm.
4. *Bone densitometry.* This is a special x-ray of the bone (usually in the forearm). It measures the density of bone and gives some idea of the risk of developing osteoporosis.

If your doctor suggests you get any of these tests, you can weigh the benefits and burdens to decide if it is worth it.

Let's start with the most common test, the mammogram.

Mammogram

I approach this part of the book with more trepidation than with all other sections put together.

Two years ago I presented the following analysis to a community group. Before I concluded my talk, a woman bolted out of her seat.

"I can't take any more of this, Dr. Murphy! I had breast cancer. I'm standing here right now because I had a mammogram. If I had skipped that mammogram, I wouldn't be here. How can you say the things you're saying?"

I'm sure there was more. I don't remember it because I was reeling from the first blow. I didn't mind her attacking my argument. But I did mind upsetting her so much.

Women in my family have reviewed this section. It makes them uneasy. They, like most other women, want to believe in mammograms. Other tests don't evoke such emotion.

Many believe the myth that mammography is a foolproof way of preventing death from breast cancer. No wonder. Consider the TV advertisement I saw in May 1994. A forty-five-year-old woman was standing next to her seventy-year-old mother. The daughter claimed that the best gift she could give her mother for Mother's Day was a mammogram. It could save her life. The announcer proceeded to state that "there is no reason a woman should die of breast cancer in 1994." The implication, of course, is that mammography can prevent *all* deaths from breast cancer. Not only is this blatantly false, it can be a very disturbing message for patients who already have breast cancer. Imagine the guilt a woman dying from breast cancer might feel when she hears that all breast cancer deaths can be prevented.

Breast cancer is unique. Doctors don't know if it's a solid tumor or a systemic disease (with many small bits of cancer spread throughout the body) when we first detect it. I, a male doctor, don't even pretend to understand the psychological effects of breast cancer. I know that body image plays an important role, but that's the extent of my insight.

The following analysis doesn't account for the psychology of breast cancer, the "human factor," as one of my sisters said. I admit that this factor is as important as any in medicine.

Now I will cautiously proceed.

Mrs. Porter, a seventy-seven-year-old woman, came to my office for follow-up of hypertension, diabetes, and arthritis. She also had memory problems that disturbed her family. We suspected early Alzheimer's disease.

A medical resident saw Mrs. Porter first and then reported to me. After telling me about her blood pressure, diabetes, and arthritis, he said, "That about covers it." After a pause, he added with a hint of pride, "Oh, yeah, I've ordered a mammogram for her."

The medical resident was conscientious about the "health maintenance" issues that doctors routinely address. Somewhere in the back of his mind was the fear of malpractice if he missed diagnosing breast cancer in its early stage.[1] And he was aware that the experts—not only one group of experts, but all groups of experts—recommend annual mammograms for women over fifty years old.[2-4]

Dr. Robert Hayward and colleagues reviewed preventive care guidelines. They noted that the American College of Physicians, the U.S. Preventive Services Task Force, the Canadian Task Force on the Periodic Health Examination, and the American Cancer Society all recommend annual mammograms beginning at age fifty.[4]

Time magazine informed us that one in ten women in this country will have breast cancer at some time in her life.[5] This is a frightening disease; clearly, everything must be done to prevent it.

In a review of mammography, Dr. Stephen Feig concluded that mammography combined with physical exam could reduce breast cancer mortality by at least 40 percent and possibly as much as 50 percent.[6]

The medical resident obviously made the right decision when he ordered a mammogram for my patient. Right?

Let's see how much mammograms really do help. Mammograms detect early cancers. The early cancers detected by screening mammograms are less likely to have already spread to lymph nodes than cancers found without screening mammograms.[7]

Dr. Jeanne Mandelblatt and colleagues used a computer program to evaluate the usefulness of mammograms. They concluded that screening mammograms for women who had cancer "extended life by 617 days for average-health women between 65 and 69 years of age and 178 days for those aged 85 years or more."[8]

Sounds like mammograms help a lot.

Enter Petr Skrabanek, the heretic who coauthored the book *Follies and Fallacies in Medicine*.[9] He has challenged the recommendation that women get regular screening mammograms.

Dr. Skrabanek critiqued four of the largest studies that supposedly showed the benefits of screening mammography.[10] He claimed that 5,000 to 68,000 women would have to be offered mammography to postpone or prevent one breast cancer death.

He concluded, "The enthusiasts in favor of mass mammography have created an atmosphere of false optimism. They have not informed the public about the very small potential benefit nor about the risks associated with screening, especially the risks of false-positive diagnoses and of unnecessary surgical operations."[10]

How can many experts be so enthusiastic about mammography while Dr. Skrabanek, who studies the same data, is so skeptical? The main reason is that the enthusiasts consider the *relative* risk reduction. Dr. Skrabanek considers your *individual* risk reduction.

Dr. Skrabanek has company. Dr. Johannes Schmidt from Zurich reached similar conclusions in 1990. He emphasized that doctors must do many mammograms to benefit one woman. In an analysis of another large study, Dr. Schmidt concluded that doctors must do 7,000 screening mammographies to prevent one breast cancer death. For each prevented breast cancer death, about 170 women suffered anxiety caused by false-positive tests and about 30 women learned their diagnosis earlier than they would have had they discovered the tumor by self-exam.[11] In his analysis, learning the diagnosis early did not change the course of the disease. This conclusion is different from the conclusion of Dr. Mandelblatt and colleagues.

Let's look more closely at the implication of the analyses of Drs. Schmidt and Skrabanek.

Assume 7,000 women have mammograms. Of the 7,000 mammograms, 200 will be positive. Of these 200, 30 will be true-positive tests (the women with the true-positive tests do indeed have breast cancer).

Dr. Schmidt claims that detecting the disease by mammography makes a difference in the life expectancy of only 1 out of the 30 patients. The other 29 patients do not really benefit from mammography. Some of these 29 patients would be cured even if they didn't have mammograms and their cancers were detected at later stages by themselves or by their doctors' physical exams. In other words, finding the cancer earlier with mammography wouldn't make a difference in the prognosis for these women. Some of the 29 patients would die from the cancer despite aggressive treatment for small breast cancers detected by mammography. In most of these women, the cancer has already spread before the first lump in the breast gets very big.

About 170 of the 200 women with positive mammograms will have false-positive tests. They will need repeat mammograms or biopsies. Some will even need surgery to make sure they don't have breast cancer.

In summary, only 1 of the 200 women with positive mammograms will increase her life expectancy because mammography detected her breast cancer early. In this one case, surgery (and perhaps chemotherapy) will cure her breast cancer.

Let's return to Dr. Mandelblatt and colleagues. When they considered all senior women (not just those they knew had breast cancer), they found "screening yielded a savings of 1.93 days for a 65- to 69-year-old woman and 0.65 days for a woman aged 85 years or more."[8] The value was less for women who had another medical problem (specifically, congestive heart failure).

In other words, if you are a healthy sixty-five-year-old woman, screening mammography will increase your life expectancy by two days. If you are a healthy eighty-five-year-old woman, screening mammography will increase your life expectancy by fourteen hours. Hmmmm. This doesn't sound like such a great deal.

In fact, it sounds like reassurance may be the best reason to get a mammogram.

Let's now consider the harm that mammograms may cause.

Done properly, mammography is a painless procedure for most women. Drs. Inger Gram (Norway) and Suzanne Slenker (Boston) reported "ninety-nine percent of the women who attended [free mammography screening] indicated a positive attitude toward mammography that had not been adversely affected by screening experiences."[12] It appears, then, that mammography is a benign procedure for all women.

Well, almost all women. Some women insist that they will never have another mammogram because of the discomfort they felt during one test. In a letter to the editor of the *Washington Post*, one woman reported the pain she had with her last mammogram. She then asked why the male hierarchy of the medical profession had not developed a similar screening test for testicular cancer.

Many women with suspicious mammograms have psychological difficulties, even after learning that they do not have cancer.[13] There is a psychological, as well as financial, cost to the false-positive tests.

The analysis of Dr. Mandelblatt and colleagues concluded that "the anxiety and unpleasantness of the procedure outweighed the potential benefits" for eighty-five-year-old women with other medical problems.[8]

We generate much needless anxiety if only one woman out of 7,000 benefits from screening mammography, or if mammography adds only a day or two to life expectancy. The psychological cost is even greater if, as Dr. Skrabanek suggests, up to 68,000 screening mammograms may be necessary to prevent one premature death from breast cancer.[10] Even assuming that Drs. Skrabanek and Schmidt are too pessimistic, the message is still the same. The likelihood of mammography changing your future is extremely small. Again, the test does provide reassurance. As we discussed in the last chapter, this is valuable for many.

Let's return to the medical resident and Mrs. Porter. I asked the medical resident, "Don't you think we ought to know how Mrs. Porter feels about mammography before we order a mammogram? Although it doesn't seem like a big deal, her daughter does have to take off a half-day of work in order for her mother to get the mammogram. Most important, she might not even want one. Let's ask her."

I told Mrs. Porter and her daughter that mammograms could detect breast cancer in its early stage but the chance of finding an early breast cancer that we could cure was very small. For the sake of simplicity—and to give the benefit of the doubt to the many proponents of annual mammograms—I said, "at least one thousand women would need mammograms to find a curable cancer that we wouldn't have found without mammograms."

Despite her memory problem, Mrs. Porter understood this concept.

She replied, "Boy, that's a lot of fuss for not much. I just don't see why everyone worries about that cancer and all. My friends worried. I just don't want to get all worried about it. It doesn't really help you, does it? No, I don't want that. You know how old I am, don't you, Doctor? Why are you so worried about me and cancer? No, let's not worry about it."

The medical resident canceled the order for her mammogram. He commented that Mrs. Porter and the experts had different perspectives. Indeed, they did.

The medical resident began exploring the perspectives of other seniors after he told them the likely benefit of screening mammograms. Mrs. Porter's perspective was more common than he expected; many women did not think mammography was worth the inconvenience and cost. On the other hand, many women thought they should get a mammogram once a year.

Mrs. Rosenthal anchored this end of the spectrum. She is a sixty-seven-year-old who had a surgical cure of breast cancer ten years before. Like the woman in the audience I described earlier, Mrs. Rosenthal was aghast that any doctor would even question the value of the test that "saved her life." She thought that without the screening mammogram she had ten years before, her cancer would have progressed undetected until it was no longer curable.

It didn't matter to her if 7,000, 70,000, or 7 million mammograms had to be done to detect one curable breast cancer. In her mind, she was the fortunate one.

Different seniors have very different perspectives. If your perspective is the same as the experts who recommend annual mammograms, ask your doctor to order a mammogram each year. Keep in mind that Medicare pays only for screening mammograms done every other year. On off years, a mammogram may cost you from $50 to $135.[14]

If your perspective resembles that of Drs. Skrabanek and Schmidt, don't worry if you miss your annual mammogram. You don't even need to worry if you miss your mammogram for the next several years.

Are you wondering why Drs. Skrabanek and Schmidt, two male heretics, should influence a woman's perspective about mammography? What do they have to lose by missing mammograms? These are fair questions.

For another perspective, consider what Dr. Maureen Roberts, clinical director of the Edinburgh Breast Cancer Project, said of mammography before she died of breast cancer in 1989:

"We all know that mammography is an unsuitable screening test: it is technologically difficult to perform, the pictures are difficult to interpret, it has a high false-positive rate, and we don't know how often to carry it out. We can no longer ignore the possibility that screening may not reduce the mortality in women of any age, however disappointing this may be."[15]

The largest study of mammography supports these skeptics' views. Canadian researchers reported that mammograms did not save lives in women under 50.[16]

The Canadian researchers have joined the chorus of others who are shouting, "The emperor has no clothes!" The chorus makes us uncomfortable. But if we are to help medicine progress, we must listen.

Flexible Sigmoidoscopy

In 1985 President Reagan enjoyed excellent health and was preoccupied with a sagging economy, the cold war, and the like. He also had a polyp in his colon. Yes, right there on the front of any newspaper you could read about the president's polyp.

Dr. Douglas McGill from the Mayo Clinic reported that "the recent torrent of telephone calls and visits by worried patients asking about colonic cancer attests to the remarkable power of the President's health to stimulate interest in a particular disease. The American Cancer Society is in the middle of a major campaign to increase public awareness of colorectal cancer. The task is surely much easier now than in the past. Most people are aware that an instrument can be used for peering into the large bowel, and this previously taboo topic is now suitable for conversation at a dinner party."[17]

The expectation of colon cancer screening is the same as that of breast cancer screening. Find a cancer in its early stage, remove it, and cure the patient. Is this expectation justified?

Experts estimated that screening persons for twenty-five years (for example, age fifty to seventy-five) reduces the chance of developing or dying from colorectal cancer by as much as 70 percent.[18–20]

Whenever you read a risk reduction this high (for example, 70 percent), assume the author is referring to the *relative* risk reduction. Indeed, your *individual* risk reduction is much lower. In fact, it is less than 0.2 percent.[18,21-23] In other words, more than five hundred people like you must have screening sigmoidoscopy before anyone will benefit.

The value of screening flexible sigmoidoscopy is probably less for seniors over age eighty. Sigmoidoscopy can detect cancer, but the discovery may have no effect on the course of the disease.[24]

What is your doctor or his assistant looking for with a sigmoidoscope? He is of course looking for cancer, but usually doesn't expect to find one in someone who has no symptoms, such as blood in the stool.

He is also looking for polyps. These are small outgrowths of the bowel wall. Doctors call one kind hyperplastic. They don't grow into cancer and they don't indicate that cancer might be present somewhere else in the colon.[25]

Doctors call the other kind adenomatous (or adenomas). They can grow into cancer. If your doctor finds one in the last part of your colon—a flexible sigmoidoscope can cover up to sixty centimeters (about one-third) of the colon—there's a good chance you have other polyps higher up in your colon.

What if your doctor doesn't find any adenomas with flexible sigmoidoscopy? Does that mean that you don't have any adenomas anywhere in your colon? Unfortunately, no. You need colonoscopy to be certain.

Colonoscopy

Experts have different opinions about the value of colonoscopy when flexible sigmoidoscopy is normal. Some reported that colonoscopy detected polyps high up in the colon of 25 percent of people who had no adenomas detected with flexible sigmoidoscopy.[26] In contrast, others reported that the type, size, and number of adenomas in the last twenty centimeters of the colon determine the risk of cancer elsewhere in the colon.[27]

I suggest that if you have no adenomas or small adenomas of a certain type, don't worry about cancer in your colon; your risk is very small. On the other hand, if you have larger adenomas, consider colonoscopy because your risk of colon cancer is higher.

What if screening sigmoidoscopy isn't as helpful as you would like? Should you have screening colonoscopy to know how the entire bowel looks?

Drs. David Ransohoff and Christopher Lang from Yale University recommended a moderate approach that may be right for most seniors. They stated, "Indeed, a case can be made for complete colonoscopic screening, particularly in persons who are old enough to have a large polyp or an early-stage cancer but young enough to benefit from early detection. One plausible approach might be to perform a single colonoscopy at the age of 60 or 65. If no adenoma or cancer is found, the person may be considered to have a very low risk of subsequent cancer and to need little or no follow-up."[28]

This sounds reasonable to me.

Assume you and President Reagan have at least one health problem in common. You have a polyp removed. What kind of follow-up should you have?

Many gastroenterologists have recommended annual colonoscopy or at least colonoscopy every other year. Is this close follow-up really worth it?

Dr. Ransohoff and colleagues concluded that up to "1,131 colonoscopies would be required to prevent one death from cancer, incurring 2.3 perforations [rupture through the colon wall], 0.17 perforation-related deaths, and physician costs of $331,000."[29] In other words, annual colonoscopy is very unlikely to benefit you.

Recent recommendations from experts suggest that if you have a polyp removed, you should wait three years to have another colonoscopy.[30] If the follow-up colonoscopy is negative, you can wait five years to have a repeat colonoscopy.[31]

Barium Enema

An alternative to sigmoidoscopy and colonoscopy is the barium enema. Studies demonstrating the value of screening barium enemas are as flawed as the studies of sigmoidoscopy.

Dr. Douglas McGill wrote, "Radiology of the colon or barium enema studies and colonoscopy are largely competitive (but frequently complementary) procedures. The literature of the last 10 years is replete with studies that have compared the relative merits of each of these techniques. In general, such studies are seriously flawed because they tend to be conducted by highly skilled advocates of one procedure, and [inadequate] methods of analysis are often used."[17]

Dr. McGill is correct. If a study reports that barium enema is the superior procedure, you can bet that the authors are radiologists. Conversely, if a study reports that colonoscopy is superior, you can bet the authors are gastroenterologists.

For example, a study in 1987 reported that "a clear preference for colonoscopy was expressed by our patients in terms of comfort and polyp detection despite higher cost. Time lost from work and post-procedure constipation were significantly less for colonoscopy than for barium enema."[32]

Now, this may be the best study ever done, but you have to wonder. Are the authors gastroenterologists or radiologists? That's correct—gastroenterologists.

Now that you're on a roll, let's try one more. Who authored the recent report "Colorectal Cancer: The Case for Barium Enema"?[33] Correct again—it was a radiologist.

If you are looking for definite directions to prevent colon cancer, consider Dr. David Eddy's advice. He suggested: yearly rectal exams to test for blood in the stool (although these are controversial—see chapter 6); flexible sigmoidoscopy every three to five years for average-risk men and women who are between fifty and seventy-five years of age; and barium enemas (instead of sigmoidoscopies) every three to five years for persons with first-degree relatives with colorectal cancer.[18]

Ultrasound of the Prostate

Doctors can now put a small probe along their fingertip during a rectal exam and get ultrasound images of the prostate. Most urologists and many radiology departments have these instruments. As with any screening test, there are enthusiasts and skeptics.

In a recent review of studies of prostate cancer, Dr. Ruben Gittes from the Scripps Clinic noted, "Some point out that there is no proof that the detection or biopsy of these early [prostate] lesions changes the clinical outlook for the patients. Unfortunately, screening transrectal ultrasonography has been marketed to the public in many cities as a lifesaving procedure."[34]

The Canadian Task Force on the Periodic Health Examination concluded that there is fair evidence to exclude transrectal ultrasonography from the periodic health examination of asymptomatic men over forty years of age.[35]

This test is not worth the extra trip to your urologist or the nearest radiology department if you have no symptoms.

Ultrasound of the Ovaries

Doctors can detect early ovarian cancer by ultrasound, either through the abdomen[36] or through the vagina.[37] However, it is extremely unusual for early detection to help improve a woman's chances of survival.[37-39] Doctors cannot yet justify routine screening for ovarian cancer.

Exercise Treadmill Test

Coronary artery disease (CAD) results when the blood vessels that supply the heart become blocked. Most people with coronary artery disease have angina, a pressure-like discomfort in the middle or left side of the chest. Angina usually occurs with exertion. Some people have it at rest. Some people with coronary artery disease may get short of breath but not have any pain. And some people with coronary artery disease have no symptoms.

If you have coronary artery disease without symptoms, you may have "silent ischemia." "Ischemia" means that the heart is not getting enough oxygen. People with ischemia are at higher risk of having a heart attack or succumbing from sudden death, a condition in which the heart unexpectedly stops beating.

The rationale for screening is the following. If you detect coronary artery disease before you have symptoms, treatment (for example, coronary artery bypass surgery) may prevent a serious heart attack or sudden death.

The exercise treadmill test, also known as the ECG stress test, is a screening test for coronary artery disease. In this test, you walk up an incline while your doctor monitors an electrocardiogram (ECG) that runs continuously during the exercise. This test may show your risk for a heart attack.[40] On the other hand, it may not.[41] Either way, it doesn't really help your doctor plan treatment for you.[42,43]

Some cardiologists recommend screening people at high risk for CAD (that is, those with two or more risk factors such as high cholesterol, hypertension, diabetes, and cigarette smoking).[44] However, without any evidence that coronary artery bypass surgery prolongs life for persons with no symptoms, it is hard to justify this screening procedure.

There are several reasons for not screening with exercise treadmill tests.[42,45] First, most people with silent ischemia usually develop symptoms before a fatal event. Therefore, tests can wait until symptoms develop. Second, the large majority of people without symptoms who subsequently die of heart disease have normal treadmill tests. Third, only cardiac catheterization (injecting dye into the arteries around the heart) predicts which patients can benefit from coronary bypass surgery.[42] A normal test in someone who actually has coronary artery disease may give the patient and his doctor false reassurance.

Mrs. Perez, an eighty-five-year-old who had a stress test to help evaluate an unusual type of chest pain, gives one other reason for skipping this test. After "going the distance" on the treadmill, Mrs. Perez gasped, "I haven't worked this hard in fifty years and I ain't gonna work this hard in the comin' fifty years. Why'd you make me do this?"

Well, I thought her chest pain was a good reason. Without chest pain, there's no good reason.

Pulmonary Function Tests

Your doctor can measure the function of your lungs with pulmonary function tests. Many doctors have portable machines in their offices called spirometers. Alternatively, your doctor might recommend that you go to a lung specialist for more sophisticated pulmonary function tests.

Some lung specialists encourage the use of the spirometer as part of the routine examination of all adults. They argue that breathing capacity is as important as other vital functions. Who can argue against this point of view? Why then shouldn't we measure pulmonary function as routinely as we measure other vital signs, such as blood pressure and pulse?

The answer is that we may not need to measure pulmonary function to give patients a message. That message is: stop smoking.

Doctors use pulmonary function tests primarily to detect disease caused by smoking. Doctors should be telling their patients to stop smoking regardless of the results of the pulmonary function tests.[46]

If you smoke and have no symptoms (except maybe a "smoker's cough") and want to know how your lungs are doing, pulmonary function tests will tell you. If you smoke and have no symptoms and want to know what to do to improve your health, then pulmonary function tests are unnecessary. You already know the answer before you even look at a spirometer.

Some people need measurements to make the message crystal clear. Pulmonary function tests will help these people.

Abdominal Ultrasound

Mr. Arnold is an eighty-six-year-old who struggles along with arthritis. Six years ago a doctor asked him to get an abdominal ultrasound. As far as I could tell, the ultrasound was a screening test. There was nothing on his physical exam at that time to suggest an aneurysm.

The ultrasound was positive. It revealed a 5-centimeter-wide abdominal aortic aneurysm (widening of the artery). Mr. Arnold's doctor recommended surgery, but he refused. He did, however, agree to have an ultrasound each year to see if the aneurysm was getting bigger. By the time I first saw Mr. Arnold, his aneurysm was 6.2 centimeters.

Doctors worry a lot when aneurysms are wider than 5 centimeters. There is roughly a 25 percent chance that a 5-centimeter aneurysm will rupture in the next five years.[47] Some doctors think we should worry about smaller aneurysms.[48] The chance of rupture—usually a catastrophic event—increases as the aneurysm grows.

Explaining the risk of a rupture, I asked Mr. Arnold to reconsider surgery. He replied, "Doc, my granddaughter is getting married next month. I want to be at her wedding. If you can guarantee that I'll make it to her wedding after surgery, I'll go for it. If you can't guarantee it, then let's forget it. You see, if this thing in my belly explodes after the wedding"—he waved his arms as if to outline a mushroom cloud—"that's okay. I'm ready."

I got the sense that the time bomb in his abdomen was more my problem than his.

Other seniors do not share his perspective. They would want a small aneurysm, which has a very low risk of rupture, surgically repaired. Small aneurysms are difficult to detect on physical exam. An abdominal ultrasound is an excellent test to detect aneurysms of all sizes.

This test is noninvasive, easy to perform, inexpensive, and does not involve harmful radiation.[49]

The Canadian Task Force on the Periodic Health Examination decided there was no conclusive evidence to either include or exclude it as a screening test.[50]

Dr. Fernando Santiago from Atlanta made a good case for including it as a screening test.[51] First, many seniors have aneurysms. For example, a study from Oxford, England, revealed that 5.4 percent of asymptomatic men aged sixty-five to seventy-four had aneurysms when examined with abdominal ultrasound. In 2.3 percent the aneurysm was 4 centimeters or more in diameter.[52]

Second, an ultrasound will detect the aneurysm in almost

100 percent of people with aneurysms tested. Third, the intervention (surgical repair of the aneurysm) is effective.

Abdominal ultrasounds, therefore, meet the major criteria for a good screening test. We use the test to look for a common disease. The test is accurate. The intervention is effective.

One way to strengthen an argument is to use a military metaphor. The medical profession is full of them. Dr. Santiago adds another. Writing about aneurysms, he stated, "These lesions are silent and deep and lethal, like the U-boats of old (a U-boat inside the belly), and like them they can be found by reflected sound waves and taken out before they torpedo the patient."[51]

There is only one problem with Dr. Santiago's argument. We don't know whether people with asymptomatic aneurysms have a greater life expectancy if operated on than if not. No well-conducted studies have shown the benefits of surgery for people without symptoms.

Screening all seniors may be too expensive for society.[53] A moderate approach is to screen seniors at high risk for aneurysms. These include seniors with hypertension, peripheral vascular disease (i.e., blocked arteries in the legs), or first degree relatives with aneurysms.[54,55] If you are like my patient and are unwilling to have surgery, there is no reason to have the screening test.

Bone Densitometry

Mrs. Frye came to the office for a routine checkup. She asked, "Do you think I need to go to the women's center?" "I'm not sure what a women's center is," I responded. "You know, it's where women get breasts and bones checked."

What could be more clear? I recalled hearing an advertisement for the women's center a week before. It sounded as if a tune-up at the women's center could add several years of pain-free living. Why not try it, especially if it could prevent osteoporosis, one of the biggest burdens of aging women?

Osteoporosis is a big problem. About 54 percent of fifty-year-old women will sustain osteoporosis-related fractures during their remaining lifetimes.[56]

The selling point for Mrs. Frye was the bone densitometer, an instrument that measures the density of bone (I'll address this more in chapter 10). If your bone is dense, your risk of fracturing your backbone or hip is low. If your bone is not dense, your risk is high. Knowledge of your risk should help you decide whether to take calcium, estrogen, or other medicines to help strengthen bones and prevent fractures.

Some experts believe that the only way to know a woman's risk of fractures is with bone densitometry.[57,58] Many studies have confirmed that low bone density predicts fractures.[59–62] Nevertheless, other experts have too much doubt about bone densitometry to recommend it for all senior women.[63–65]

The real question is, Do you need to know your bone density to decide whether or not to take estrogen or other medicines to strengthen bones and prevent fractures?

It depends on how you view the benefits and burdens of these medicines. I will discuss their value in chapter 10. If you think these medicines are worthwhile, don't bother with bone densitometry. Take the medicines.

If the burdens of these medicines outweigh their benefits for you, don't bother with bone densitometry. You won't take the medicines anyway.

If you are on the fence, think about bone densitometry. The results may help you decide what to do about these medicines.[66]

But I suggest you read chapter 10 before rushing off to the nearest women's center.

Summary

If you have no symptoms when leaving your doctor's office, think twice before you schedule a test that may take up half of a day (transportation, waiting, having the test, etc.). These tests are very unlikely to help you. They may just cause anxiety.

On the other hand, they may give you peace of mind if you are worried about cancer.

The value of these complex tests increases if you have a strong family history for a certain disease. For example, if your mother and sister died of breast cancer, you should seriously consider mammography. If you have relatives with aneurysms, consider a screening abdominal ultrasound.

You may have more risk factors than just a strong family history of disease. The more risk factors you have, the more likely you are to benefit from one of these tests.

Before you decide to proceed with one of these tests, ask yourself if it's really worthwhile. The evidence showing that these tests make a difference is sparse. Your peace of mind may be the most important reason to get a test.

Part III

RISK REDUCTION

8

Medicines

Up to this point, I have referred to your doctor as a diagnostician (someone who uses the physical exam and laboratory tests to make diagnoses) and counselor.

Now I ask that you think of your doctor as a healer, someone who provides something to make you feel better or help prevent disease. Granted, that something may be reassurance, a caring touch, or a shared story. For the next few chapters, however, that something is medicine.

The benefits of medicines are risk reduction and symptom relief. Even without these benefits, medicines may help you psychologically.

The burdens are costs, side effects, and inconvenience. Even without these burdens, medicines may harm you psychologically.

Individuals weigh the benefits and burdens differently. You

must understand the benefits and burdens to decide if you are taking the right medicine for you—or if you need medicine at all.

The Value of a Prescription

Mrs. Bowen is a seventy-six-year-old who came to see me two months after she had seen my colleague, Dr. Day. Before greeting her, I reviewed Dr. Day's notes. He had covered everything in his initial visit. I mean everything, and then some. How was I going to improve on Dr. Day's care?

I assumed that Mrs. Bowen was dissatisfied with something about her first visit with Dr. Day. Otherwise, why would she make an appointment to see a different doctor two months later? I figured it must have been bad chemistry.

Was it a personality clash? Did Dr. Day wear colors she didn't like? Did Dr. Day remind her of a banished family member? I decided to ask her.

"Mrs. Bowen, I've had a chance to review Dr. Day's thorough evaluation of your medical history. Do you mind telling me why you didn't keep your appointment with Dr. Day?"

"Of course I will," she responded enthusiastically. "I like Dr. Day. He asked about a lot of things that doctors don't usually bother with, and I like that. And he called me to tell me about the test results. That was nice, too. But you know, he didn't do anything for me."

"What do you mean he didn't do anything for you?" I inquired. I was confused. I felt tempted to say, Are you kidding? Dr. Day spent twice as much time with you as most doctors would and thought about your problems four times as much as most doctors would. And you don't think he did anything for you?

I resisted this temptation.

"He didn't do anything for me," she repeated. "He didn't give me any medicine. Why would I come to a doctor if I didn't need any medicine? My old doctor used to give me medicine for my stomach. What was the name of that stuff? Anyway, it worked for the fifteen years I doctored with him. It was a blue pill. I don't know if they make it anymore, but it worked." She continued to describe other nostrums she had taken over a lifetime.

What Mrs. Bowen was really looking for was a prescription.

She had little time for chatter about preventive health care. Her interest in the possible diagnoses that explained her symptoms was fleeting. She appreciated inquiries about different dimensions of her health. But none of these made the doctor-patient interaction complete.

She wanted a prescription.

If Dr. Day had prescribed a medicine—anything, it didn't have to be something strong—Mrs. Bowen would have thought Dr. Day was a good doctor. Since he didn't prescribe a medication, Mrs. Bowen thought he was inadequate.

I predicted that Mrs. Bowen would doctor-shop until she found a prescription. I wrote a prescription for aspirin, one a day (see chapter 9). Never mind that Mrs. Bowen could get aspirin over the counter. From her perspective, the doctor-patient interaction was complete because the doctor had written a prescription for her.

For every senior who wants to take more medicine, there are probably five (or more) who want to take fewer medicines. One senior who was taking seven different medicines beamed when I told him we could get him down to two or three. Indeed, he looked and felt better after each month he tapered off a different medicine.

Potential Benefits of Medicines

All medicines have potential benefits. The most obvious benefit is symptom relief. For example, your joints may ache and you take a pill to relieve the pain. Or you breathe with difficulty and you spray medicine into your lungs to make breathing easier.

The other benefit is risk reduction. For example, you may take aspirin to prevent a heart attack, estrogen to prevent osteoporosis, or a water pill to lower your blood pressure to prevent a stroke. These medicines don't relieve symptoms, but they may give you peace of mind because you think they are protecting you.

Your assessment of symptom relief is not like your assessment of risk reduction. For symptom relief, you are the best judge of the value of medicines. But when it comes to risk reduction, you probably have little idea of the value of medicines.

Don't worry. You're not alone. A study by Dr. Lachlan Forrow and colleagues from Boston revealed that many doctors don't even know your individual risk reduction with medicines to treat hypertension and high cholesterol.[1]

In later chapters, I will discuss the likelihood that specific medicines can reduce your risk of various problems.

Potential Burdens of Medicines: Costs

All medicines have potential burdens. The most obvious burden is cost. Although insurance programs (Medicaid, Medicare, health maintenance organizations, special senior discount plans, etc.) may subsidize some costs of your medicines, you may still have large out-of-pocket payments.

The costs are particularly burdensome for seniors who have fixed incomes and are taking many medicines. Many seniors take three to twelve different medicines each day.[2–4] These are just prescription medicines. What about over-the-counter products?

Drs. Daniel Everitt and Jerry Avorn from Boston reported that up to 60 percent of seniors' medicines are over-the-counter products and that seniors frequently don't report them to a physician or nurse.[2]

The costs can be high. Most doctors do not discuss the costs of medicines with their patients. Yet costs are very important for most people.

If you're taking a medicine that is twice as expensive as another medicine that works just as well, you should know about it—and then you should do something about it. I'll discuss what to do in the last chapter.

Potential Burdens of Medicines: Side Effects

Side effects are another major burden that receives much attention in the media,[5] in books,[6-8] and in the medical literature.[2,3,9] Side effects are indeed a big problem.

About 12 percent to 25 percent of hospitalized seniors have drug-induced illness.[3] Many senior outpatients attribute new symptoms to medicines.[10]

Side effects are the reason that many medicines made the "do not use" list in Dr. Sidney Wolfe and the Health Research Group's best-seller, *Worst Pills, Best Pills: The Older Adult's Guide to Avoiding Drug-Induced Death or Illness*.[6] I agree with Dr. Wolfe, who stated, "The best medicine may be no medicine. If a drug is needed, the choice should be made by the active and informed participation of the patient with a sympathetic and unhurried physician."[6]

On the other hand, there are practically no medicines that are universally bad. Many patients do better with medicines on the "do not use" list than with medicines on the "safe to use" list.

Mrs. Collins is a seventy-two-year-old woman with anxiety.

She had been on Xanax, a blackballed medicine on the "do not use" list, for three years. Other medicines didn't help as much as Xanax. Believe me, she had tried them all.

One day she was extremely anxious. She told me she had been feeling that way for two weeks. I tried to determine if something new was bothering her or if her Xanax wasn't working anymore.

I suggested she increase the dose of Xanax for a few days. She quickly replied, "Oh no, I can't do that. I had to stop taking Xanax." She then opened her purse, pulled out Dr. Wolfe's book, and plopped it on my desk. "This book said Xanax is bad for me."

Eventually I convinced Mrs. Collins that Xanax was safe for her. It had been safe for three years. She started taking Xanax again and soon felt much better.

In later chapters, I will discuss side effects of medicines only briefly. There are three reasons. First, whenever your doctor starts you on a new medicine, he should mention the most common side effects. (He is unlikely to discuss your individual risk reduction, though—that's why I will discuss this issue.)

Second, a thorough discussion of medicine side effects is a book in itself. The *Physicians' Desk Reference (PDR)*,[11] the *AARP Pharmacy Service Prescription Drug Handbook*,[8] and *Best Pills, Worst Pills*[6] are good examples of these references.

Third, I can summarize the message about side effects with a simple caution: Whenever you have a new symptom, be suspicious of your medicines. A story about a family member illustrates this point.

Mr. McCarthey is a ninety-two-year-old relative of mine who began hallucinating for no apparent reason. Other relatives hospitalized him so he could have the usual tests to sort out the problem. No one found a good explanation.

In three days he had returned to his usual state of good

health. After returning home, he called long-distance to tell me about his hallucinations.

"You know, Doc, something strange happened. One minute I was dreaming about the beaches of Hawaii and I've never been there. The next minute I saw people dancing on the end of my bed—and they were naked. Boy, I'll tell you. It's as if they were right there."

I asked my relative about his experience in the hospital and the tests. No clues. I asked him about his medicines.

"Well, Doc, I haven't been taking anything for years. My ulcer is better, and I don't need my blood pressure pills anymore. Oh, I did have a little cough syrup because of the cold I had before going to the hospital. What was it? Oh, yeah, Robitussin."

Robitussin? No, how could it be? The PDR states that Robitussin consists of guaifenesin and "no serious side effects from guaifenesin have been reported."[11]

Let me report one. Six months later my relative had another rendezvous with the sparsely clad beach dancers. Sure enough, he had taken Robitussin for a cough. The hallucinations subsided. He has had no Robitussin since and has not seen any dancers (he tells me that he sometimes wants to take Robitussin even without a cough).

Be suspicious of *all* medicines when new symptoms arise.

Other Potential Burdens of Medicines

Inconvenience is another burden of medicines. Many seniors need help keeping track of medicines they take two, three, or four times a day. It becomes almost a part-time job when someone is taking many medicines.

Taking medicine can be a psychological burden for some people. Pills are subtle reminders that you have an illness or are worried that something bad might happen to you.

I believe that some of my patients refuse to take medicines as a defense mechanism. They don't want reminders that they have or could have a disease.

One last burden appears trivial, but it's important for some seniors. Medicines can be hard to swallow.

Weighing the Benefits and Burdens

Many seniors want to trust their doctors to make all of the medical decisions for them. They want their doctors to paint the decisions in black and white: Yes, you need this medicine. No, you do not need this medicine. The complete trust in doctors can be comforting and make life a little easier.

One day I saw a senior for the first time and encouraged him to weigh the benefits and burdens of a medicine he had taken for years. Suddenly, he realized that his decision was different from the decision of the doctors he had seen for years. He said, "Perhaps I should be a part of this decision. Perhaps I should be a part of many decisions about health care."

I want to encourage you to be a part of decisions about your medicines. You, not just your doctor, must weigh the benefits and burdens. After all, you are the one taking the medicine. Of course you will ask your doctor for guidance, but you should make the final decision.

I suggest the following guidelines for deciding whether or not to take a medicine.

1. If you take a medicine to reduce the risk of something bad happening to you, ask yourself:
   a. What is the likelihood the medicine actually reduces your risk?
   b. What do you pay out of pocket for the medicine?
   c. Are there less expensive alternatives?
   d. How likely are the major side effects?

e. How many times a day do you need to take the medicine?
2. If you take a medicine to control symptoms, ask yourself:
   a. Is there a medicine that works better?
   b. What do the alternative medicines cost?
   c. How likely are the major side effects of the alternatives?
   d. Do you need to take the medicine as frequently as prescribed if your symptoms are under good control?
   e. Do you need to take the medicine at all if your symptoms are under good control?

When you weigh the benefits and burdens for yourself, you may come up with a different choice than your doctor's.

Summary

Symptom relief and risk reduction are the benefits of medicines. Medicines may help you psychologically even if they don't relieve symptoms or reduce your risk of disease. You are the best judge of the effectiveness of medicines.

Cost, side effects, and inconvenience are the burdens of medicines. Medicines may harm you psychologically even if they are inexpensive, have no side effects, and are easy to take. You are the best judge of the burdens of medicines.

Seniors weigh benefits and burdens differently. You must understand the benefits and burdens to decide if you are taking the right medicine for you. Perhaps you don't need the medicine at all.

9

An Aspirin a Day?

We will start with the most common medicine, aspirin.

The benefits of daily aspirin are: reduction of your chance of a fatal heart attack by 0.1 percent, and reduction of your chance of fatal colon cancer by 0.02 percent.

The burdens include a slightly increased risk of stroke (no more than 0.1 percent increase) and a minimal cost. The major side effect, stomach irritation, is unusual in people taking only one aspirin a day.

The benefits of salicylates, the active chemicals in aspirin, have been know for centuries. In an editorial response to the recent investigations of aspirin, Dr. John Mills from Boston wrote, "In 1763 the Reverend Edward Stone of Chipping Norton submitted a brief letter to the Royal Society in which he described his discovery of the benefit of willow bark for the treatment of ague . . . True, the analgesic [pain-killing] property of willow bark, which contains salicylates, was known by Hippocrates as well as the Indians of North America, but it was Stone's letter that stimulated the clinical and pharmacologic investigation of salicylates . . . By the 1960s, aspirin had become the most widely used pharmaceutical product in the world, with an annual production in the United States of over 15,000 tons."[1]

You can imagine how many tons drug companies produce in the 1990s, when everyone takes aspirin not only to relieve pain but also to prevent heart attacks.

Preventing Heart Attacks

Will an aspirin a day prevent a heart attack? Many people think so.

Three large studies help answer this question. Two are studies of male physicians. The other is a study of female nurses.

In a report of the U.S. study of physicians, the authors reported, "There was a 44 percent reduction in the risk of [heart attack] in the aspirin group. A slightly increased risk of stroke among those taking aspirin was not statistically significant . . . No reduction in mortality from all . . . causes was associated with aspirin use."[2] The British study of physicians revealed no significant difference in rates of heart attacks or strokes between physicians taking aspirin and those taking placebo.[3] There was no significant difference in all-cause mortality. The study of nurses aged thirty-four to sixty-five years concluded that the use of one to six aspirin a week is associated with a reduced risk of heart attack.[4]

Let's take a closer look at this benefit of aspirin. The media focused on the 44 percent reduction in heart attacks. That's an impressive reduction. Who wouldn't want to take this simple precaution, an aspirin a day, to reduce the risk of a heart attack by almost half?

Dr. Robert Kaplan from San Diego explained why the 44 percent reduction exaggerates the value of aspirin.[5] He noted that ten patients in the aspirin group died from heart attacks, whereas twenty-eight patients in the placebo group died from heart attacks. Okay, aspirin appears to protect against fatal heart attacks.

But now consider deaths from all causes, including stroke. There were eighty-one deaths in the aspirin group and eighty-three in the placebo group. What the researchers and media didn't emphasize is that there were actually more deaths due to stroke, sudden death, and other causes combined in the aspirin group.

What if heart attacks, but not other causes of death, are your only interest? Isn't a 44 percent reduction still very impressive? Yes, until you understand that 44 percent is the *relative* risk reduction.

Your *individual* risk reduction is nowhere near 44 percent. It is 0.1 percent instead.

Dr. Kaplan explained, "The chances of not dying of a [heart attack] were 99.9 percent in the aspirin group and 99.8 percent in the placebo group. With all causes of death considered, the great majority of the participants (98 percent in each group) were alive at the time the final results were published."

Dr. Kaplan concluded, "These data hardly justify the bold claims made in the popular media about the life-extending benefits of aspirin."[5]

The Canadian Task Force on the Periodic Health Examination shares Dr. Kaplan's skepticism. They concluded there is weak evidence to use aspirin to prevent heart attacks.[6]

Your doctor, however, may not be aware of the critiques of the aspirin studies. He may just remember the 44 percent reduction of heart attacks and therefore be enthusiastic about recommending an aspirin a day.

Even doctors who have studied the critiques recommend an aspirin a day. For example, Dr. James Dalen, editor of the *Archives of Internal Medicine,* stated, "In my opinion, aspirin therapy is indicated in the U.S. men aged 50 years or older and in women after menopause."[7]

The burdens of aspirin are minimal. One small dose of aspirin a day is very unlikely to cause side effects, and the cost is negligible.

Preventing Colon Cancer

Miss Green is a sixty-six-year-old with rheumatoid arthritis. At one point she was taking large doses of aspirin for her arthritis. She had to stop because the aspirin irritated her stomach.

She asked me if she should start taking low doses of aspirin.

"I've read in the paper that an aspirin a day is good for you. It saves lives, right?"

Well, in some cases, Miss Green, an aspirin a day might . . .

"It wasn't just one paper, Doctor. I saw it in several papers. It was a big study. Looked like aspirin really helped."

Okay, Miss Green, but I think . . .

"I think I should start one a day. I don't think it will irritate my stomach the way it used to. Not with one a day."

I slowed Miss Green down enough to explain to her about her individual risk reduction for heart attacks. I told her what I wrote in the first part of this chapter.

She responded, "Oh, I'm not so worried about heart attacks. I'm worried about colon cancer. My mother died of colon cancer. Yeah, the newspaper said aspirin protects against colon cancer. I'm sure you're familiar with all of that."

No, Miss Green, you caught me off guard. I had to make hospital rounds early that morning. Didn't even get to read the paper.

This was one of those embarrassing moments when the patient knew more than the doctor about the medical literature. The story hit the newspapers before the medical journal containing the study hit my desk.

Aspirin preventing colon cancer? I recalled a different study that reported that daily aspirin may cause a slightly higher mortality rate from colon cancer.[8] But I didn't know what Miss Green was talking about.

I forget how I responded. It was probably something like, "Yes, that's an interesting finding. There may be something to that report. It's a little early to tell. We certainly ought to consider an aspirin a day." Maybe I was even more vague.

I've had a chance to look at the story that made the news. Dr. Michael Thun and colleagues from Atlanta reported that low dose aspirin could reduce the risk of colon cancer mortality by about 40 to 45 percent.[9] This, of course, is the relative risk reduction. Your individual risk reduction is 0.02 percent.

Summary

Aspirin can benefit you by: reducing your chance of a fatal heart attack by 0.1 percent, and reducing your chance of fatal colon cancer by 0.02 percent.

Aspirin might harm you by slightly increasing your risk of stroke (no more than 0.1 percent increase). The cost is minimal. One aspirin a day causes side effects only infrequently.

The benefits and burdens appear to be very small. Maybe an apple a day would do more for your health.

10

Osteoporosis

Fractures are a major problem for seniors, particularly women. Seniors with weak bones can fracture their hips or backbones with minimal trauma. In fact, some people will get fractures even without trauma. For example, a backbone can collapse when someone is just sitting still. Some seniors can fracture a hip just by walking. However, most fractures occur because someone falls or is bumped or hit in some other way.

Many seniors over eighty years old have thin bones. Their bones look like tissue paper on x-rays. Doctors call this osteopenia. Your doctor may have told you that you have thin bones after he looked at your x-ray. This does not mean that you have osteoporosis.

Osteoporosis is a clinical definition. Osteopenia is an x-ray finding. The clinical definition of osteoporosis is that someone has had two or more vertebral (backbone) compression fractures, where the vertebrae (backbones) collapse. The fractures may occur suddenly, causing intense back pain. Or they may occur gradually, causing seniors to lose height and develop stooped postures (the "dowager's hump").

Explaining this condition requires a brief physiology lesson.

Bone is dynamic; it is constantly changing. Some cells tear down bone; others build it back up. Because of this dynamic process, the bones you have now are different than the bones you had a year ago.

If these two processes (tearing down and building up) remain in balance, the density of the bone remains stable. If the processes are not in balance, the density of the bone changes.

After menopause, women lose this balance. Over the years, their cells tear down more bone than they build up. As a result, their bones become less dense. We call this bone loss.

This also happens in men, but to a much smaller extent.

If seniors lose much bone, they are at greater risk of fracturing their backbones or hips. Fractures can be very uncomfortable and disrupting, and seniors rightly want to prevent them. In this chapter, we will look at the benefits and burdens of medicines that prevent bone loss.

Mrs. Allen is a ninety-two-year-old with osteoporosis. Life has been good to Mrs. Allen. Her husband of sixty-five years remains healthy. They have five children, all very successful and supportive of their parents. Their home has a beautiful view of Denver and the Rocky Mountains. They enjoy cultural events and still participate in civic affairs.

But age is taking its toll. After her last vertebral fracture, Mrs. Allen had difficulty recovering. Her fear of falling made her a prisoner in her own home. Eventually, she felt confident using her walker. Finally, she got out for walks. Life looked better again.

Mrs. Allen needed encouragement more than anything else. She needed to hear how much she had improved. I gave her pep talks whenever I could.

One day she shared a psychological burden she had carried since the day of her first fracture. She lamented, "Things were going so well until I first hurt my back. I could go anywhere and do anything. I wasn't like this at all. My husband and I did whatever we wanted. He wonders why I can't get around like before. He doesn't understand why I still need this walker. I know it's my fault. None of this would have happened if I had taken those medicines."

"What medicines?" I interjected.

"Those medicines to keep my bones strong. Isn't that what calcium and hormone pills do? Yes, if I had done a better job of taking care of myself, I wouldn't be in this mess."

Mrs. Allen blamed herself for her brittle bones and fractures. Somewhere she got the message that she could have prevented fractures from osteoporosis. Should Mrs. Allen feel guilty? Could she have prevented her fractures?

The staples of prevention of osteoporosis have been calcium and estrogen, the female hormone that diminishes at menopause. This chapter will outline the benefits and burdens of each of these. In addition, it will highlight the benefits and burdens of etidronate, vitamin D, fluoride, and calcitonin, medicines that doctors use to prevent bone loss in people who have osteoporosis.

A word of caution is necessary. Do not assume that the results of available studies apply to most seniors (that is, those seventy years or older). Most studies of osteoporosis involve women near menopause. These women are usually forty-five to sixty years old. When studies refer to postmenopausal women, they refer to women who are usually fifty to sixty-five years old. Unfortunately, we don't have good studies of osteoporosis prevention in the population where fractures are a large problem —women over seventy years old.

Calcium

Studies show that most older women are in "negative calcium balance." In other words, over the years women lose more calcium from their bones than they gain. Does this have much to do with hip or back fractures? We don't know.

Some studies show that calcium supplements increase the density of bone.[1-4] Does this mean that denser bone is stronger and less likely to fracture? Not necessarily.[5,6] Other studies show that calcium supplements don't increase the density of bone.[7-9] Only a few studies suggest that calcium supplements decrease the risk of fractures.[10,11] One of these studies indicates that you can reduce your risk of a fracture by 3 percent if you take calcium with vitamin D.[11]

An *Internal Medicine News* report in 1986 stated, "Although there is no denying that fractures are an important public health problem in older white women, inappropriate publicity has created a climate in which some physicians have become evangelical in their recommendations for exercise and calcium supplementation. This situation creates 'a setup for abuse,' said Dr. John Meuleman, of the University of Florida College of Medicine."[12]

Is Dr. Meuleman full of sour grapes, or is he encouraging healthy skepticism? I believe it's the latter.

Now let's consider the burdens. The wholesale price of a month's supply of calcium ranges from $2.00 to $6.50. The costs of some brands are three times the costs of other brands. Ask yourself, Why pay three times as much if you don't know that calcium supplements prevent fractures? If you knew that calcium supplements did indeed prevent fractures and that the trade brands worked better than generic drugs, the extra cost might be worth it. With current knowledge, it is hard to justify the extra costs.

Side effects are unusual unless you take huge quantities of calcium. If you've had kidney stones, avoid calcium supplements.

Estrogen

Estrogen is the female hormone that diminishes at menopause. It affects many parts of the body; bone is only one of them. To weigh the benefits and burdens of estrogen, you need to consider how it affects the heart and uterus as well as bone.

Let's first consider its effect on bone. Evidence that estrogen prevents fractures in postmenopausal women is strong. The important question is, How much does estrogen help?

Many studies show that estrogen replacement increases bone density.[3,13-19] Again, we don't know that denser bone is stronger bone. Fortunately, other studies focus on the rate of fractures with estrogen replacement.

One of the larger studies indicates that estrogen decreases your individual risk of a hip fracture by less than 1 percent.[20] Your individual risk reduction is actually 0.23 percent according to this study. In other words, about four hundred women would have to take estrogen to prevent one hip fracture.

Some studies suggest that long-term use of estrogen lowers your risk of fractures.[21-23] The best estimate of your individual risk reduction is 4 percent if you use estrogen for a long time (up to seventeen years).[22]

Women who start taking estrogen after age sixty or seventy may not benefit at all.[19,24] If you start taking estrogen right after menopause, your individual risk reduction is as little as 1 percent (likely) or as high as 15 percent[21] (unlikely).

Lowering the risk of fractures is only part of the estrogen

story.[25] Another benefit of estrogen is the prevention of heart disease. Studies reveal reduced mortality from heart disease for women who take estrogen.[26-28] Estrogens reduce your individual risk of heart disease by about 2.4 percent.[29]

Although recent studies suggest that estrogens slightly decrease your risk of stroke (by less than 1 percent),[30,31] other studies suggest that estrogens slightly increase your risk of stroke.[32]

In addition to reducing the risk of fractures and heart attacks, estrogen relieves menopausal symptoms such as sweats, hot flashes, and vaginitis.

Unfortunately, estrogen use involves some burdens. Estrogen increases the risk of cancer of the uterus. Taking progesterone with estrogen may decrease the risk of uterine cancer. Some doctors recommend that women who have used estrogens should have routine gynecologic surveillance.[33] Surveillance does not mean a brief chat with your gynecologist. It means a dilation and curettage (D and C), a procedure that most women would avoid if it wasn't necessary.

Estrogen supplements may cause a slightly increased risk of breast cancer.[34-36] Some studies, however, report no increased risk of breast cancer.[37,38] The association between estrogen supplements and breast cancer appears to be negligible.

Side effects are a major problem. In one study, breast tenderness occurred in 47 percent of the postmenopausal women taking estrogen.[3] Vaginal bleeding (usually less than the amount during a period) occurred at some time in 52 percent of women who had not had a hysterectomy and were on estrogen.[3]

Many doctors think that estrogen also increases a woman's risk of blood clots, but a recent study shows that estrogen doesn't cause blood clots.[39]

The wholesale price of a month's supply of estrogen ranges from eight dollars to fifty-five dollars.

How do you weigh these benefits and burdens? Drs. Lee Goldman and Anna Tosteson help simplify the decision in their analysis.[29] They claim that your chance of preventing a hip fracture (0.36 percent) is about the same as your chance of inducing breast cancer (0.30 percent) if you take estrogen. These two competing factors cancel each other out.

Your chance of preventing a fatal heart attack (2.4 percent) is the same as your chance of dying from cancer of the uterus (2.4 percent) if you take estrogen. However, the chance of dying from cancer of the uterus may be much smaller than 2.4 percent if you see your gynecologist regularly.

Goldman and Tosteson conclude that if the risk of uterine cancer is indeed much lower with gynecologic exams, the reduced risk of heart disease with estrogen outweighs all other effects on life expectancy.[29]

Women who have had hysterectomies do not need to worry about uterine cancer. If they have no symptoms on estrogens, they have nothing to lose—and something to gain—by taking estrogens.

What if you already have osteoporosis? Or what if you have already fractured your hip and worry that it might happen again? Is there anything you can do to prevent other fractures? The rest of this chapter will focus on four medicines that doctors use to prevent fractures in people who already have osteoporosis.

Etidronate (Didronel)

Three recent studies show promise for etidronate.[40–42] One indicates that you can reduce your individual risk of a vertebral fracture by 5 percent if you take etidronate for two years.[40] It is difficult to determine your individual risk reduction from the other studies, but the authors did find a decrease in fracture rates after only one to two years.[41,42] Had either of these studies been longer (say, ten years), the benefit of etidronate might have been even more striking. On the other hand, the benefits might have been minimal.[43] We don't know yet.

The burdens of etidronate appear minimal. You don't have to take it every day. Instead, you take it in cycles. For example, you would take it for thirteen consecutive days every thirteen weeks.[40] If you took etidronate fifty-two days a year, the whole-sale price of this medicine would be $210. However, for cyclical etidronate to work, women need to take calcium and potassium phosphate during different cycles.[40] The costs of these are usually minimal.

Etidronate had few side effects in these studies, so this po-tential burden is minimal.

Vitamin D

Vitamin D may increase the density of bone,[44,45] but recall that denser bone may not be stronger bone. Some studies show no decreased fracture rate in people taking vitamin D.[46,47]

The largest study, however, shows that vitamin D does prevent fractures.[48] Dr. Murray Tilyard and colleagues from New Zealand studied 622 women who had one or more verte-bral compression fractures.[48] Their results show that you can decrease your risk of a vertebral fracture by 14 percent if you take vitamin D.

The dose of vitamin D used in this study (50,000 interna-tional units twice a day) was much higher than the dose you might take in your multiple vitamin pills. The dose in your vita-min pill is probably only 400 international units.

The wholesale prices for a month's supply of the higher doses of vitamin D are as follows: Engocalciferol 50,000 units, three dollars for generic and seventeen dollars for the trade brand.

Vitamin D has very few side effects.[48] You want to avoid high doses of vitamin D if you've had kidney stones.

Fluoride

We once thought fluoride had a lot of promise because it could build up bone. Dr. Lawrence Riggs from the Mayo Clinic has reminded us to be suspicious about bigger bones. He stated, "Fluoride is the only agent stimulating bone formation that consistently produces large gains in vertebral mass, but there is controversy about whether fluoride-treated bone has normal strength."[5]

A study by Dr. Riggs and colleagues shows that fluoride did not prevent fractures in women with osteoporosis. It did cause a lot of side effects.[49]

You should use fluoride for your teeth, not for your bones.

Calcitonin (Calcimar)

In the mid- to late 1980s I couldn't open a medical journal without seeing an advertisement featuring a certain older woman. She had a stooped posture and appeared to be in pain. The advertisement suggested that a shot of calcitonin would make her feel better and prevent fractures.

I'm sure many doctors believed it. I did. Then I looked a little closer.

The company that produced calcitonin based this massive marketing campaign on one study published in 1984.[50] Would you believe that the same company funded the study? You might expect that this study would show that calcitonin helped to prevent fractures.

Guess again. There was no difference in fracture rates between women who took calcitonin and those who did not.

How about the burdens of calcitonin? This medicine has to

be taken as a shot (often painful) or as a nose spray.[51] The wholesale price for a month's supply is about $160.

Summary

Evidence that calcium supplements prevent fractures is sparse. Costs are reasonable. Side effects are rare.

If you are fifty to sixty years old, there is roughly a 1 percent chance that estrogen will strengthen your bones and thus prevent fractures. If you start to take estrogen when you are older, there is probably less than a 1 percent chance that estrogen will prevent fractures. On the other hand, there is a 2 to 3 percent chance that estrogen will prevent heart attacks. There is less than a 1 percent chance that you will develop cancer of the breast or uterus from taking estrogen.

Costs of estrogens are reasonable. You can take estrogen three different ways. Side effects are frequent. In some women, they are mild; in others, they are very bothersome.

If you have osteoporosis, consider taking etidronate and vitamin D. You have a 5 to 15 percent chance of preventing fractures if you take one of these medicines. Costs are reasonable. Side effects are infrequent.

Forget fluoride.

If you have severe osteoporosis and are at the end of your rope, consider calcitonin. It might help a little, but it is inconvenient (sometimes painful) and expensive.

11

Hypertension

Hypertension (high blood pressure) is the most common reason for patients in the U.S. to see a doctor and to receive medicines.[1]

The major risks of hypertension—stroke and heart attacks—are well known. But hypertension also causes kidney failure and damage to large and small blood vessels throughout the body. Many doctors have called hypertension the "silent killer" because it usually does not cause symptoms.

People with hypertension want to lower their blood pressure so they can reduce their risk of strokes, heart attacks, kidney failure, and blood vessel disease. This chapter will focus on the benefits and burdens of lowering blood pressure.

Mrs. Thomas is an eighty-three-year-old who readily admits that she is always anxious. She has hypertension. One medicine has controlled this for years. I saw her one Thursday morning; she was fine except for her usual worries.

"Do you need a refill of your medicine, Mrs. Thomas?" I asked before saying good-bye.

"No, I'm all set, Doctor," she replied. She felt relieved that I had asked about one of her concerns. "You know I wouldn't let those run out."

Yes, I did know that. But this time she and I were both wrong. She ran out of her medicine on Saturday. I was not on call that weekend.

On Monday morning, my colleague, the doctor who had been on call, reported that Mrs. Thomas had called four times over the weekend. "She thought she was having a stroke," he told me.

My heart sank. Strokes are bad enough for anyone. It would be devastating for Mrs. Thomas. "Did she have one?" I asked, fearing the answer.

"No, she was just worrying," he reassured me.

I saw Mrs. Thomas at her life-care community later that morning. She looked the same. I could see that she was eager to tell a story.

"Doctor, you don't know what kind of weekend I've had. I thought I was going to have a stroke. It was awful! I ran out of my medicine on Saturday. I don't know how it happened. It was just awful. I tried to call you but you weren't on call. I called Dr. Martin because I knew I had to get the medicine. Well, I finally got it this morning. Do you know how close I came to having a stroke? My daughter checked my blood pressure on Sunday afternoon. It was already up to one hundred and seventy. And then yesterday, Doctor, it was just awful."

After pausing to take an extra breath, Mrs. Thomas stared at me and exclaimed, *"One hundred and ninety!* Yesterday it was one hundred and ninety. Doctor, I thought it was all over. We have to check it this morning. I know it's better because I got the medicine this morning."

She was right. It was lower. Was I ever relieved when I read 150. Mrs. Thomas sighed as if I had just said, Good news, Mrs. Thomas. Our diagnosis was wrong. You don't have cancer.

Mrs. Thomas worries more than the average senior. However, many seniors share some of her beliefs about high blood pressure.

First, she believed that she would very likely have a stroke if her blood pressure rose above a certain level. Second, she believed she wouldn't have a stroke if her blood pressure remained below a certain level. Third, she believed her blood pressure was lower only because she had taken her medicine.

In summary, she believed the myth that her medicine would save her from a stroke.

History of Antihypertensives

Some history is necessary to understand why Mrs. Thomas and so many others fervently believe in the power of medicines that lower blood pressure. Doctors call these medicines antihypertensives.

A provocative essay, "The Evolution of Antihypertensive Therapy" by Drs. Ichiro Kawachi and Nicholas Wilson from New Zealand,[2] reveals insights about the medical profession and the pharmaceutical industry that apply to many areas of health care.

Doctors recognized the risks associated with hypertension in 1925. Drug companies introduced antihypertensives in the

1950s. These medicines were extremely effective in treating malignant hypertension, the severe type of hypertension that causes acute medical problems.

If antihypertensives worked so well for malignant hypertension, why not try them for lesser degrees of the disease? Kawachi and Wilson wrote, "After all, studies of the natural history of raised blood pressure, including the Framingham Heart Study, had shown that the risk of death rose steadily from the lowest to the highest levels of blood pressure. Reflecting on the implications of their study, the Framingham investigators wrote in 1972: 'The usual medical practice focuses on the treatment of ill people, [however] the prevention of cardiovascular diseases may actually require the evolution of a new breed of physicians . . . Such practitioners must come to regard the occurrence of stroke, coronary heart disease, congestive heart failure and peripheral vascular disease . . . as a medical failure rather than the starting point of medical treatment.' "[2]

In 1972 the National Heart and Blood Pressure Education Programme began a massive campaign to educate the American public about the risks of hypertension. The "new breed of physicians" were encouraged to treat lower and lower degrees of hypertension.

Kawachi and Wilson continued, "By 1980 the pharmacological treatment of hypertension, even at the lowest levels of elevation, had attained the status of a 'standard procedure.' The Joint National Committee report, published in that year, recommended that all patients with diastolic blood pressures above 90 mmHg ought to be treated, 'even in uncomplicated' cases. Defined in this way, nearly 20–30% of the population in many Western countries now had levels of blood pressure requiring drug treatment."[2]

The medical profession willingly accepted the arbitrary cutoff, which suggested that people with diastolic blood pressure above 90 mmHg had disease and that people with diastolic blood pressure below 90 mmHg did not have disease.

This arbitrary cutoff created the demand for medical treatment and for a supply of drugs to treat hypertension.[2]

Several large studies in the 1970s and 1980s, all of which had major flaws, supported the recommendation to treat diastolic blood pressures above 90 mmHg. Without analyzing these studies, you can assume they reported *relative* risk reductions and thus exaggerated the value of antihypertensives for individuals.

Researchers from England published the largest study with a good design, the British Medical Research Council (MRC) study,[3] in 1985. Kawachi and Wilson called that a "watershed year" for reopening the debate about the benefits of antihypertensives.

Kawachi and Wilson summarized the results of this study. "The MRC trial concluded that, on average, 850 patients with mild hypertension would need to be treated for a year to prevent one stroke. Furthermore, there was no overall difference in total mortality or coronary heart disease incidence between the placebo and active treatment groups."[2]

Debates about the value of treating mild hypertension have raged ever since. The latest consensus suggests that individuals with "high normal" blood pressure (that is, systolic blood pressure between 130 and 139 mmHg or diastolic blood pressure between 85 and 89 mmHg) should take measures to reduce their blood pressure.[4-6]

According to Kawachi and Wilson, "The persistence of an established procedure has often little to do with its intrinsic worth, but is dependent on the power of the interests that sponsor and maintain it . . . Rather than question the intrinsic value of treating mild hypertension, the medical profession has diverted attention towards the need to develop more effective drugs with fewer side effects."[2]

The pharmaceutical industry is of course very interested in hypertension. Imagine 20 to 30 percent of the population taking a medicine to lower blood pressure. Profits for most drug companies would be handsome indeed.

Don't get me wrong. Drug companies greatly contribute to health care and medical advances. They invest large sums in research and development. They educate practitioners. And they provide medicines to people who might otherwise be unable to afford them.

However, you must recognize the strong influence drug companies have on the practice of medicine. Kawachi and Wilson noted, "Several studies have indicated that a physician's prescribing behavior is directly influenced by the promotional activities of drug companies, which include the use of sales representatives, direct mailings, the donation of free drug samples, advertising in medical journals and sponsorship of seminars and conferences."[2]

These are strong influences indeed.

Drug companies try to convince doctors that their product is best because it either is more effective, is easier to use (for example, is taken once a day instead of twice a day), is less expensive, or has fewer side effects. As Kawachi and Wilson noted, "There has been increasing attention paid by the industry to 'quality of life' issues in drug therapy. The result has been to divert attention away from the more fundamental question of whether current practice is justified in the first place."[2]

The more basic question can be answered by the one group that has been excluded from the debate. That group consists of you, the consumers.

If your decision to take antihypertensives is to be truly informed, you must first understand the benefits and burdens.[7]

Benefits of Lowering Blood Pressure

A recent study by Dr. Stephen MacMahon (United Kingdom) and colleagues summarizes the benefits of lowering blood pressure. They analyzed all of the large studies together, for a total of 37,000 people.

They report the *relative* risk reduction from lowering blood pressure. If a group of people lower their diastolic blood pressures by 5 mmHg, they will have 34 percent fewer strokes and 21 percent fewer heart attacks. If they lower their diastolic blood pressures by 7.5 mmHg, they will have 46 percent fewer strokes and 29 percent fewer heart attacks. And if they lower their diastolic blood pressures by 10 mmHg, they will have 56 percent fewer strokes and 37 percent fewer heart attacks.[8]

No wonder there has been a massive campaign to reduce blood pressure. Keep in mind, however, that the relative risk reductions are much more impressive than your individual risk reduction.

What is the chance that you can prevent a stroke or heart attack if you lower your blood pressure with medicine? Let's look at the few studies that have focused on seniors.

The largest and most eagerly awaited is the Systolic Hypertension in the Elderly Program (SHEP). The SHEP Cooperative Research Group studied 4,736 persons with hypertension aged sixty years and older. According to this study, you can decrease your individual risk of a stroke by 3 percent if you lower your blood pressure with medicine. You can decrease your individual risk of a heart attack by 1.5 percent if you lower your blood pressure with medicine.[9] It is likely that the benefit would have been greater if the study had been longer (for example, ten years instead of five).

The European Working Party on High Blood Pressure in

the Elderly is another large study that sheds light on the value of antihypertensives for seniors. This study found that the overall mortality rate was no different between the active treatment group and the placebo group. The mortality rate from heart attacks and strokes alone was lower in the treatment group (12.0 percent after seven years) than in the placebo group (18.4 percent).[10]

According to this study, you can decrease your individual risk of a fatal heart attack or stroke by 6.4 percent if you lower your blood pressure with medicines. On the other hand, you would increase your individual risk of dying from something else (participants in this study died from illnesses other than heart attack and stroke) by 6 percent if you took medicine to lower your blood pressure.

The study-with-the-best-name award goes to the Swedish Trial in Old Patients with Hypertension (STOP-Hypertension). According to this study, you can decrease your individual risk of a stroke by 3 percent if you take medicine to lower your blood pressure. You can decrease your individual risk of a heart attack by less than 1 percent if you take medicine to lower your blood pressure.[11]

The most recent study, the Medical Research Council Trial of Treatment of Hypertension in Older Adults, confirmed the results of the previous three studies. According to this study, you can decrease your individual risk of stroke by 2.7 percent if you take medicine to lower your blood pressure. You can decrease your individual risk of heart attack by 2.4 percent.[12]

The four studies reviewed here used good old-fashioned medicines in the treatment groups. These included diuretics (water pills) and a class of medicines called beta-blockers.

Doctors commonly use newer medicines to treat hypertension. We know that the newer medicines are as effective in reducing blood pressure,[13–15] but we don't know if they protect better against stroke or heart attacks than the older medicines. Large studies of the newer medicines for seniors haven't been done.

In summary, antihypertensives do prevent strokes and heart attacks. Although your chance of preventing a stroke is low (1 to 6 percent), you may feel that the benefits are worth the burdens.

Burdens: Costs of Antihypertensives

New medicines are emerging faster than stories about health care reform. The list of antihypertensives is a long one and grows by the month. As of May 1994, there were approximately ninety different antihypertensives.

Doctors divide antihypertensives into nine classes. The costs of medicines in certain classes are much higher than the costs of medicines in other classes. For example, the wholesale price of a month's supply of the newer, more expensive drugs is sixty dollars, whereas the wholesale price of a month's supply of the older, less expensive drugs is three dollars. Drug companies frequently advertise the expensive drugs and rarely advertise the inexpensive drugs. They want us to believe that the supposed advantages of the newer medicines are worth the extra cost.

Does this mean that the new medicines are much better than the old ones? No. They all work, and there is little difference in the frequency of their side effects.[14] Furthermore, there is little difference in the quality of life people have while taking different types of antihypertensives.[16] But drug companies have no reason to advertise medicines that cost as little as two cents a day. The drug companies do much better when people are using medicines that cost two dollars a day.

Dr. Gregory Magarian from Portland really upset the apple

cart in a recent review of a long forgotten antihypertensive, reserpine.[17] I remember talking about reserpine when I was a medical resident. We wouldn't prescribe that deadly poison. A well-entrenched myth was that reserpine causes depression in seniors. I believed the myth.

Dr. Magarian pointed out the fallacy of my thinking. He emphasized that when doctors prescribe proper doses of reserpine, depression is rare and probably no more common than that seen with other antihypertensives.

Dr. Magarian presented convincing arguments that reserpine, a true fossil in hypertension management, is actually as good as any other medicine. He concluded, "Reserpine has many desirable features: 1) it requires only once-a-day dosing; 2) the combination of reserpine and a [water pill] has always been comparable to or better than the other drugs with which it has been compared; 3) it is effective and well tolerated . . . in elderly patients . . . 4) its long-term effect allows for sustained blood pressure control even when doses are inadvertently missed; 5) it has few side effects, including a very low risk of inducing depression . . . 6) . . . is not associated with elevations in total cholesterol; 7) has no adverse effect on glucose tolerance . . . 8) it [keeps the left side of the heart from expanding]; and 9) it is remarkably inexpensive."[17]

A one-year supply of reserpine may cost you as much as a one-week supply of a newer medicine. Other experts agree that reserpine may be the most cost-effective antihypertensive.[18] I'm not trying to sell reserpine. I *am* trying to sell the idea that the newer, expensive medicines may not be necessary. If you're tired of paying twenty-five dollars a month for a medicine that doesn't make you feel any better, think about asking your doctor to consider a change (see chapter 22).

This is especially true if your doctor is a medical resident. A recent study shows that medical residents select more expensive medicines to treat hypertension than do their faculty supervisors.[19]

Since there are many ways to treat hypertension, you and your doctor could consider changing to a different medicine if cost is a burden for you. If future studies show that the newer medicines protect you better than the older medicines,[20] then the extra costs may be worth it to you.

Burdens: Increased Mortality?

Is it possible to lower blood pressure too much? Could low blood pressure lead to increased mortality? Although none of the large studies of antihypertensives reach this conclusion, some other studies suggest that overzealous treatment of hypertension may be unhealthy.

Several studies suggest that low blood pressures lead to increased mortality.[21-23] These findings may be the result of the effects of illness and disability in the population. They do not necessarily mean that lowering blood pressure in an otherwise healthy group of seniors will lead to increased mortality.

However, two studies suggest that too much of a good thing may cause problems. People who decrease their diastolic blood pressure below 84 mmHg are at increased risk of heart attacks.[23,24]

Burdens: Side Effects

Side effects are common with these medicines. About 5 percent[25] to 20 percent[26] of participants in studies of antihypertensives withdraw because of side effects. (Of course, side effects with placebo are also common.[27]) Usually the side effects are mild,[28] and seniors are probably no more susceptible to side effects than younger patients.[29]

Since there are so many options for treatment, seniors can find at least one medicine that is effective and causes no side effects. The search for the right medicine may require experimenting with different medicines.

Is Hypertension Really Hypertension?

Believe it or not, you may be taking an antihypertensive and not even have hypertension.

Dr. Norman Kaplan from Dallas, a leader in hypertension research, claimed that the number of overtreated patients is already high and "will certainly grow and become an increasingly serious problem in clinical practice."[1]

How can this be?

First, the one or two blood pressure readings that were slightly elevated in your doctor's office don't mean that you have hypertension. Your blood pressure may have been up because you were seeing a doctor.

Dr. Kaplan notes, "In various surveys, as many as half of those with office diastolic blood pressure above 95 mmHg despite treatment with two or more drugs have pressures persistently below 95 or even 90 out of the office."[1] We call the falsely elevated high blood pressure detected in the doctor's office "white coat" hypertension. Because of the chance of this occurring, don't agree to take a medicine after only one (or possibly two) blood pressure readings, unless your blood pressure is extremely high.

Second, the criteria for hypertension are changing. For example, some groups of experts recommend starting antihypertensives if the diastolic blood pressure is 90 mmHg or higher after three to six months of repeated blood pressure readings and the use of nondrug therapies, such as weight reduction.[4] Other groups recommend starting antihypertensives at lower diastolic blood pressures.[6]

Treatment for Life?

Doctors used to think that someone with hypertension needed treatment for life. Not so. If your blood pressure has been well controlled on antihypertensives for years, consider either reducing the dose of your medicine or stopping it altogether. Many patients do this anyway.[30] It might be better for them to do this with their doctor's guidance.

If you reduce or stop your medicine and your blood pressure rises, you can resume your medicine. You don't lose anything by experimenting. Contrary to what my patient, Mrs. Thomas, thought, strokes don't occur because the blood pressure sneaks up above a certain level. It is the prolonged elevation of blood pressure—years of elevation—that increases the risk of stroke.

Who Should Be Most Concerned About Hypertension?

Dr. Edward Fries from Washington, D.C., a leading expert in hypertension, advises people with diabetes, kidney failure, or other evidence of damage from hypertension (for example, an enlarged heart) to pay close attention to even mild hypertension. However, he concluded that, "Aside from these exceptions, most of which are infrequent among marginal hypertensive subjects, there is little evidence that [patients with very mild hypertension] will achieve enough benefit to justify the costs and adverse effects of antihypertensive drug treatment."[31]

Treating Hypertension Without Drugs

Exercise,[32] weight reduction,[33] and restricting alcohol intake to moderate amounts (approximately two drinks a day)[34] can lower blood pressure. Seniors with hypertension who can achieve these goals ought to consider this nondrug treatment as their first approach.

What about reducing salt intake? Recall my concern about the salt shaker (see introduction). That's what made me wonder about the messages doctors and the media send to you every day.

Mr. and Mrs. Kay are unique. They are both ninety-two and are in very good health. After sixty-seven years of marriage, they are still able to laugh with each other and at each other. One day the levity lifted, and they exposed the underbelly of their marriage.

Mrs. Kay cooks without salt. She worries about Mr. Kay's high blood pressure and does not want to do anything to aggravate it. Mr. Kay insists on using table salt because without it he "can't taste a damn thing . . . and my wife's one of the best cooks in town." She thinks he's setting himself up for problems with his hypertension. He thinks she needs something to worry about.

Mr. and Mrs. Kay were forty-two years old when the salt hypothesis began to emerge in 1944. Proponents of the salt hypothesis claimed that high salt intake was a major cause of hypertension. According to the salt hypothesis, if you decrease your salt intake, you decrease your blood pressure and therefore decrease your risk of stroke and heart attack. Mrs. Kay believes the salt hypothesis; Mr. Kay does not (or maybe he does and he just doesn't want to do anything about it).

Thomas J. Moore chronicled the emergence and fall of the salt hypothesis in *The Washingtonian* in 1990.[35] This intriguing history started in 1944, when a researcher at Duke University found that patients hospitalized with severely elevated blood pressure improved when they followed a rice diet. Another researcher, Lewis K. Dahl, picked up on this observation and surmised that salt restriction was the key. Dahl then showed that high salt intake could cause high blood pressure in rats. But what about man?

Enter serendipity. A friend of Dahl's returned from South America after studying a primitive tribe. Moore recounted, "Dahl wanted to know how the tribe got salt and if they used it. At first the answer seemed unpromising. 'They all carry it around in small bags,' Dahl was told. But the next comment was to trigger a worldwide research program. 'It is used for money, never on food. Too valuable, you know.' "

In the jungle of the upper Amazon rain forest, scientists found that the Yanomamo tribe's people had no high blood pressure. The salt hypothesis took off. Supporters of the hypothesis promoted it with evangelical fervor.

Other studies, however, did not support the salt hypothesis. Sir George Pickering, a leader in hypertension research, studied hundreds of patients in England and found no relationship between the amount of salt they consumed and their blood pressure. Moore continued, "The famous government study of heart disease and stroke in Framingham, Massachusetts, for example, found no relationship between salt consumption and high blood pressure. Data from an important federal survey of a cross section of 20,000 Americans showed little or no effect."[35]

The controversy led to the Intersalt study, which Moore called "arguably the biggest and best such international study ever conceived." This study of 10,079 men and women in fifty-two communities in thirty-two countries revealed "a very weak and minor link between salt and high blood pressure." Moore added, "But when the figures were adjusted for two other known factors linked to high blood pressure—weight and alcohol consumption—the relationship vanished."[35]

Moore suggested that the salt hypothesis crashed and burned with the publication of the Intersalt study in 1988. The medical community, with lightly salted egg on its face, was slow to publicize the crash.

Moore's story, published in 1990, is incomplete. In 1991 the phoenix rose from the ashes. M. R. Law and colleagues from London reported that the association of blood pressure with sodium intake is higher than the Intersalt study indicates. Furthermore, the association increases with age and initial blood pressure.[36] They analyzed studies from twenty-four communities and data from 47,000 people. They did not include data from the Intersalt study in their analysis.

Dr. Law's results suggested that salt reduction may be most helpful for older people who have high blood pressure.

Should Mr. and Mrs. Kay let table salt—or salted foods in general—interfere with blissful dining? Let us assume that Mrs. Kay is correct: the salt hypothesis is true. What is the likelihood that Mr. Kay can avoid, or at least delay, a stroke or heart attack by following his wife's advice?

Let's review a few definitions before proceeding. We use two numbers to measure blood pressure. The top number is the systolic pressure; the bottom number is the diastolic pressure. If your systolic blood pressure is above 160 (for example, 180/80), you have high blood pressure. If your diastolic blood pressure is above 90 (for example, 150/98), you have high blood pressure. One high blood pressure reading doesn't mean much. Repeatedly high blood pressures mean that you have hypertension. The unit we use to measure blood pressure is millimeter of mercury, symbolized by mmHg.

Dr. Law and colleagues claimed that "moderate dietary salt

reduction would, after a few weeks, lower systolic blood pressure by an average of 5 mmHg, and by 7 mmHg in those with high blood pressure (170 mmHg); diastolic blood pressure would be lowered by about half as much. It is estimated that such a reduction in salt intake by a whole Western population would reduce the incidence of stroke by 26% and of [coronary artery disease] by 15%."[37]

Let us give Law and colleagues the benefit of the doubt again. The *relative* risk reduction might be 26 percent or 15 percent. But Mr. Kay's *individual* risk reduction (or your individual risk reduction) is much lower.

Medicines reduce blood pressure twice as much as dietary salt restriction reduces it. Therefore, let's assume that dietary salt restriction will reduce your risk by 2 percent.

If Mr. Kay dutifully follows his wife's advice, he has a 2 percent chance of delaying a heart attack or stroke. He has a 98 percent chance of having no benefit other than pleasing his wife. With moderation (light sprinkles, not handfuls of salt), he could probably please both his wife and himself.

Summary

If you have hypertension, lowering your blood pressure will decrease your risk of stroke by about 3 percent and decrease your risk of a heart attack by less than 1 percent. You may increase your risk of serious problems (probably by no more than 1 to 2 percent) if you lower your blood pressure too much.

Hesitate to take medicines if you've had only one or two elevated blood pressure readings in your doctor's office. If you need medicine to control your hypertension, don't assume that the medicine your doctor prescribes for you is the right one.

Some medicines are very inexpensive. Others are very expensive. The inexpensive medicines probably work as well as the expensive ones.

Side effects of medicines are common. By trying different medicines, you should find one that causes no side effects.

Don't assume you need to be on medicine for the rest of your life. Be willing to ask your doctor to try different approaches. One approach may be to stop taking your medicine.

The options for treating hypertension are numerous. Consider weight reduction and exercise first. By restricting the salt in your diet, you may decrease your risk of a heart attack or stroke by about 2 percent.

12

Cholesterol

There's a good chance you are one of the millions who have checked their cholesterol level in the last year or two. And there's a good chance that your level is higher than you would like. You may have changed your diet in hopes of lowering your cholesterol.

Fifteen years ago few people thought about the cholesterol in their diet. Today people wonder how much cholesterol they are eating with every bite they take. Most food producers and restaurants—even fast food chains—have jumped on the low-fat bandwagon. Almost everyone wants to know his cholesterol level. I recall a ninety-four-year-old who was in excellent health. He came to the office just to have his cholesterol level checked.

High cholesterol is a well-known risk factor for heart disease. Since the prevalence of heart disease increases in seniors, shouldn't cholesterol reduction be a major health concern?

Yes, it should be a major concern for those with a public health perspective. It's possible that many seniors could lengthen their lives or improve the quality of their lives by reducing their cholesterol intake. Studies to answer this question are under way. Recent studies give hope that people with cholesterol buildup in the heart can actually reverse the disease with medication.[1,2] Could the same be true of dietary restraint?

Your question should be, What are the chances that reducing cholesterol will improve my life or increase my life expectancy? What is my individual risk reduction associated with lowering cholesterol?

Cholesterol reduction will improve your life if it prevents diseases that cause symptoms. If it prevents coronary artery disease, you are less likely to have chest pain or shortness of breath as a result of this disease. Unfortunately, none of the available studies report your individual risk reduction for symptoms. Several studies do indicate your individual risk reduction for death when you lower your cholesterol with medicines.

Assume your cholesterol is still hovering around 250. You may wonder if you should take a medicine or modify your diet to lower your cholesterol. You think you'll feel more secure with a cholesterol level below 220. This chapter will focus on the benefits and burdens of lowering cholesterol with medicines and diet.

Mr. Wilson is a seventy-four-year-old who appeared to be in good health. An unusual cough was his only symptom when he first came to my office. Actually, it was a gagging sensation in his throat that bothered him. I referred him to a pulmonologist (lung specialist) and an otolaryngologist (ear, nose, and throat specialist). One of them suggested that Mr. Wilson see a gastroenterologist (esophagus, stomach, and intestine specialist) to make sure the problem wasn't in his esophagus. We were all puzzled.

As we four doctors were scratching our heads, Mr. Wilson gave us a very important clue. He came to the emergency room with severe chest pain. Within an hour we knew he had suffered a heart attack. Enter a couple more specialists.

Eventually a heart surgeon replaced two of the arteries that supply Mr. Wilson's heart. His first two weeks after the operation were stormy because he was bleeding from an ulcer in his stomach. After the ulcer quieted down, he did very well.

We worried about so many other problems that we almost forgot to think about the complaint that first brought him into the office. Finally, I asked, "Mr. Wilson, have you had that gagging sensation that you told me about when you came to the office the first time?"

"No, come to think of it, I haven't had that problem since I came to the hospital," he responded. "I hope I don't have to worry about that anymore," he continued. "What do you suppose it was?"

"It was probably your heart, Mr. Wilson. The fact that you haven't had that problem since you had the heart surgery indicates your heart was the problem. I doubt it will bother you anymore since you've had heart surgery," I tried to reassure him.

"Do you think it all happened because of my cholesterol? The cardiologists told me my cholesterol was pretty high. They want to start me on some medicine to lower the cholesterol. What do you think? I sure don't want to go through that heart surgery again."

I didn't think Mr. Wilson needed to hear about the burdens and benefits of cholesterol-lowering medicines at that moment. And I didn't want to say anything that might contradict the cardiologists. "Yes, I think that would be a good idea. I'm sure we can find some medicine that you'll be able to take without any problem."

One of the cardiologists wrote a prescription for Mr. Wilson. When I saw Mr. Wilson two weeks after we discharged him from the hospital, he was slowly regaining his energy. Two months later he was thriving. The medicine that lowered his cholesterol was the only regular medicine he needed to continue. He was able to get off two heart medicines and one medicine for his stomach.

One month later he returned to my office with a sinus infection. After prescribing an antibiotic, I asked, "Will you need refills for your cholesterol medicine?"

He looked at his wife, who also had elevated cholesterol, and then looked back at me. "Doctor, I'm not sure how to tell you this, but I'm not sure I need to keep taking that medicine for cholesterol." His wife nodded. "I'm not sure it's really going to help me. I mean my cholesterol level isn't that high. What do you think?"

"Well, Mr. Wilson, I'm not sure what to think. Some experts would exhort you to take medicine. Others would tell you not to worry. Let me tell you about the cholesterol battle. Then you can decide if you want to continue the medicine."

The Cholesterol Battle

On one side are the experts who encourage cholesterol reduction for everyone who might be at risk for heart disease. You probably have heard their message at your doctor's office, on the television, at shopping malls, etc. The most recent recommendation from a panel of experts advocates even more aggressive control of cholesterol.[3] On the other side are the critics who say that we've gone overboard with the cholesterol craze.

One of these critics is Russell Smith, author of *The Cholesterol Conspiracy*.[4] Dr. Douglas Vaughan from Boston reviewed this book in the *New England Journal of Medicine*. He wrote,

"This book argues that American physicians have been duped by greedy drug companies and a misguided research establishment into believing that high levels of cholesterol are dangerous and require treatment. The American public is now suffering the consequences of this enormous hoax by having their diets unnecessarily modified, and many citizens are being subjected to unpleasant and dangerous treatments to lower their serum cholesterol levels. Are conspiratorial forces at work? The authors of this book would have readers believe that greed and subterfuge are behind the national preoccupations with cholesterol, and they go as far as to describe it as deception on a Hitlerian scale. . . . Unfortunately, this book is laced with paranoia and hearsay."[5]

Another leading critic is Thomas J. Moore—recall that he is the heretic who said we didn't need to worry about salt in our diets. In the September 1989 issue of *The Atlantic Monthly*, Moore attacked what he called the "cholesterol myth."

Moore's criticisms of the National Cholesterol Education Program sparked a heated debate.[6] I will highlight the arguments about seniors using medicines to lower cholesterol.

Is Elevated Cholesterol a Risk Factor for Seniors?

Moore charges that although elevated cholesterol is a risk factor for middle-age persons, it is not a risk factor for seniors.

Early results from the large Framingham study suggest that elevated cholesterol is not a risk factor for seniors. However, more recent results show that elevated cholesterol is indeed a risk factor for seniors. The relationship between cholesterol level and risk of heart disease applies to persons aged sixty to seventy years as well as to younger persons.[7]

Other studies confirm that the risk of heart disease increases as a person's cholesterol level increases. Researchers found this association in a study of men aged sixty-five years and older,[8] a study of men sixty to seventy-nine years of age,[9] and a study of men forty to sixty-nine years of age.[10]

How much does elevated cholesterol increase your individual risk of heart disease? If a middle-aged man had a very high cholesterol level, he would have a 2 to 6 percent higher chance of a heart attack over the next twenty years than if his cholesterol level were only mildly elevated.[11]

Does this mean that your risk of death is lower if your cholesterol is low? Not necessarily. Some studies show that the risk of death increases with abnormally low and high levels of cholesterol.[12,13] The association between cancer and low cholesterol partially explains the increased mortality rate for people with low cholesterol. It doesn't fully explain it.[13]

If your cholesterol is normal, don't assume you can decrease your individual risk of heart disease by lowering your cholesterol to ranges below normal.

The Benefits of Lowering Cholesterol with Medicine If You Are at Low Risk of Heart Disease

Moore's next charge is that there is no evidence that lowering total cholesterol lowers total mortality. Moore and other critics are correct when considering people who are at low risk of heart disease.

In 1989, Dr. Allan Brett from Boston reviewed two of the largest studies of drug therapy for high cholesterol.[14] Although both studies were of middle-age men who had no symptoms, the results give some idea of your individual risk reduction. In brief, the overall mortality rates were the same in the drug and in the placebo groups. Without studies of cholesterol reduction in seniors, we don't yet know if these outcomes apply to seniors.

In the first study,[15] 9.8 percent of the patients who were given placebo had major heart problems. In contrast, 8.1 percent of the patients treated with cholestyramine, a drug used to lower the cholesterol level, had major heart problems.

Based on this study, your individual risk reduction for major heart problems is the difference between 9.8 percent and 8.1 percent, or 1.7 percent. This means that only 1.7 percent of people benefit from medicine; the other 98.3 percent do not.

In the second study,[16] 4.1 percent of the men who were given placebo had major heart problems. In contrast, 2.7 percent of the men treated with gemfibrozil, another drug used to lower cholesterol, had major heart problems.

Based on this study, your individual risk reduction for heart attacks is the difference between 4.1 percent and 2.7 percent, or 1.4 percent. In other words, only 1.4 percent of people benefit from the medicine; the other 98.6 percent do not.

Dr. Brett highlighted two of the biases that I talked about earlier. First, the researchers, editors, and the media published the relative risk reductions, which ranged from 19 percent to 39 percent, depending on the group of patients analyzed. These are much more impressive than your individual risk reductions of 1.4 percent and 1.7 percent. Second, the researchers highlighted the findings they were hoping for and downplayed the unexpected findings. For example, although patients taking a placebo were more likely to die of heart disease, patients taking a medicine were more likely to die of causes other than heart disease. As I noted above, the total mortality rates, that is death from all causes, were the same in the placebo and drug groups. Neither the researchers, the editors, nor the media emphasized this point.

Some could argue that seniors might benefit more than middle-age men from cholesterol reduction, though researchers haven't established this in any large study. The jury is still out, and we expect some better information in the near future.[17] However, your individual risk reduction is likely to be small.

Several experts reviewed all of the studies that compare the benefits of medicines with the benefits of placebo.[18–21] These experts found the same results discovered in the two studies mentioned above. Medicines that lower cholesterol decrease your chance of having a heart attack (either fatal or nonfatal) but increase your chance of dying from other causes.

Dr. Lee Goldman and colleagues from Boston provide a different way of looking at the benefits of lowering cholesterol with medicine. In their cost-effectiveness analysis, they estimate the number of dollars needed to treat a lot of people to benefit one person. The benefit would be adding one year to that person's life.[22]

Consider men aged seventy-five to eighty-four years with cholesterol levels between 250 and 299. Assume they have no other risk factors for heart disease. The cost to treat enough men like this so one may live a year longer is $210,000. Many seniors would need treatment for many years to benefit one person.

Low-risk men and women (who don't smoke, don't have hypertension, etc.) with cholesterol levels between 200 and 300 would increase their average life expectancy by about ten days if they reduced their cholesterol levels 5 to 33 percent with medicine. High-risk men and women with cholesterol levels between 200 and 300 would increase their average life expectancy by about three years and two months if they reduced their cholesterol with medicine.[23]

Is mortality the only concern? What about people who develop heart disease but don't die from it? Do people who take medicine to lower cholesterol have better health while alive?[24]

It is probably true that they have fewer symptoms from heart disease. But do they have fewer symptoms from other diseases? If cholesterol-lowering medicines contributed to more deaths from other causes (for example, cancer and violent deaths), could it be that they also cause more symptoms such as depression? The studies don't make this clear,[25,26] but the possibility exists.[27]

In summary, if you are at low risk of heart disease, taking a medicine to lower your cholesterol will not make you live longer or give you a better quality of life.

The Benefits of Lowering Cholesterol with Medicine If You Do Have Heart Disease

Medicines that lower cholesterol are more likely to help if you already have heart disease or if you are at high risk of heart disease.[3,28]

Some studies show that medicine to lower cholesterol can actually help open up partially blocked arteries. One study shows that patients who lower their cholesterol with medicine have improved blood flow through their heart arteries after only two and a half years.[1]

Lowering cholesterol is much more cost-effective for people with heart disease than it is for people without heart disease.[22] Consider men aged seventy-five to eighty-four years with cholesterol levels above 250. Assume they have heart disease. The cost to treat enough men like this so that one may live a year longer is $15,000 to $25,000 (much less than the $210,000 for those without heart disease).

People with heart disease can reduce their mortality rate from 6 percent to 8 percent by lowering their cholesterol level with medicine.[21,29] This, then, is the likelihood that Mr. Wilson would benefit from medicine to lower his cholesterol.

The Benefits of Lowering Cholesterol with Medicine If You Have Other Risk Factors for Heart Disease

Many people with elevated cholesterol levels have other risk factors for heart disease. For example, they smoke, have hypertension, or are overweight.

Could lowering cholesterol and addressing the other risk factors (e.g., lowering blood pressure, losing weight, etc.) help prevent a heart attack?

A couple of large studies report very puzzling and disturbing results. One study from Finland shows that multiple interventions in middle-aged men may do more harm than good.[30] For example, more heart attacks occurred in the group of men whose doctors advised them about diet, smoking, and exercise.[30,31]

In another study, doctors prescribed medicines to lower blood pressure and cholesterol when necessary. Overweight participants lost weight. These interventions lasted about ten years. Nevertheless, the mortality rate from heart disease was no different from the rate for middle-aged men who did not have multiple interventions.[32]

The largest study from the U.S. is known as "Mr. Fit" (Multiple Risk Factor Intervention Trial).[33] The first report from this study focused on the first six to eight years of intervention.[34] Mortality from heart disease and from all causes did not differ significantly between men assigned to special interventions and men assigned to their usual sources of health care.

The most recent report from Mr. Fit describes the mortality findings after 10.5 years (an average of 3.8 years after the end of the intervention).[33] Men who had their usual care had a 0.6 percent greater chance of dying than men who had special interventions. The difference is much less than expected.

More Critics
The critics of the cholesterol craze are growing in numbers. Dr. Michael Oliver from London claims that multiple interventions have become increasingly difficult to justify. He states, "This runs counter to the recommendations of many national and in-

ternational advisory bodies, which must now take the recent findings from Finland into account. Not to do so may be ethically unacceptable."[35]

In the same issue of the *British Medical Journal*, Drs. George Smith and Juha Pekkanen go a step further. They propose a moratorium on the use of cholesterol-lowering medicines until further studies show that they produce greater benefit.

They claim "the cholesterol lowering enterprise threatens to turn a large percentage of the healthy population into patients, at a substantial cost to the [National Health Service in Britain]."[27]

For example, based on the guidelines of a new study in Europe (EXCEL),[36] one-third of the population of Britain would be eligible for the study because of "high" cholesterol levels.[27] They also note that in the initial results from this study the medicine group has a higher mortality rate than the placebo group.[27]

The medicine used in the EXCEL study is lovastatin. It represents a new generation of cholesterol-lowering medicines that can lower cholesterol levels by 20 to 40 percent.[37] The medical journals are full of advertisements for these new medicines—some ads run for six consecutive pages. Your doctor can't miss them. Although we have no evidence that these medicines will decrease mortality and disease associated with high cholesterol, their use is widespread.

Recall one of the earlier studies that showed no change in total mortality from lowering cholesterol with medicine.[15] Clofibrate was the medicine used in this study. What has happened to the use of clofibrate since the results of that study were published? It has plummeted.

What about the use of the newer medicine, lovastatin, which, based on the initial results of ongoing studies, is no more effective in reducing mortality than clofibrate? It has skyrocketed.

Drs. Smith and Pekkanen note, "The prevalence of use of

cholesterol lowering drugs in 1988 was about eight times higher in the United States than in Britain. In the United States total prescriptions decreased from the late 1970s to early 1980s because of large reductions in the prescription of clofibrate. Between 1983 and 1988 total prescriptions increased fivefold. The rapid increase was due to the introduction of . . . lovastatin and the greatly increased prescription of gemfibrozil."[27]

Gemfibrozil was the medicine used in one of the other large studies that showed no decrease in total mortality by lowering cholesterol.[16]

Will history repeat itself? Will millions of people take the new medicines before large studies report that these medicines, like their predecessors, do not decrease total mortality?

Perhaps there should be a moratorium on the use of these medicines until researchers prove more benefits. A moratorium is justified if the burdens of these medicines are significant. What are they?

Burdens of Cholesterol-Lowering Medicines: Costs
The wholesale price of a month's supply of medicines to lower cholesterol ranges from $8 to $140. The newest medicines are the most expensive. Monitoring the cholesterol level and liver function (see below) with blood tests may add extra out-of-pocket costs.

Burdens of Cholesterol-Lowering Medicines: Side Effects
The least expensive medicines are unfortunately the ones that are most likely to cause side effects.

Niacin frequently causes flushing. About one-third to one-half of patients who try niacin eventually stop taking it because of this annoying side effect. Cholestyramine frequently causes gastrointestinal symptoms, such as nausea, bloating, and constipation. Furthermore, it is unpalatable.

Side effects with the other medicines are much less common. However, they can all cause abnormal liver function. Therefore, patients who take these medicines should have a blood test three or four times a year.[38] This means extra visits to your doctor's office even though you feel fine. The inconvenience of these extra visits—not to mention the extra needle sticks—may be trivial burdens but are burdens nonetheless.

The Benefits of Lowering Cholesterol with Diet

Dieting is demanding. One expert notes that modest reductions in cholesterol require intensive counseling from a variety of health care professionals.[39]

It's likely that your individual risk reduction with cholesterol reduction—1.4 percent and 1.7 percent in the studies—would be even smaller if the studies involved diet therapy. If you have no risk factors for coronary artery disease, you may have only a 1 percent chance of living longer by following a strict low-cholesterol diet.

The chance of reducing your risk of a heart attack by dieting may be higher than 1 percent (perhaps as high as 7 percent) if you already have coronary artery disease. Researchers from London reported that patients with coronary artery disease were less likely to have a heart attack or die if they followed a low-cholesterol diet.[40] For some, the 1 percent chance of increased life expectancy would be worth the sacrifice of a diet. For others, it would not. You, not the experts who recommend that everyone lower their dietary cholesterol,[41] must weigh the benefits and burdens.

Another question you could ask is, How much time are you likely to add to your life by reducing the cholesterol in your diet?

Researchers from Boston estimated that twenty- to sixty-year-old persons at low risk (do not smoke, do not have high blood pressure, and have a good cholesterol profile) can expect a gain in life expectancy of three days to three months from a lifelong program of dietary cholesterol reduction.[42] Persons at high risk can expect to gain eighteen days to twelve months. Researchers from San Francisco estimated that Americans would increase the average life expectancy three to four months if everyone restricted their intake of dietary fat.[43]

The benefits of restricting cholesterol in your diet appear real. But are they worth the sacrifice? That is a question that only you can answer. Assume that you do want to reduce the cholesterol in your diet. The next question is, How strict should you be?

A step-one diet, that is mild to moderate reductions in cholesterol intake, has little effect on the cholesterol level.[44] A strict diet is necessary to lower your cholesterol. Is such a change in your lifestyle worth the benefits discussed above?

Entire books focus on detailed diets. If following these diets gives you a sense of control over your destiny, they are worth the sacrifice. If they do not make you feel better and are a nuisance, why bother?

Keep it simple. Drink skim or 1 percent milk. Cut down on butter and margarine. Balance red meat with white meat or fish. And eat more fresh fruit and vegetables.

Some experts might claim that this advice is going overboard. For example, Professors T. Ulbricht and D. Southgate from London argue that there is no evidence of a relation between total fat consumption and heart disease incidence.[45] They suggest that doctors restrict advice to eat less fat to those who are obese or who have high cholesterol levels.

Julia Child would probably agree with the professors from

London. In a *Newsweek* interview (May 27, 1991), Child said, "I do not believe in this meatless, dairyless, butterless society." The interviewer stated, "Americans seem susceptible to every food and diet fad," and then asked, "Are you fighting a lost cause?" Child responded, "I hope not. I'm hoping that people will take an adult approach to food. Why do people prefer to believe the latest television ad or the latest scare in the newspaper? It's a childlike approach. Why not take food as an adult and enjoy the pleasures of food because it's certainly one of our most innocent pleasures."

Seniors who have been enjoying Child's gustatory delights for the last three decades would do well to heed her call for moderation.

Summary

If your cholesterol level is high and you don't have heart disease, lowering your cholesterol with medicine will probably not change your individual risk of death from all causes.

It may decrease your risk of death from heart disease by 1 to 2 percent. On the other hand, it may increase your risk of death from other causes by the same amount.

If your cholesterol level is high and you have heart disease, lowering your cholesterol with medicine should decrease your risk of death from heart disease by about 6 to 8 percent.

Older medicines are inexpensive but frequently cause side effects. Newer medicines are expensive but cause very few side effects.

If you take a newer medicine to lower cholesterol, you should have a blood test about three to four times a year to check for liver function abnormalities.

Significant reductions in cholesterol levels without medicines require a strict diet. Your individual risk reduction from a strict diet is likely to be less than 1 percent if you don't have coronary artery disease. It is likely to be less than 7 percent if you do have coronary artery disease.

I explained these benefits and burdens to Mr. and Mrs. Wilson. Mr. Wilson smiled and said, "Thanks, Doctor, but I think I'll hold off on the medicine for a while. Maybe later."

13

Arrhythmias

The human heartbeat is not perfectly regular twenty-four hours a day. All seniors have some extra heartbeats. Most extra heartbeats occur sporadically and cause no problem. You may have many extra heartbeats during a day and not be aware of them. If your heart has extra beats that closely follow one another, you may have palpitations. If your heart has a spell of nothing but extra beats (abnormal heartbeats that come too fast), you may pass out. Worse yet, you may die.

The heart can have many kinds of abnormal rhythms, which doctors call arrhythmias. One of the most common arrhythmias in seniors is atrial fibrillation. Doctors call this a-fib for short.

The heart has special cells that control its rate and rhythm. When these pacemaker cells aren't doing their job, other cells pitch in. These other cells, however, don't have the rhythm that the pacemaker cells have. When the heart relies on these other cells to set the rhythm, the rhythm is chaotic. This is atrial fibrillation.

If you check your pulse and it feels irregular, there's a good chance you have a-fib. If you have a-fib, your heart rate may be fast (that is, greater than one hundred beats per minute), normal (sixty to one hundred beats per minute), or slow (less than sixty beats per minute).

Many people change from a normal heart rhythm to a-fib and back to normal. Doctors say they are "bouncing in and out of a-fib." Some of these people have palpitations when they change from a normal heart rate and rhythm to a-fib. Some never know that they are changing. The people with symptoms (for example, palpitations) should of course seek help to alleviate those symptoms.

What should those people without symptoms do? The first part of this chapter will focus on those people with asymptomatic a-fib. Although the a-fib may not cause symptoms, it may predispose these people to strokes.

The questions are: Should people with a-fib take a medicine that decreases the frequency of a-fib? and Should people with a-fib take a blood thinner (Coumadin) to prevent strokes?

The second part of this chapter will focus on extra beats called premature ventricular contractions (PVCs). All seniors have simple PVCs—PVCs that occur alone and infrequently.

Many seniors also have complex PVCs, for example, three back-to-back PVCs. These may be a warning of much longer strings of PVCs. Ventricular tachycardia is the arrhythmia where identical PVCs follow one another in rapid succession. It may cause the heart to stop beating. Ventricular fibrillation is more chaotic than ventricular tachycardia. It will definitely cause the heart to stop beating. The question is, Can medicines that reduce complex PVCs prevent lethal arrhythmias?

My father is a sixty-seven-year-old retired internist. He has had a-fib for about four years. Occasionally the irregular rhythm causes palpitations. When that happens, he lies down and the discomfort subsides. Infrequently, he takes medicine to slow his heart rate.

One day we had this conversation.

"Dad, have you thought about taking Coumadin for your a-fib?" I asked, realizing that this was a silly question to ask an internist. Of course he had thought of it.

"Of course I have, Don, but I decided not to."

"Why not take it?" I pursued. "Recent studies show that it can help. I mean, it can reduce the risk of a stroke."

"That may be, but I still don't think it's worth it. Not for me, anyway. I've read the editorials in the medical journals. They're pretty enthusiastic about the results of the studies. Still, I don't think it's worth it. First of all, my a-fib is infrequent. I believe the risk of stroke is small with infrequent a-fib. If my risk of a stroke is only one or two percent anyway, how much can I really reduce this risk with Coumadin? And the second reason is that I don't want to spend a lot of time going into the doctor's office just to get a blood test. Those are two good reasons, I think. Oh, I almost forgot the other reason. I've been in too many emergency rooms when people who are anticoagulated come in with serious injuries. What might have been a bruise turns into a serious internal bleed. And I've seen a lot of patients on Coumadin bleed from their gastrointestinal tract. I don't want to take that risk. I may change my mind later, but that's how I feel about it now."

"Okay, Dad, I can see why you've decided not to take

Coumadin. But what if future studies show that the benefits are greater than they appear to be now? Would you reconsider?"

"Sure I would."

Antiarrhythmics for A-Fib: Benefits and Burdens

We call medicines that suppress an arrhythmia an antiarrhythmic. Antiarrhythmics do not get rid of arrhythmias entirely. Instead, they decrease their frequency. Quinidine is an antiarrhythmic doctors use frequently to suppress a-fib. Indeed, quinidine does decrease the frequency of a-fib.[1] But does it help the people who take it?

One study shows that the mortality in the quinidine-treated group is about three times higher than in the placebo group.[1] Thus, although quinidine is effective in suppressing a-fib, it may lead to increased total mortality.[2]

Doctors have used another medicine, digoxin, for many years to control the heart rate in people with a-fib. Just when I thought I could count on this tradition, critics asked me to open my eyes.

Drs. Rodney Falk and Jeffrey Leavitt from Boston reviewed the use of digoxin for a-fib and noted, "It is remarkable that digitalis, and its successor digoxin, have remained so popular for so long. It is perhaps more remarkable that only now are we beginning to realize that some of the firmly held beliefs about the properties of this drug are no more than medical myths rooted in a less scientific age."[3]

If you're taking quinidine or digoxin for a-fib, consider stopping them to see if you feel any different without these medicines.

A newer antiarrhythmic, amiodarone, may be a good choice for treating chronic a-fib. Recent studies suggest that low dose amiodarone decreases your risk of death by about 3 percent and causes few side effects.[4] Amiodarone is a medicine that doctors have used in higher doses for more serious arrhythmias. I expect it will take some time for most primary care doctors to feel comfortable using it for a-fib.

Blood Thinners for A-Fib: Benefits

The reason your doctor may prescribe warfarin (Coumadin), a blood thinner, for a-fib is that you are more likely to form a blood clot in your heart if you have a-fib. The blood clot can break off and go to your brain, causing a stroke. If you take a blood thinner, this may decrease the chance that you will form a blood clot. Doctors call the process of thinning the blood with medicine anticoagulation.

How great is the risk of stroke in people who have a-fib? It depends on your age and other risk factors. Some experts believe the risk is very low for people under age sixty with a-fib and no other heart disease.[5]

Others believe it is higher.[6] For example, there may be a fivefold increase in stroke incidence in people with a-fib who do not have rheumatic heart disease (problems with heart valves from rheumatic fever) and a seventeenfold increase in stroke incidence in people with rheumatic heart disease.[7]

The risk is higher in people who have hypertension, congestive heart failure, a history of previous blood clots,[8] or a history of previous heart attacks.[9]

The overall mortality rate for people who have a-fib is about twice that of the mortality rate for people without a-fib.[10] In summary, most studies show that the risk of stroke is higher in people with a-fib.

If you have a-fib, the question that concerns you is, Does anticoagulation (that is, taking warfarin) decrease your risk of stroke? A related question is, Does aspirin reduce your risk of stroke? Aspirin affects platelets, the blood cells that promote blood clots. Since aspirin makes the platelets less likely to stick together, it can decrease the chance of forming blood clots.

Four large studies have reported the value of warfarin in preventing strokes.[11] These studies show that you can reduce your individual risk of stroke by 2 to 5 percent if you take Coumadin.[12–15] However, the risk of serious bleeding, the major side effect with anticoagulation, is about 1 to 2 percent higher for people taking Coumadin.

Aspirin may be safer because it doesn't cause as much significant bleeding. One study shows that you can reduce your individual risk of stroke by 3 percent if you have a-fib and take aspirin.[12] However, it doesn't appear that seniors over age seventy-five will get this benefit.[16]

Dr. John Cairns from Ontario summarized these studies in the following way. "A patient over the age of 50 years with chronic atrial fibrillation has an annual stroke risk in the range of 5%, and this may be substantially reduced with a conservative-dose warfarin regimen. The risk of bleeding with such regimens is low, the absolute increment of major bleeding being under 1% per year, and of fatal bleeding much lower. Hence, for every 1,000 patients treated with warfarin, the expectation is prevention of 15–50 occurrences [of stroke] at a cost of about 5 major bleeds per year. The risk/benefit ratio appears to be very much in favor of warfarin therapy although persisting [bleeding] risk necessitates prudent institution of such therapy."[17]

Blood Thinners for A-Fib: Burdens

The wholesale price for a month's supply of Coumadin (2.5 mg a day, a common dose) is twenty dollars. Depending on your insurance, you may have extra out-of-pocket costs for the frequent laboratory tests that are necessary to monitor your blood.

You might consider frequent trips to the doctor's office for blood tests a burden. On the other hand, you might consider the protection you get a benefit.[18] If the results of your blood test have been stable, you probably don't need to have a blood test more often than once every two months. If you need adjustments in your dose of medicine, you may need blood tests as frequently as once a week.

Antiarrhythmics to Prevent Sudden Death: Benefits?

Sudden death is the term doctors use to describe a sudden, unexpected death. When a healthy man falls over on the golf course and stops breathing, he has sudden death. Occasionally sudden death results from a massive blood clot in the lung. More frequently sudden death results from an arrhythmia, such as ventricular tachycardia or ventricular fibrillation. Is there any way you can prevent sudden death? In other words, can you prevent lethal arrhythmias?

Doctors have assumed that people with frequent PVCs are more likely to have sudden death. Therefore, people with frequent PVCs seem like the best candidates for preventive measures.

Is our assumption correct? Are people with asymptomatic PVCs at increased risk for sudden death?

One large study shows that people with PVCs and no symptoms are not at increased risk of sudden death.[19] But let's assume that people with frequent PVCs are at increased risk of sudden death despite the results of this study. Could they lower their risk of sudden death to that of the general population by suppressing their PVCs?

The most important study addressing this question is the Cardiac Arrhythmia Suppression Trial (CAST). The results of CAST were very surprising to the medical community.[20]

CAST evaluated the effect of three antiarrhythmics (flecainide, encainide, and moricizine) in patients with asymptomatic or mildly symptomatic ventricular arrhythmia after heart attacks. Everyone expected some benefit from these medicines; they just didn't know how much to expect.

Everyone was mistaken. In 1989 the authors reported that patients on antiarrhythmics had a higher mortality rate than patients taking placebo.[20] Because of these surprising results, the researchers prematurely stopped the part of the study involving encainide and flecainide.

In an editorial response to the CAST report, Dr. Jeremy Ruskin from Boston advised doctors to reserve judgment on antiarrhythmics until we knew the results of the part of the study involving moricizine.[21]

It doesn't appear that moricizine will fare much better than the other two antiarrhythmics. Moricizine is ineffective in suppressing sustained ventricular arrhythmias—and actually makes some rhythms worse—in patients with heart disease who do not respond to other medicines.[22,23]

Okay, so the new medicines aren't the wonder drugs we had hoped for. What about the older medicines, quinidine and procainamide? These medicines probably make no difference for seniors with heart disease and ventricular arrhythmias.[24]

The lesson is clear. If you have PVCs and no symptoms, be reluctant to start a medicine to suppress those extra heartbeats.

Antiarrhythmics for Symptomatic Arrhythmias

Let's assume you have symptoms, such as palpitations. If you take an antiarrhythmic and it makes you feel better, then keep taking it.

But what if you don't feel better on the medicine? Has your doctor told you that you need to stay on the medicine because your tests show that the medicine decreases the frequency of your PVCs? Keep in mind that tests can be misleading. The frequency of PVCs may increase or decrease regardless of medicines.[25] If you don't feel better on the medicine, hesitate to continue it just because tests suggest that you have fewer PVCs.

Antiarrhythmics: Burdens

The wholesale price for a month's supply of antiarrhythmics ranges from $14 to $160.

All antiarrhythmics have one potential side effect in common: they can make rhythms worse.[26] This is true for the old standbys to treat a-fib, such as quinidine, as well as the new medicines to treat ventricular arrhythmias.[22,23,27]

Major side effects occur in 18 to 24 percent of patients taking the older medicines and in 44 to 49 percent of patients taking some of the newer medicines.[27]

Summary

If you have asymptomatic a-fib, antiarrhythmics such as quinidine may decrease the frequency of a-fib. However, these medicines may also increase your risk of death because they can cause more serious arrhythmias. Newer treatments for a-fib, such as low-dose amiodarone, may decrease your risk of death by about 3 percent.

If you have a-fib, you can decrease your risk of stroke by 2 to 5 percent if you take Coumadin (warfarin) to thin your blood. If you take Coumadin, you have about a 1 percent chance of a serious bleeding complication. The cost of Coumadin is reasonable. The frequent blood tests necessary to monitor Coumadin therapy do not bother most people.

Aspirin may decrease your risk of stroke by about 3 percent

if you have a-fib. This benefit may not apply to seniors older than seventy-five years. One aspirin a day is inexpensive, convenient, and very unlikely to cause any side effects. The net benefit of aspirin is about the same as the net benefit of Coumadin.

If you have asymptomatic PVCs, antiarrhythmics to suppress the PVCs will likely cause more harm than good. This is true whether the PVCs are simple or complex and whether they are infrequent or frequent. These medicines can cause fatal arrhythmias. Costs can be high. The burdens of antiarrhythmics clearly outweigh the benefits if you have asymptomatic PVCs.

If you have symptoms with PVCs (or ventricular tachycardia), the benefits may outweigh the burdens. You should judge the benefits more on how you feel than on the results of electrocardiograms or other tests.

14

Diabetes

Many seniors have diabetes. Doctors classify diabetes as Type I or Type II. We often call Type I diabetes insulin-dependent diabetes, because people with this disease require insulin to control their blood sugar. Insulin shots are necessary because the pancreas doesn't produce enough insulin on its own.

We often call Type II diabetes non-insulin-dependent diabetes. People with Type II diabetes may or may not need insulin. Most do not. They can control their blood sugar through weight loss or with oral medicines, also known as oral hypoglycemics or oral agents.

The pancreas of a person with Type II diabetes produces enough insulin. The problem is that many of the cells in the body don't respond normally to the insulin that is circulating in the bloodstream. Weight loss and oral agents help the cells respond normally to insulin.

If a diabetic's blood sugar is too high, he may have symptoms such as thirst, frequent urination, and fatigue. He would of course want whatever medicine (insulin or oral agents) necessary to control his blood sugar and lessen symptoms.

Diabetics can also have symptoms related to complications from the diabetes. The complications include retinopathy (eye disease), cardiomyopathy (heart disease), gastroenteropathy (stomach and intestine disease), nephropathy (kidney disease), and neuropathy (nerve disease).

Can diabetics prevent these complications with adequate blood sugar control (keeping the blood sugar less than 200 mg/dl)? The normal blood sugar range is about 60 to 140 mg/dl. Maintaining good blood sugar control is not easy for many seniors. It requires frequent monitoring of blood sugar and may involve frequent changes in the type or dose of medicine they take.

Many seniors need a good rationale for committing to this lifelong process. If good blood sugar control prevented the complications of diabetes, this would be the rationale.

Unfortunately, evidence that good blood sugar control prevents complications in Type II diabetes is scant. Seniors who worry about minor fluctuations in their blood sugar are probably worrying unnecessarily. Controlling blood sugar enough to prevent symptoms may be a reasonable goal for many seniors.

Mrs. Samuels has Type II diabetes. Doctors treated her with insulin at one time, but she no longer requires it. She claimed that an oral agent adequately controls her blood sugar. I wondered how she knew her blood sugar wasn't in the 250 to 350 mg/dl range just because she didn't have symptoms—some people with blood sugar measurements as high as 350 mg/dl don't have symptoms.

"Mrs. Samuels, do you monitor your blood sugar at home?" I asked.

"No, I don't bother with that," she replied.

"Did you ever check your blood sugar at home? Or did you ever check your urine to see if you had sugar in it?" I persisted.

"Yes, I used to do it all the time. First, I checked my urine for years. I didn't have a problem with that. Then I started checking my blood sugar. But you know what? I got so tired of poking myself all the time that I just quit. It didn't seem like it was worth it. My hand got real sore after a while. Haven't checked anything since then except when I go to the doctor."

"Would you be willing to check your urine just to make sure your blood sugar isn't getting too high?" I asked.

"Okay, if you think it would help," she replied.

Glucose Monitoring

Should Mrs. Samuels return to the old-fashioned way of monitoring blood glucose with a urine dipstick? Or should she use the more modern approach, pricking her finger and testing the blood with a glucometer?

Dr. Udaya Kabadi from Phoenix made a strong case for the old-fashioned approach by arguing the following.

First, glucometers are not always accurate, particularly for seniors with poor vision and poor coordination.[1]

Second, most seniors with Type II diabetes do not have wide fluctuations in their blood sugar levels. Therefore, there is no need to check for these fluctuations by measuring the blood glucose level on a daily basis.

Third, doctors should not change a senior's insulin dose as frequently as he might change a younger patient's dose. The risk of hypoglycemia (low blood sugar) is greater in seniors who make frequent insulin adjustments based on their blood glucose monitoring.

Finally, urine glucose testing may be as effective as blood glucose monitoring with fingersticks and a glucometer. Dr.

Kabadi wrote, "Since urine glucose testing is simple, convenient, and noninvasive, it may result in better compliance by the patient. Moreover, it is 8–12 times less expensive than self-monitoring of blood glucose. Therefore, we believe that urine glucose testing may be a more appropriate and cost-effective option for routine usage in management of diabetes in the elderly."[1]

Other experts agree that urine testing is a reasonable monitoring strategy for patients with Type II diabetes.[2]

However, some clearly disagree. For example, Dr. John Morley and his colleagues from Los Angeles wrote, "With the [changes in kidney function] that occur in diabetes and with aging, together with a heightened awareness of the need for better control than that indicated by merely measuring urine glucose spillage, it is now clear that there is little place for urine testing in the management of diabetic patients. Home blood glucose monitoring should be offered to every elderly diabetic patient who has sufficient visual acuity and is capable of learning the procedure."[3]

Dr. Loren Lipson from Los Angeles wrote, "Because of the high prevalence of . . . diabetes in the elderly, physicians must routinely screen *all* older patients for disorders of [blood sugar], and must control blood glucose levels in elderly diabetic patients in order to prevent both short- and long-term complications. Even though the diabetes in the elderly tends to be Type II . . . it is still important to control the [blood sugar levels] and to keep them from becoming excessive. Some clinicians are not concerned about [blood sugar levels] in the elderly as high as 300 mg/dl, since 'these people are old and will not live long enough to die of their complications.' This approach has little merit, for it increases the risk of both acute and chronic complications in elderly diabetics."[4]

Is the close monitoring advocated by Dr. Lipson, Dr. Morley, and colleagues necessary? Read on and decide for yourself.

If the evidence is strong that you can prevent complications with good blood sugar control, then you would likely want to closely monitor your blood sugar so that you could control it better. If the evidence is weak, then it may not be worth it to you to closely monitor your blood sugar.

Several caveats are in order. First, there are excellent physiologic reasons to assume that tight blood sugar control will prevent complications.[5-7] However, convincing physiologic reasons don't always pass muster.

Recall what happened in the CAST study (chapter 13) when people with PVCs (extra heartbeats) reduced the number of extra beats with medicine. From a physiologic point of view, it made sense that reducing PVCs would reduce the risk of dying. But that's not what happened. It actually increased the patient's risk of dying. Doctors would not have expected this result based on their knowledge of physiology. A large study of outcomes was necessary to uncover the truth. The same may be true for blood sugar control and diabetes.

The second caveat is that the analysis of diabetic complications will be different from those in preceding chapters.

A diabetic complication is not as easy to measure as events such as strokes, heart attacks, and deaths. Doctors know when a patient has had a stroke or heart attack (and with all that schooling, they can also recognize when a patient has died). These are outcomes that we can measure with a "yes" (it happened) or a "no" (it didn't happen) response.

In contrast, we measure diabetic complications in degrees. It is therefore hard to determine your individual risk reduction from the studies. I won't even try. Instead, I will summarize the studies in general terms. This should give you an idea of whether tight blood sugar control is worth it for you.

The third caveat is that definitive answers are not right around the corner. After reading the evidence, you might think,

"Gee, I'm not sure what to do. I guess I'll just wait a few more years for the good studies to finish so I can get better answers." Don't hold your breath.

Drs. Michael Stern and Steven Haffner from San Antonio explained why few good studies have been done and why waiting for definitive studies may be like waiting for Godot. They stated, "There are remarkably few prospective epidemiologic studies of diabetes. This is quite unlike the situation in [heart] disease epidemiology, where there is an almost countless number of such studies. A principal reason for this lack is the much lower rate of occurrence in the general population of diabetes compared with [heart] disease. This lower incidence mandates that either very large populations be studied or that very prolonged durations of follow-up be used to achieve statistically meaningful results."[8]

Such studies are hard to do. The doctors added, "Population-based, prospective studies of diabetes complications are rarer still . . . To date, randomized clinical trials designed to test whether tight control of diabetes can reduce the risk of complications such as retinopathy have involved relatively small numbers of cases and have given equivocal results."

But there is hope. The Diabetes Control and Complications Trial,[9] recently reported in the media, shows that tight control of blood sugar in Type I diabetes can prevent complications. Unfortunately, we don't know if we can apply the results of this study to people with Type II diabetes.

In short, it is going to be a long time before you will have a lot of good information about reducing complications of Type II diabetes.

Finally, the fourth caveat is that you need to consider another kind of blood test if you want tight control of blood sugar. We call this blood test the hemoglobin A_{1C}. It tells us what kind of control a patient has had over the preceding six to eight weeks. It is more accurate than other clinical information.[2,10]

Type I diabetics who seek tight control may need to follow their hemoglobin A_{1C} levels every three to four months.[10,11] Type II diabetics may not need this extra test because a fasting blood sugar level (a blood test taken after abstaining from food for eight hours) is usually sufficient to determine their blood sugar control.[12]

Preventing Eye Disease

Tight control of blood sugar for only a few years probably doesn't prevent eye disease. The Kroc Collaborative Study Group reported that tight control for eight months (with continuous insulin infusion through a pump) unexpectedly caused progression of eye disease compared to standard control with daily insulin injections.[13] After two years, however, both groups had the same amount of eye disease. The longest follow-up in a study is five to seven years. After this length of time, tight control does seem to prevent eye disease for Type I diabetics.[14,15]

Eye disease is the complication that researchers have studied most. Yet the evidence that tight blood sugar control prevents eye disease for seniors has been woefully lacking.[16] This may be changing. A recent study suggests that tight control can also prevent eye disease in seniors with Type II diabetes.[17] Another study shows that seniors with a high hemoglobin A_{1C} level (and thus higher blood sugar levels) have more eye disease than seniors without a high hemoglobin A_{1C} level.[18]

The best way for diabetics to prevent eye disease is to have regular eye exams by an ophthalmologist. Laser therapy can reduce the rate of vision loss by 50 percent among patients with early eye disease.[19]

Preventing Nerve Disease

Tight blood sugar control does not improve nerve function over the short-term (that is, four months).[20] It may improve nerve function over a longer period (that is, eight months).

Researchers are studying a new class of medicine for treatment of neuropathies. Early studies show favorable but small benefits with these new medicines.[20] The benefit of one of these medicines (sorbinol) appears unrelated to blood sugar control.[21] Therefore, we cannot assume that the standard oral agents will have the same effect simply because they lower the blood sugar.

Preventing Foot Ulcers

Diabetics prevent foot ulcers more by careful inspection of their feet than by tight blood sugar control.

Dr. John Morley and colleagues wrote, "At every visit to their physicians, elderly diabetic patients should take off their shoes and socks and have their feet examined. Although the loss of manual dexterity in older diabetic patients can make this a tedious, time-consuming process, careful attention to the feet of diabetic patients represents one of the most cost-effective preventive medicine approaches. Elderly diabetic patients should not cut their own toenails, as more often than not they finish up cutting themselves."[3]

Preventing Kidney Disease

Control of blood pressure is probably more important than tight control of blood sugar in decreasing the rate of loss of kidney function.[16,22] A couple of studies show that intensive insulin therapy may slow deterioration of kidney function in Type I diabetes.[23,24] No studies have shown that tight control in Type II diabetes prevents kidney disease.

Other therapies may slow the progression of diabetic kidney

disease. These include taking antiplatelet drugs (for example, aspirin) and restricting protein intake. We do not know if these will really help.[16,25] Recent studies suggest that captopril, a member of a class of drugs called ACE inhibitors, prevents kidney disease in Type I diabetics.[26,27]

Preventing Complications in General

Some people who have had diabetes for years do not develop complications, regardless of their blood sugar control.[28] Alternatively, a few people with well-controlled diabetes develop complications after only a few years of the disease. Some diabetics will develop complications because of genetic predisposition. Others do not have the genetic predisposition and will develop complications only if they have poor control of their blood sugar levels.

The important question is, How do we identify the group in which a particular person belongs? Currently, we can't.

In summary, there is little evidence that tight blood sugar control—or even moderate blood sugar control—significantly decreases the risk of complications from diabetes. Controlling blood sugar certainly prevents symptoms. It will probably be decades before we know which Type II diabetics can prevent complications by controlling blood sugar.

Burdens of Medicines That Lower Blood Sugar

The wholesale price of a month's supply of oral hypoglycemics ranges from four dollars to sixty-six dollars. The newer medicines tend to be more expensive. Most doctors agree that the newer medicines are more suitable for seniors than many of the older medicines.

Monitoring sugar in the blood or urine also involves out-of-pocket costs.

If a diabetic's blood sugar gets too low, he may lose consciousness. Before this, he may get sweaty, feel hungry, and become confused.

Patients with good blood sugar control are at increased risk for developing mental impairment before they develop the usual symptoms associated with low blood sugar.[29] The blood sugar doesn't have to get too low before it can affect a diabetic's thinking.

Diabetic Diets

Many people believe that the body responds to sugar the same way it responds to cholesterol. If you eat a lot of cholesterol, your blood cholesterol level rises. If you eat a lot of sugar, your blood sugar level rises. Neither are necessarily true.

The amount of sugar you eat is only one factor in a very complex process. Your blood sugar level depends on many factors, including several hormones and the amount of sugar stored in your liver. The process is even more complex in people with diabetes.

Everyone should watch the amount of sugar they eat for two simple reasons. One, excess sugar can cause tooth decay without good dental hygiene. Two, excess sugar causes weight gain. Moderate gains in weight (five to ten pounds) should not cause undue anxiety. There is little evidence that moderate weight gain adversely affects health in later years.[30] Significant weight gain (twenty pounds or more) is unhealthy.

Diabetics should watch their sugar intake for two other reasons. If sugar intake does cause the blood sugar level to rise, a diabetic may have symptoms. Some patients report that they just don't feel right when their blood sugar is elevated. Most seniors, however, cannot feel a difference between a blood sugar of 140 mg/dl (considered the upper range of normal) and one of 240 mg/dl (a mild to moderate elevation). Some cannot even feel a difference when their blood sugar is as high as 340 mg/dl. The second concern is complications. Does a strict diabetic diet prevent complications of diabetes?

Drs. Francis Wood and Edwin Bierman from Seattle reviewed the value of diabetic diets. They stated, "Dietary management of diabetes mellitus is stressed in current textbooks and articles on treatment of the disease. Diet in diabetes has had a distinguished, controversial, 3500-year history, and through the years, tradition, as opposed to scientific evidence, has had a remarkable influence on the prescription of dietary therapy for diabetes."[31]

One of the traditional beliefs is that sweets are bad for diabetics. A recent review article suggested that this belief has little foundation. Dr. John Bantle from Minneapolis noted that diabetics have traditionally been discouraged from eating sugar for fear of elevating their blood sugar.[32] However, studies showed that simple sugars (i.e., sweets) do not cause greater rises in blood sugar than complex sugars such as bread, potatoes, and rice.[32] Recognizing this, the American Diabetes Association recently said it was okay for diabetics to include modest amounts of sweets in their diets.

But wait! Before storming the soda fountain, consider one other controversy. An opposing viewpoint emphasizes the harmful effects of moderate amounts of sweets. Dr. Clarie Hollenbeck and colleagues from Stanford noted that sucrose, a simple sugar that sweetens food and drink, has been shown to increase cholesterol in some studies.[33] They claimed that this may be reason enough to limit sucrose consumption.

If you still have a hankering for a Hershey bar or soda, please review your individual risk reduction associated with cholesterol reduction. Then enjoy sweets without feeling guilty.

Summary

If you have Type II diabetes, you can aim for adequate control or for tight control. Keeping the blood sugar in the 200 to 250 mg/dl range is adequate control. This may be enough to prevent symptoms from high blood sugar (for example, thirst, frequent urination, blurred vision, fatigue).

Keeping the blood sugar under 150 mg/dl (or perhaps 200 mg/dl) is tight control for seniors with Type II diabetes. Tight control prevents symptoms from high blood sugar. However, tight control increases the risks of symptoms from low blood sugar (if it should fall below 50 mg/dl for example). We don't know if tight control of blood sugar prevents complications for Type II diabetics, but recent studies suggest that good control may prevent eye disease.

Monitoring blood sugar is necessary to achieve tight control of blood sugar. It involves regular fingersticks. Monitoring urine sugar is probably not adequate to allow for tight blood sugar control but is adequate to allow for enough control to prevent symptoms from high blood sugar. It is less expensive (and less painful) than monitoring blood sugar.

Oral agents usually suffice to control blood sugar for Type II diabetics. The costs of these medicines are reasonable, with some more expensive than others. They may cause symptoms by lowering the blood sugar too much. Type II diabetics who require less than 20 units of insulin a day can probably change to an oral agent.

A diabetic diet may or may not be important for you. If your blood sugar does not fluctuate much, following a strict diabetic diet may not be worth the sacrifice.

Part IV

SYMPTOM RELIEF

15

Angina and
Congestive Heart Failure

U p to this point, I have discussed seniors who have no new symptoms. But what if you have new symptoms? Don't you want everything possible to eliminate, or at least relieve, those symptoms?

Yes, of course you do. But you still need to weigh the benefits and burdens of tests and treatments. Let's start with one of the most common symptoms, angina.

Angina is the chest discomfort people feel when an inadequate amount of oxygen goes to their heart muscle. Usually blockage of coronary arteries (the arteries that supply the heart) is the reason for the inadequate supply of oxygen. Occasionally spasm of an artery causes angina. Angina usually occurs with exertion but may occur at rest. Many seniors have some degree of angina.

A heart attack results if the oxygen supply to the heart muscle is inadequate for too long. In this case, there is permanent muscle damage.

Tests for Angina

Often tests are unnecessary to diagnose angina. If your chest discomfort is typical of angina, your doctor will be able to make the diagnosis based on your symptoms. Sometimes the diagnosis is difficult because the chest discomfort is not typical of angina. If so, tests may be necessary to make the diagnosis.

An exercise treadmill test (see chapter 7), a first step in the diagnosis, allows your doctor to view changes on your electrocardiogram while you exercise. If your coronary arteries are blocked, your doctor should see characteristic changes in your electrocardiogram. The treadmill test is not always accurate—it can produce false-positive and false-negative results. If your doctor is still uncertain about the diagnosis, he may advise a special x-ray that lets him see your heart muscle while you are stressing it (either with exercise or special medicines).

If these tests don't provide a diagnosis, your doctor may advise cardiac catheterization, a test that allows a cardiologist to see the outline of the coronary arteries. This test involves a catheter that the cardiologist threads into the heart. It may require hospitalization.

Before you agree to have cardiac catheterization, you should ask one question: Are you willing to have heart surgery? If not, you do not need cardiac catheterization just to confirm that you have blockage of your coronary arteries. Your doctor could try medicine to relieve your chest discomfort without knowing the anatomy of your coronary arteries.

Nonmedicine Treatment for Angina

People who have had heart attacks benefit from cardiac rehabilitation, a program of gradually increasing exercise.[1,2] People with angina but no history of heart attacks may also benefit from exercise, though the benefit may not be significant.[3]

If you have angina, you can decrease your risk of a heart attack by 2 to 3 percent if you follow a low-cholesterol diet (see chapter 12).

Medicines for Angina

Mr. Henry is a ninety-three-year-old who looked very healthy the first time I saw him. He had two symptoms. First, he thought his memory was failing. It wasn't. Second, he felt tired most of the time. The only remarkable finding from his history and physical was that he was taking four different medications for his heart.

"Mr. Henry, tell me about your heart condition," I inquired.

"Well, I had the bypass surgery in 1980. I've been doing fine ever since. These medicines keep everything under control," he replied.

"When was the last time you had chest pain?" I pursued.

"Not since before the operation," he informed me.

"Do you think you've done so well because of these medicines? Or do you think that you would do okay without some of them?"

"I've wondered about that, Doctor."

"Are you willing to see how you will do without one of these medicines?"

"Yes, if you think it's okay. My other doctors thought I needed them, but I'm willing to see what happens without them."

One by one, we peeled away his heart medicines. After six months, he was taking no medicines and had no angina. Although he still worried about his memory (it was as sharp as ever), he felt much better, because he had more energy.

You can take medicines for angina three different ways as an outpatient. First, you can take oral medicines (pills, tablets, capsules). Second, you can dissolve medicines under your tongue (sublingual pills). Third, you can wear a patch on your skin.

The oral medicines and skin patches are most useful for preventing angina. Some of the sublingual pills can also prevent angina. Most people with angina use nitroglycerin sublingually when they have angina.

If you need to go to the hospital because of severe angina, you may need medicines in your veins.

The wholesale price for one hundred pills to treat angina ranges from forty-one dollars to sixty-nine dollars.

Surgery for Angina

Doctors use two approaches to clear obstructed coronary arteries. The first is open-heart surgery. Doctors call this operation coronary artery bypass grafting (CABG). In this operation, the surgeon replaces the blocked coronary arteries with veins from the patient's legs. Several studies report that seniors over eighty years old respond well to this major operation.[4-6]

The second procedure is a newer one called percutaneous transluminal coronary angioplasty (PTCA). Like cardiac catheterization, it involves a catheter that the doctor threads into the heart. An inflated balloon at the end of the catheter opens up the blocked artery. Many studies indicate that PTCA is useful for seniors regardless of their age.[6-9]

Any invasive procedure can cause complications. However, seniors should not let the potential complications discourage them. Major complications are unusual for seniors who are in good shape.[10] If medicines don't control angina, surgery may be the best option for seniors who have the will to endure the stress associated with major surgery.[11]

Suggestions for Seniors with Angina

1. Consider tests such as cardiac catheterization only if there is a good chance that the results will help you. For example, if surgery is an option, catheterization may be necessary. If surgery is not an option, catheterization is probably unnecessary.
2. If you need medicine besides an occasional nitroglycerin tablet, ask for ones that are most convenient and least expensive. Be willing to try different combinations of medicines.
3. If your angina is infrequent and you are on several medicines, consider stopping one or more of them (one at a time) or decreasing the doses with a doctor's supervision. See if you really need your medicines rather than assume you must stay on the same medicines indefinitely.
4. If your angina is severe despite medicines, consider surgery, even if you are older than eighty.

Congestive Heart Failure

People with congestive heart failure (CHF) have shortness of breath. With early stages of CHF, people get short of breath with exertion. With later stages, they get short of breath at rest. CHF is not one disease. Rather, it is a manifestation of different diseases, including coronary artery disease, hypertension, diabetes, and valvular heart disease.

Tests for CHF

Usually the diagnosis of CHF is evident by a chest x-ray. Occasionally other tests are necessary to determine if the shortness of breath is from heart disease rather than some other cause. Special tests may be necessary to determine what kind of heart disease causes the CHF. For example, your doctor may get an ultrasound of your heart if he suspects a problem with a heart valve.

Nonmedicine Treatment for CHF

Salt restriction may be necessary for patients with more advanced stages of CHF. Doctors often attribute flares of CHF to "dietary indiscretion" when they can't find any other cause.

I don't believe this is fair to many patients. The truth may be that people have flares of CHF, and doctors will never know why some flares occur. Doctors should not assume that their patients are surreptitiously eating bags of salted potato chips. Moderation of salt intake, not abstinence from salt, is a good guide for people with CHF.

Rest is important for patients with flares of CHF. Unnecessary physical exertion adds stress to a heart that is already failing to pump effectively.

Medicines for CHF

There are four general classes of medicines for CHF. The first class consists of medicines to treat the underlying problem, for example, medicines for high blood pressure or coronary artery disease.

The second consists of diuretics (water pills). These are the mainstay of treatment for CHF. Lasix (furosemide) is the most common diuretic for CHF.

The third class consists of inotropic agents—medicines that make the heart squeeze harder. Digitalis, a drug that was extracted from the foxglove plant over two hundred years ago, is an inotropic agent. Unfortunately, newer inotropic agents have not lived up to their promise.[12]

The fourth class consists of vasodilators—medicines to open up blood vessels. ACE inhibitors, medicines commonly used to treat hypertension, are becoming a cornerstone of the treatment of CHF.[13]

Now, how effective are these medicines? I will not dispute the value of diuretics. They work. Doctors usually select a more expensive diuretic (for example, Bumex) only when the less expensive diuretic, Lasix, does not suffice.

I will dispute the value of digitalis for stable CHF. This is an important medicine to critique because it's widely used. Many seniors take digitalis.[14] Although it is inexpensive and easy to take (it comes in a once-a-day dose), it has the potential for causing life-threatening arrhythmias.[15] Most important, most patients with stable CHF may not need digitalis. Many studies suggest that at least 80 percent of people on digitalis do as well when they stop taking it.[16–22] However, two recent studies suggest that patients have more problems when they stop taking digitalis than when they were taking the drug.[23,24]

ACE inhibitors, such as Vasotec (enalapril) and Capoten (captopril), can relieve symptoms and increase longevity for patients with CHF.[25–27] Patients with severe CHF can reduce their one-year mortality rate by about 15 percent with enalapril.[27] Patients with moderate CHF can reduce their three-year mortality rate by about 4 percent with enalapril.[26]

Surgery for CHF

Surgery is an option when diseased heart valves are the cause of CHF. Seniors over eighty years old do well with open-heart surgery for valve replacement.[28] Some experts believe that surgery is the treatment of choice for adults with certain kinds of valve disease.[29] Others believe that doctors should try balloon valvulo-plasty, a procedure like cardiac catheterization (this doesn't re-quire surgery), before considering surgery.[30] Most experts agree that balloon valvuloplasty relieves symptoms for seniors who are too ill for open-heart surgery.[31,32]

Suggestions for Seniors with CHF

1. Question the need for special tests if you already know you have CHF and you know the cause of it. This is espe-cially true if you are hospitalized with a flare of CHF. Many special tests are available, and the temptation to use them is great. Question if they will really make a differ-ence.
2. Don't blame your problems on excessive salt intake.
3. Consider stopping digitalis if you have stable CHF.
4. If you have mild or moderate CHF, and you consider a 4 percent risk reduction in mortality worthwhile, start an ACE inhibitor.
5. If you have disease of your heart valves, consider valve replacement or valvuloplasty if your symptoms are not controlled with medicines.

16

Chronic Obstructive Pulmonary Disease

Doctors call the chronic lung disease caused by smoking "chronic obstructive pulmonary disease" (COPD). Many seniors refer to this as emphysema. Most people with COPD have part emphysema and part chronic bronchitis.

Emphysema occurs when the small air spaces in the lung lose their elasticity and do not force air out of the lungs, thus trapping air inside. Chronic bronchitis occurs when the airways get irritated and produce a lot of phlegm. This causes a recurring cough.

Most people have COPD as a result of tobacco use. However, some seniors with long-standing asthma can have problems very similar to seniors with COPD.[1,2]

Tests for COPD

Pulmonary function tests (PFTs; see chapter 7) are usually necessary to diagnose COPD. Repeated PFTs to assess the progress of the disease are unnecessary for many people with stable COPD.[3,4] The same is true for chest x-rays. Chest x-rays alter the management in only 4 percent of patients hospitalized with an exacerbation of COPD.[5] Measuring the oxygen content of the blood with a pulse oximeter can help determine the severity of the COPD.

Nonmedicine Treatment for COPD

Smoking cessation is paramount.[6] However, many patients with COPD continue to smoke. Other measures may be helpful, including exercise training directed at the arms and legs,[7] administration of oxygen, and psychosocial support, which can reduce the anxiety associated with shortness of breath.[8]

The value of respiratory muscle training is unclear. Although pulmonary rehabilitation does improve the exercise tolerance of some patients with COPD,[8] it may yield little benefit in others.[9]

Medicines for COPD

Mrs. Jackson is an eighty-four-year-old with COPD. She takes many medicines, including oxygen at home. She worried about the number of her medicines and wondered if "some might be working against others."

"Would you like to see how you do off of one of your medicines, Mrs. Jackson?" I asked.

"Please," she pleaded.

"Do you think the theophylline makes you feel any better?"

"I've been on it for years, but I can't say that taking it makes me feel any better," she informed me.

We decided that she should taper off theophylline. She returned to my office a month later.

"How did it go?" I asked eagerly, expecting that she had felt the same after stopping theophylline.

"I had to go back on the theophylline. I got more short of breath and felt like I needed it. I felt better once I started it again."

Did I consider the experiment a failure? No. I felt bad that her symptoms had gotten worse after she stopped the theophylline, but I believe the experiment was worth it. She and I both knew that the medicine relieved her symptoms—whether it was a placebo effect or not didn't really matter. Before this experiment, we didn't know if she really benefited from this medicine. Indeed, most seniors I take off theophylline don't notice a difference.

Doctors use five general classes of medicines for COPD: theophyllines; inhaled bronchodilators; medicines that help clear mucus; steroids; and antibiotics.

Theophylline has been a keystone of COPD treatment for years. Recently, its use for patients with asthma and COPD has become controversial.[10–13] Although there are good physiologic reasons theophylline should help patients with COPD,[14,15] studies haven't shown that theophylline does indeed help patients feel better. Even intravenous aminophylline may not benefit patients hospitalized with exacerbations of COPD.[16]

Some patients benefit symptomatically in the absence of objective improvement. Therefore, a trial of theophylline is worthwhile in patients with severe irreversible COPD.[10] It should be discontinued if there is no objective or subjective improvement.

Another reason to question the routine use of theophylline is that seniors are at high risk for side effects from the drug.[17] Theophylline can cause life-threatening arrhythmias. To decrease the risk of serious side effects, your doctor needs to monitor the level of the drug in your bloodstream.

The wholesale price of one hundred theophylline pills ranges from eighteen dollars to sixty-six dollars.

Inhaled bronchodilators are the medicines that give COPD patients the greatest relief. After inhaling a couple of puffs from a canister, people with COPD and asthma usually breathe much easier.

Doctors typically prescribe two puffs every four hours. Many patients follow these instructions, though more frequent use of certain bronchodilators would make them feel better. If you have COPD and get relief from inhaled bronchodilators, you ought to use them more frequently as long as you don't feel jittery or feel your heart going faster than usual. The medicines in inhaled bronchodilators also come in tablet form.

A recent study from Montreal suggests that patients with asthma who used inhaled bronchodilators more frequently were at an increased risk of death or near death.[18] Media reports of this study worried a lot of patients with asthma and COPD.

Don't assume the results of one study of asthma patients applies to different patients with COPD. This one study should not discourage you from using a medicine that may relieve shortness of breath. On the other hand, if you don't get much relief from these medicines, there is no reason to use them every four hours.

There are different types of inhaled bronchodilators. Doctors frequently treat patients with more than one type of inhaled bronchodilator. The wholesale price of one inhaler ranges from eleven dollars to forty-one dollars.

Mucolytics are the medicines that help clear mucus. Until recently, doctors prescribed mucolytics only infrequently. Recent studies suggest that these medicines may relieve symptoms of COPD.[19] These medicines are worth trying if you feel you cannot clear your mucus.

Doctors routinely use intravenous steroids to treat patients hospitalized with exacerbations of COPD. Oral steroids (for example, prednisone) help prevent relapses after patients leave the hospital.[20] The use of oral steroids for patients with stable COPD has been controversial, though there is probably some benefit.[21]

Long-term steroid use has its downside. It can cause side effects such as osteoporosis and swelling.

Antibiotic use for exacerbations of COPD is also controversial.[22,23] Most doctors will prescribe antibiotics if there is a hint of infection.

Surgery for COPD
Although some medical centers perform lung transplantation, this is not a reasonable option for most patients with COPD. There are no other surgical options for this disease.

Suggestions for Seniors with COPD

1. Consider pulmonary function tests to determine the diagnosis and long-term prognosis. Frequent follow-up pulmonary function tests are unlikely to help you unless you need measurements to help you stop smoking.
2. Try to stop smoking. Join a program that specializes in smoking cessation.
3. If you take theophylline and are not sure that it makes you feel better, consider stopping it to see how you feel.

4. If you don't take theophylline, consider a short trial to see if it makes you feel better.

5. Use inhaled bronchodilators more often than every four hours if they help you breathe and do not cause side effects.

17

Osteoarthritis

Pain from arthritis is the most common symptom reported by seniors. About 44 percent of seniors over eighty years old have some degree of osteoarthritis,[1] the most common type of arthritis. The incidence increases as the population ages.[2]

Tests for Arthritis

Doctors diagnose arthritis by history, physical exam, and x-rays. Occasionally, they need special tests, such as blood tests and specimens of the joint fluid, to determine the kind of arthritis you have. Most tests, not all, are necessary when your doctor doesn't know the diagnosis. The treatment is different for different types of arthritis. For example, doctors use different medicines for osteoarthritis, gout, and rheumatoid arthritis. In general, these tests are not cumbersome or expensive.

Nonmedicine Treatment for Osteoarthritis

A supervised fitness walking program can improve physical endurance, improve functional status, decrease arthritis pain, and decrease the need for medicines.[3] Weight loss reduces the risk of developing arthritis pain[4] and decreases pain once it has started.[5,6]

Changing furniture may help relieve arthritis pain. For example, raising the level of chairs or toilet seats can reduce pressure on the hips and knees that is generated when pushing off the seats to stand up.

Weight loss may be an unrealistic goal for seniors whose disabilities limit exercise. If so, medicines are necessary for pain control.

Medicines for Osteoarthritis

Nonsteroidal anti-inflammatory drugs (NSAID) and salicylates (aspirin) are the most popular analgesics for arthritis pain. Stomach irritation is a frequent side effect of these medicines.[7,8] You may respond to one of the NSAIDs and not to others. Similarly, you may have stomach irritation with some and not others. In general, however, the differences between medicines are subtle.[9]

The wholesale cost of a month's supply of NSAIDs ranges from three dollars (generic ibuprofen) to over one hundred dollars for some of the trade names. The newer medicines are more expensive but are easier to take (once- or twice-a-day doses) and may cause less stomach irritation.

Extra Strength Tylenol (acetaminophen) is as effective as NSAIDs in reducing the pain of mild to moderate osteoarthritis.[10] Furthermore, it is less expensive and less likely to cause side effects than NSAIDs.

Stronger analgesics are necessary if NSAIDs, salicylates, and acetaminophen do not control the pain.

Surgery for Osteoarthritis

Joint replacement can relieve intractable pain and markedly improve function.[11] These operations are now routine for seniors in their eighties. Seniors in their nineties who are otherwise healthy may also benefit from joint replacement.

Suggestions for Seniors with Osteoarthritis

1. If you can exercise without hurting your joints, try it.
2. If you can lose weight, try it.
3. If you need analgesics, start with one that is mild and inexpensive (Extra Strength Tylenol).
4. If Tylenol doesn't suffice, ask for a NSAID that is inexpensive. A generic preparation should work as well as a trade name.
5. Be willing to try different NSAIDs until you find one that relieves pain, is affordable, and causes no side effects.
6. If milder analgesics don't suffice, and you do not want surgery, ask your doctor for stronger analgesics (for example, narcotics).
7. If medicines don't control your pain, don't wait too long to see an orthopedic surgeon to discuss joint replacement. Many seniors dramatically improve with surgery and rehabilitation.

18

Dyspepsia

Dyspepsia—chronic or recurrent upper abdominal pain or nausea—is the medical term for upset stomach. There are three general causes of dyspepsia. The first is ulcers. The second is esophageal reflux (which produces heartburn). The third is cancer (for example, of the stomach and pancreas).

I will discuss dyspepsia from ulcers and esophageal reflux. Dyspepsia from esophageal reflux is about twice as common as dyspepsia from ulcers.[1]

Tests for Dyspepsia

Doctors diagnose the cause of dyspepsia with two kinds of tests. The first is endoscopy. This test allows doctors to look at the stomach and intestines with a flexible scope. The second test is an x-ray of the esophagus, stomach, and intestines after they have been filled with barium.

How important is it to know the exact cause of dyspepsia?

Should your doctor pursue all studies until he is confident of the diagnosis? One expert panel recommends endoscopy only for patients who fail to respond to a trial of antacids.[1] This is a reasonable approach.

What if you decide to wait and you miss something serious like a cancer? If this is the case, your symptoms will recur. You can then have the test. Waiting two to three months to see if your symptoms resolve is unlikely to affect your prognosis if you have stomach or pancreatic cancer.

Early tests may tell you if you have ulcers, gastritis (general irritation of your stomach), reflux, or some other common problem. Does it matter? In 1993, the answer was, Not really. We thought that treatment was similar for all of these conditions, which are all caused by too much acid in the stomach or esophagus. Therefore, a trial of antacids without tests seemed appropriate. In 1995, the answer became, Yes, it might matter. Endoscopy may be necessary to make sure you don't have a chronic bacterial infection that is associated with ulcers.[2] The treatment for this infection includes three different antibiotics for a total of two weeks.[3] Enthusiasm for this treatment is growing among experts. Some even suggest that all patients with peptic ulcers should have this treatment.

I'm not suggesting that everyone with dyspepsia line up at the gastroenterologist's office for endoscopy. If your symptoms are infrequent and are relieved with the usual medicines, endoscopy is probably not worthwhile. However, if your symptoms recur or do not respond to the usual medicines, endoscopy is probably appropriate.

Nonmedicine Treatment for Dyspepsia

Many people think that dietary changes will cure ulcers. Although dietary changes may decrease acid production in the stomach, there is little evidence that dietary changes alone improve symptoms caused by ulcers.[4] Reducing alcohol intake and stopping smoking will help, but may not be enough. Medicines are usually necessary.

Dietary changes do help with esophageal reflux,[5] which occurs when stomach contents flow up into the esophagus, causing heartburn. See the list of suggestions at the end of this chapter for appropriate dietary changes.

Medicines for Dyspepsia

Several different kinds of medicines relieve dyspepsia. I will divide them into three groups: antacids, which you can buy over the counter; H_2 blockers, such as Tagamet (cimetidine) or Zantac (ranitidine); and miscellaneous medicines.

Antacids contain either aluminum, magnesium, or calcium. Some antacids contain two of these elements. Magnesium-based antacids can cause diarrhea. Aluminum- or calcium-based antacids can cause constipation.

You can combine different types of antacids to reduce side effects. For example, if you take an aluminum-based antacid and develop constipation, you can combine it with a magnesium-based antacid to offset the constipation. Antacid tablets are as effective as liquid antacids. Lower doses of antacids are usually effective, are inexpensive, and only infrequently cause significant side effects.[4] However, these medicines might not be as effective for esophageal reflux. Some studies suggest that placebos are as effective as antacids in people with esophageal reflux.[5]

The H_2 blockers are very popular. Your doctor is likely to prescribe one of these if you see him for dyspepsia. None of the H_2 blockers has a clear advantage over the others.[6] They cause few side effects. Confusion is one of the side effects,[7] but this occurs very infrequently. H_2 blockers are more expensive than antacids. The wholesale price of one hundred pills ranges from $88 to $160.

The miscellaneous class contains one medicine that people have used for two hundred years—bismuth compounds—and several others that are very new. Except for Pepto-Bismol, they are expensive. Doctors usually reserve misoprostol (Cytotec) for patients who have peptic ulcers as a result of taking nonsteroidal anti-inflammatory drugs. Sucralfate (Carafate) is an option that costs less than most H_2 blockers. Omeprazole (Prilosec), the newest and most expensive medicine, is effective for many patients whose symptoms are not relieved by antacids or H_2 blockers.

Most of these medicines cure approximately 80 percent of peptic ulcers after four weeks of therapy.[4] Some have even higher cure rates.

Assume your symptoms subside in four to eight weeks. Should you do anything to prevent recurrence of ulcers? If you smoke and drink much alcohol, you are at high risk of recurrence and probably should take H_2 blockers (at reduced doses) to prevent recurrence of ulcers.[8,9] Even if you don't smoke or drink, you can reduce your individual risk of recurrence by about 20 percent if you continue taking H_2 blockers.[10]

Several different treatments are effective in preventing recurrence of ulcers.[10] Antacids taken with meals are as effective as H_2 blockers and sucralfate, but have to be taken three times a day and cause more minor adverse effects.

Surgery

Surgery is an option for patients with frequent recurrence of ulcers[8] and for patients with esophageal reflux who do not respond to conservative therapy.[11] Surgery is necessary for patients who have persistent bleeding from ulcers.

Suggestions for Seniors with Dyspepsia

1. If dyspepsia is a new symptom, consider a trial of medicine before having endoscopy or barium x-rays. A blood test (complete blood count) may be necessary to make sure you are not bleeding from your stomach or intestines.
2. If dyspepsia persists for a month despite medicine, then consider tests to diagnose the cause of dyspepsia.
3. If you have reflux, you should avoid large meals; avoid lying down after meals; avoid fat, chocolate, and caffeine; elevate the head of your bed with blocks; and stop smoking.
4. If you need medicine, consider antacids. If high doses of antacids cause problems such as diarrhea or constipation, you should combine different kinds of antacids to reduce these side effects. If the side effects continue, then consider prescription medicines like the H_2 blockers.
5. If cost is not a major concern but convenience is, consider the newer medicines that you can take once (Prilosec) or twice (H_2 blockers) a day.
6. If you need an H_2 blocker, ask for the least expensive one.
7. Consider surgery for reflux symptoms (heartburn) that are debilitating.

19

Urinary Incontinence

U rinary incontinence is the involuntary loss of urine. It may
occur as a small leak, a gusher, or as anything in between.
Drs. Neil Resnick and Subbarao Yalla from Boston proposed a
clever way to remember the transient causes of incontinence:[1]

Delirium or confusional states
Infection (i.e., urinary tract infection)
Atrophic urethritis or vaginitis (caused by lack of estrogen)
Pharmaceuticals (many types of drugs can cause inconti-
nence)
Psychological disorder, especially depression
Endocrine disorder (high calcium or high blood sugar)
Restricted mobility (for example, bed rest from a hip frac-
ture)
Stool impaction (severe constipation)

When doctors treat the underlying condition, the incontinence usually resolves.

There are three general types of chronic incontinence. The first is urge incontinence, where the bladder is hyperactive and has a mind of its own. Patients usually feel an urge to void but they can't get to the bathroom fast enough. The second is stress incontinence, where the muscles that should stop the flow of urine are weak. Patients usually leak urine when they cough, laugh, or bend over. The third is overflow incontinence, where the bladder never really empties itself. Patients usually feel like they don't empty their bladder, and urine tends to dribble out frequently throughout the day. Many seniors have a combination of these types of chronic incontinence.

Mrs. Abrams, Mrs. Falk, Mrs. Moore, Mr. Price, and Mrs. Tulley all stated that things were going fine when I asked, "How have you been doing lately?" When I tried to focus the conversation by asking, "Do you have any new symptoms I should know about?" the seniors all responded that everything was okay.

Oh, really? I thought. Why don't I get even more specific? I decided to ask about individual symptoms. Doctors call this the review of symptoms.

"Have you ever had a problem with control of your urine?"

"Well, now that you mention it . . ." And the stories flew.

Incontinence is an embarrassing problem. It has taken a long time for it to come out of the closet, but this is finally happening.[2]

The success of a recently published book illustrates the point. Kathryn L. Burgio, Ph.D., K. Lynette Pearce, R.N., and Angelo J. Lucco, M.D., wrote a book titled *Staying Dry: A Practical Guide to Bladder Control.* You can imagine that publishers were not beating down the authors' doors to get the rights to publish their manuscript. Indeed, the book had a slow start.

Then it happened. Someone commented on the book in a letter to Ann Landers. A flood of inquiries followed. Book sales soared. The popularity of this book confirms what all geriatricians suspect: incontinence is a big problem.

Tests for Incontinence

A group of experts recommend the following for a core evaluation: history (a thorough voiding history is very important), physical exam, urinalysis, a few blood tests, and a post-void residual (PVR).[3] Your doctor (or a specialist) determines the PVR by inserting a catheter into your bladder shortly after you void.

This basic evaluation can determine the cause of incontinence for most patients. Even if your doctor isn't sure about the diagnosis after this limited evaluation, he should have a good enough idea that he can start treatment. If the treatment doesn't work, he can refer you to a urologist.

More complicated cases require special tests such as cystoscopy (viewing the bladder through a scope) and urodynamic tests (measuring the function of everything related to the flow of urine). A urologist performs these procedures.

Nonmedicine Treatment for Incontinence

If you have incontinence, these two paragraphs should be good news. The nonmedicine treatment for incontinence may be the most effective nonmedicine treatment for any symptom a senior might have. It consists of bladder training and pelvic muscle exercises.

Distraction (thinking about other things besides the nearest bathroom) and prompted voiding (urinating on a schedule) are two examples of bladder training. Kegel exercises strengthen the pelvic muscles around the bladder. Next time you void, stop the urine in midstream. You will be doing a Kegel exercise.

Many studies show these and similar techniques are very effective for treating urge and stress incontinence.[4-8] Bladder training can benefit nursing-home residents as well as seniors who are independent.[7] Some seniors need coaching to do the bladder training and maintain an exercise program. An interested nurse can be very helpful.[9]

Medicines for Incontinence

If bladder training and Kegel exercises fail to control incontinence, various medicines may be effective. If a medicine doesn't help, your doctor is unlikely to keep you on that medicine. Therefore, excessive costs or side effects are usually not problems for patients with incontinence.

Surgery for Incontinence

There are many different surgical procedures that may be used to treat incontinence. Surgery may be necessary to reposition the bladder, to remove an obstruction, to replace or support severely weakened pelvic muscles, or to enlarge a small bladder. Doctors usually reserve surgery for patients with stress incontinence. The highest reported cure rate is 94 percent.[10]

Suggestions for Seniors with Incontinence

1. If you don't want to discuss the problem with your doctor—or if your doctor doesn't seem to want to deal with the problem—try to understand incontinence by reading literature for patients. I suggest *Urinary Incontinence in Adults: A Patient's Guide.* For a copy, write to:

   Agency for Health Care Policy and Research
   Executive Office Center

2101 East Jefferson Street, Suite 501
Rockville, MD 20852

Ask for publication number AHCPR 92-0040

2. Try bladder training first. If your doctor or nurse cannot guide you, consider trying on your own. The book by Dr. Burgio and colleagues is an excellent guide. For a copy, write to:

The Johns Hopkins University Press
701 West Fortieth Street
Baltimore, MD 21211

3. If you need medicines, be willing to try different ones. If you take estrogen, you may need to wait four to six weeks to know if it will relieve your symptoms. You don't need to wait this long to know if other medicines will help.

4. Do not assume you are too old for surgery.

20

Dementia

Dementia is a memory disorder that interferes with some-one's life. Many seniors have problems recalling the name of a familiar person or object. As long as these short-term memory lapses don't interfere with anything, you can ignore them. When memory lapses begin to interfere with daily activities, dementia may be the cause.

Dementia is common in the oldest seniors. Studies estimate that 24 to 47 percent of community-dwelling seniors over eighty have dementia.[1-3]

Alzheimer's disease is the most common cause of dementia; multiple small strokes are the second most common cause. Some people have both Alzheimer's disease and small strokes. We call this mixed dementia. Other causes are much less frequent.

Most causes of dementia are irreversible. The problems just

get worse with time. Occasionally patients have dementia that treatment can reverse. For example, depression, thyroid disease, vitamin B_{12} deficiency, and various medicines can cause memory problems. Memory can improve when doctors treat these problems.[4] Most geriatric textbooks suggest that reversible causes of dementia are more frequent than they really are. The unfortunate reality is that seniors with a gradual onset of dementia—and who are on no medicines that are causing side effects—rarely have reversible dementia.

Mrs. Parker lives in a nursing home and has had Alzheimer's disease for five years. Mr. Johnson is her fifty-five-year-old son.

One day Mr. Johnson asked if we could have a family conference. We arranged one.

At the conference we exchanged pleasantries and I reviewed Mrs. Parker's few medical problems. Nothing new had arisen in the last six months. Mrs. Parker was as stable as anyone could expect. In fact, she had gone months without any agitation or other behavioral problems. I couldn't understand why Mr. Johnson had requested a family conference when his mother was doing fine. He then informed me.

"Doctor, I know that you and other doctors think that Mother has Alzheimer's disease. But are you sure? Don't you think we need another CAT scan or some other test? And even if she does have Alzheimer's disease, isn't there a medicine that will improve her memory?"

At first I thought that Mr. Johnson's concerns reflected his stress. He couldn't reconcile himself to his mother's condition and was hoping for a miraculous cure. Then I realized the source of his concerns. He was responding to stories he had read in the press.

Weeks before the family conference, Mr. Johnson read a story in the *Washington Post* about a woman who was cured after having dementia for four years. Dr. Robert Friedland from the National Institutes of Health, the author of the *Post* story, reported the same story in the *Journal of the American Medical Association*.[5]

It is a remarkable story about a seventy-four-year-old woman who doctors thought had Alzheimer's disease. After four years of progressive deterioration, she enrolled in a study at the National Institutes of Health. An extensive evaluation revealed normal-pressure hydrocephalus, a rare brain disease that causes dementia. She had a shunt placed in her brain (that is, a tube to relieve the pressure from too much fluid) and eventually recovered her memory.

What was the moral of this story? Don't leave any stones unturned. What looks like Alzheimer's disease may not be Alzheimer's disease. Instead, it may be something that doctors can reverse.

Mr. Johnson and his family got the moral of this story. If doctors could cure another senior with presumed Alzheimer's disease, why couldn't doctors cure his mother? Their second hope—that a medicine could improve the memory of people with Alzheimer's disease—was also based on a news story.

In 1986 Dr. William M. Summers and colleagues from Los Angeles reported that a drug called THA (tacrine) improved the memory and function of patients with moderate to severe Alzheimer's disease.[6] Furthermore, THA didn't cause serious side effects.

The press splashed this news across every front page.[7] Mr. Johnson and his family followed the saga of THA. They had hope.

They didn't realize that Dr. Summers's study created an unusual amount of controversy. Five years after the publication of Summers's study, Dr. Arnold Relman, editor of the *New England Journal of Medicine,* published a series of commentaries about the THA saga.

In one of them, representatives from the Food and Drug Administration wrote, "The fact that Dr. Summers may not have set out intentionally to mislead anyone does not alter the fact that the misrepresentation of his work, appearing as it did in a prominent medical journal, had serious undesirable effects. Setting in motion premature requests for wide distribution of the drug, it caused those who care for the victims of Alzheimer's disease needless anguish, leading them to believe that their loved ones were being denied access to a drug of established efficacy and value. Some, driven by this anguish, went so far as to secure supplies of tacrine from unreliable and frequently illicit sources, often at considerable effort and expense."[8]

The anguish is real. The title of a classic book in this field, *The 36-Hour Day* (The Johns Hopkins University Press), says it all. Others have described caring for loved ones with Alzheimer's disease as an "unending funeral." No wonder family members look for hope wherever they can find it. Is there any room for diagnostic moderation amidst this anguish? Yes. In fact, moderation, not false hope, is your best guide.

Tests for Dementia

Many seniors with dementia can hide their memory problems in casual conversation. Doctors look for dementia with a series of questions called a mental status exam.[9] Some mental status exams are very short[10]; others are long.

The history is the most important part of the evaluation. Routine laboratory tests can help uncover reversible causes of dementia. However, an overemphasis on these tests is unlikely to help and may detract from recognition of more common causes of suffering.[11] Patients with reversible dementia may improve but rarely return to normal.[11]

Many experts echo this caution about excessive testing.[12–15] A consensus conference from the National Institutes of Health concluded that "the laboratory tests that are used should be individualized based on the patient's history and results of the physical and psychological examinations. Overtesting may expose the patient to discomfort, inconvenience, excess costs, and the likelihood of false-positive test results that may lead to additional unnecessary testing. Undertesting also has hazards, for example, in elderly persons, in whom medical diseases may have nonspecific presentations, such as dementia."[16]

Nonmedicine Treatment of Dementia

This is the essence of treatment for dementia. Although doctors play a key role in the treatment of dementia,[17,18] it is others who make the biggest difference in delaying nursing-home placement[19] or improving the quality of life of nursing-home residents.

The nonmedicine treatment of dementia is beyond the scope of this book. Your local chapter of the Alzheimer's Association can provide valuable information.

Medicines for Dementia

Doctors have used the following classes of medicines to treat dementia: cerebral vasodilators (medicines that open up the blood vessels in the brain); cholinergics (medicines that replace chemicals thought to be low in patients with Alzheimer's disease); miscellaneous other medicines; and medicines that treat the symptoms associated with dementia.

Doctors have used cerebral vasodilators for years to treat

dementia.[20] Hydergine is the most popular medicine from this class. Its effect may be to enhance the metabolism in the brain rather than open blood vessels.[21] There is little evidence that Hydergine or any other medicine from this class makes much difference. However, a trial for patients with early dementia is reasonable. If improvement is not clear within a month, stop the medicine.

THA represents the cholinergics. Dr. Summers's report prompted much enthusiasm for this class of medicines.[22] Other studies suggest there is modest to moderate improvement with THA.[23–26] On the other hand, some studies found no significant improvement with THA.[27,28] Furthermore, some patients develop hepatitis on THA. We can conclude that if THA does help with dementia, its long-term effect is modest, though some patients do have significant short-term benefits.

Doctors have used miscellaneous other medicines to treat dementia, but none have shown much promise. However, many researchers are hopeful that experimental medicines now being developed can slow the progression of dementia. Mr. Andrew Skolnick summarized the state of the art in a recent report in the *Journal of the American Medical Association*. He interviewed one expert, Dr. Thomas Crook, and wrote, "While Crook says that chances are good for finding a treatment that has a 'slight but reliable beneficial effect,' he says the chances of finding a therapy over the next 5 years that produces a dramatic effect appear small."[29]

When these new medicines arrive on the marketplace, ask yourself the following questions: How much do they cost? What is the likelihood they will benefit your loved one? and What is the likelihood they will cause side effects? Consider THA (tacrine), which arrived on the market in October 1993. The benefit is that there is a reasonable chance (I would estimate 30 percent) that it will improve memory in a patient with Alzheimer's disease. The burdens include a cost of approximately $3.50 a day, the inconvenience of frequent blood tests (at least for the first eighteen weeks), and the potential for side effects.

I must confess that I have changed my thinking about tacrine in a short period of time. I was very skeptical when it arrived on the market. However, my colleagues and I have seen some remarkable success stories since we started treating patients with tacrine. Whether these improvements are temporary or more lasting remains to be seen. Most patients and their families believe that the burdens of tacrine are worth the potential benefits. I agree that it's worth a try for most seniors with mild to moderate Alzheimer's disease.

The fourth class of medicines used in dementia address symptoms, not the dementia itself. Doctors commonly use sedatives to suppress disruptive behavior.[30,31] Some people refer to these medicines as "chemical restraints." New federal regulations discourage the overuse of these medicines in nursing homes. Many seniors with dementia and agitation respond better to gentle reassurance than to sedatives. Some, however, need small doses of sedatives because gentle reassurance either does not suffice or is not a reliable option (for example, in nursing homes with a shortage of staff).

Surgery for Dementia

Fetal tissue transplants may help patients with Parkinson's disease, but there is nothing on the horizon for patients with the common causes of dementia.

Suggestions for Families of Seniors with Dementia

1. If the dementia is relatively abrupt in onset, assume that the cause is something other than Alzheimer's disease.

Seek attention from a specialist if your primary care doctor insists that it is Alzheimer's disease.

2. If the dementia is gradual in onset, don't get your hopes too high that a doctor can find a reversible cause. Your loved one very likely has Alzheimer's disease or another irreversible cause of dementia.

3. Get literature from the Alzheimer's Association.

4. Seek help from support groups.

5. Get respite care if you can—you need to take care of yourself in order to provide the best support for your loved one.

6. Ask your doctor if he knows of any local studies that your family member might participate in as a subject.

7. If you try a medicine, consider the cost, side effects, inconvenience, and likelihood that it will help your loved one. If you don't notice a significant improvement in a few months, stop the medicine.

Part V

WHAT MATTERS MOST

21

Health Outside
Your Doctor's Office

Good health involves more than the absence of disease. The healthiest seniors have more than healthy bodies. They enjoy health in other parts of their lives. Some have healthy social lives. Some have healthy spiritual lives. Some have healthy sexual lives. And some have all of these and more.

The healthiest seniors attend to all dimensions of their lives—physical, spiritual, mental, social, and emotional. They all add to health. We develop these parts of our health outside the doctor's office.

The stories of a few senior superstars illustrate that seniors are never too old to attain health in all areas of their lives. Emulating these people would lead to frustration for most seniors. I present their stories in hopes that they will encourage seniors with voids in their lives. You see, these superstars were not superstars in their fifties and sixties. They got better as they got older.

Exercise

Mr. Rollings is an eighty-four-year-old gentleman who appeared very fit when I first met him. He came to the office because he had an important "camping trip" coming up. He wanted to make sure that a certain symptom didn't get out of control on the trip. Camping trip? Was he the oldest den master in the country or what? I asked him about this camping trip. It turns out he was planning more than a leisurely stroll through the Rocky Mountain National Park. He was preparing to be the first person over sixty-five to climb Mount Aconcagua in Argentina.

What does Mr. Rollings do to get in shape? Runs hundred-meter dashes, of course. He was excited about his upcoming eighty-fifth birthday because he would qualify for the eight-five-and-over division. His fastest time as an eighty-four-year-old was only 0.4 seconds shy of the world record for the under-eighty-five division. He knew he could break the world record for the eighty-five-and-older division. After that, he had to find a higher mountain to climb. It was the one in Argentina.

You probably share my thoughts about Mr. Rollings. Here is a health fanatic who has pushed himself his entire life and just happens to run fast. Yes, he did happen to be fast. But he did not begin pursuing these goals until he was sixty-six years old. While his health held up, he thought he was never too old to reach for the top.

Mr. Rollings is not alone. Dr. Paul Spangler, a retired California surgeon, runs marathons at age ninety-one and has already set his world records.[1] Dr. Spangler, who describes himself as "just an ordinary guy," started running at age sixty-seven.

Few will have a chance to run in Mr. Rollings's or Dr. Spangler's footsteps. But many will have a chance to pursue the goals of Mrs. Morris, another senior superstar. Mrs. Morris lives in a long-term-care facility. The last hundred-meter dash she ran was eighty-five years ago in a country school parking lot in Maine.

She has severe arthritis and early Parkinson's disease and used to spend most of her day in a wheelchair. She tried to get around with a walker but fell frequently. One time she broke her hip and ended up in the hospital for three weeks. After that she resigned herself to living in her bed and wheelchair. She gave her walker to a friend. A current myth suggests that people like Mrs. Morris are beyond benefiting from exercise. Fortunately, this myth is falling by the wayside.

In 1986 gerontologists wanted to study the effect of exercise on the strength of frail seniors like Mrs. Morris.[2] Mrs. Morris volunteered to be in the study. For sixteen consecutive weeks she performed modest exercises. For example, she had to flex her hip, lifting her leg up while it had five-pound weights attached to the ankle. She had to repeat this ten times per session and had three sessions per day. This was not strenuous exercise, even for Mrs. Morris. It just took time and concentration.

After sixteen weeks of this program, the researchers found that the muscle mass in Mrs. Morris's leg had actually increased. More important, she was functioning much better. She was using her walker again. The researchers followed Mrs. Morris for a year and discovered that she and many others who participated in the study were falling much less frequently than they used to. Without these simple exercises, Mrs. Morris would still be in her wheelchair or in bed.

Seniors like Mrs. Morris and Mr. Rollings, and everyone in between these two extremes, benefit from exercise. The intensity and location of the exercise program don't make a big difference.[3] Many types of exercise, whether high intensity or low intensity, home based or group, help seniors stay fit and are safe. Regular exercise may enhance a senior's sense of well-being, improve self-image, sleep patterns, and bowel function, and reduce anxiety.[4]

Physical inactivity is a problem in our country. Less than 20 percent of adult North Americans perform optimal amounts of physical activity.[5] Some investigators believe that much of the decline attributed to aging is disuse atrophy resulting from inactivity.[5]

Denver has a cardiologist who is a zealot about reducing heart disease with exercise. His prescription is simple—sweat and enjoy it. If you don't like jogging, don't jog. If swimming is too boring, don't swim. But find something you enjoy and sweat.

I believe we should change this prescription for many seniors. The prescription should be: Move and enjoy it. If you take walks and enjoy them, walk regularly. If you're in a wheelchair like Mrs. Morris and can move your arms and legs, find a way to move them regularly and enjoy it. And if you're fortunate enough to have Mr. Rollings's or Dr. Spangler's good health, and you enjoy climbing mountains or running marathons, then do it regularly.

Spirituality

Before Mrs. Naylor died suddenly in her apartment, I saw her once every four months to make sure her congestive heart failure was under control. I didn't know her very well, but well enough to know that she was unique. She always seemed content. Shortness of breath, rising rents, unfriendly neighbors—none of these bothered her.

One day I told her I wanted to understand why seniors grow old gracefully. I asked her why she was so content despite the burdens she carried.

"I have a good family," she began. I acknowledged that this certainly makes a difference for everyone.

"And I have a strong faith," she continued. She was looking to me to say, Thank you very much, that's the end of this discussion, but I didn't say a word, allowing her to elaborate.

"It's quite simple, Doctor. I've had a strong faith all of my life. I try to reach out to others even when I'm having problems myself. When I help others, even if it's just to greet them with a warm smile, I don't get so carried away with my problems. And my church has always been a real joy for me."

Mrs. Naylor did not pretend to be a Mother Teresa from Calcutta, a hall-of-fame senior superstar. But Mrs. Naylor's death left a big void in her community. She had touched many lives.

Here is a reality the medical profession must acknowledge. A trip to the doctor's office meant very little in Mrs. Naylor's life. Changes in medicines, electrocardiograms, and x-rays were all trivial. It was going to church and reaching out to others that made her feel healthy.

The medical profession does not typically concern itself with spiritual matters. Geriatrics is a good example of how the profession downplays the importance of spirituality in seniors' health. Geriatrics, one of the newest subspecialties in internal medicine and family practice, prides itself on making comprehensive evaluations. By using a team approach, geriatricians evaluate multiple dimensions of seniors' lives.

A cardiologist evaluates the heart; a neurologist evaluates the nervous system; and a general internist evaluates many physical aspects of the patient. But a good geriatrics team will also evaluate social, psychological, financial, environmental, and other aspects of a patient's life. Functional assessment, a comprehensive evaluation of a patient's functioning, is the "technology" of geriatrics.[6] The scope is broad.

It is noteworthy that very few functional assessment techniques include evaluation of a senior's spirituality. Even the most

enlightened, open-minded geriatrics team can fail to acknowledge the importance of spirituality in health.

David and Susan Larson from Duke University have ex-
plored the exclusion of spirituality in health research. They note,
"Historically, however, researchers have made but slight forays
into the area of religious commitment. Our own investigations
have documented that religious commitment is seldom studied,
and that when it is, it is often studied only in terms of denomination, which demonstrates little in clinical effects. Yet when studied with measures designed to assess the depth of a person's faith,
such as frequency of worship-service attendance, of prayer and
Scripture reading, or of questions raised about one's relationship
with God, religious commitment is associated with clinical benefits."[7]

Although your individual risk reduction associated with
spirituality may be small, it may be greater than that associated
with cholesterol reduction and other preoccupations of the medical profession.

Other investigators have linked spirituality with mental and
physical health[8] as well as with recovery from illness. For example, religious belief may be associated with lower levels of depres-
sive symptoms and quicker recovery from surgical repair of
broken hips.[9]

It appears to be the depth of religious commitment that
makes a difference.[7] The denomination—Catholic, Protestant,
Jewish, or one of the Eastern religions—makes little difference.

Mrs. Steiner illustrates that one is never too old to develop
spiritually. I share this story with some reservation. It requires a
confession of parental weakness and a peek at a world of which I
have no knowledge or expertise—the supernatural.

When I first met Mrs. Steiner she was bedridden and received nourishment through a feeding tube connected to her

stomach. Multiple strokes had paralyzed her. Her speech was slow and slurred. Her face was pale. We knew that she was bleeding from an ulcer in her stomach. Despite her illness, she was determined to be hospitable to all who entered her room. With every ounce of energy she could muster, she turned her head, locked eyes on the visitor, parted her lips, and said hello.

The nurses told me something strange had happened. Mrs. Steiner had always been cantankerous. She had alienated most of her family and the nursing staff. Ever since she had returned from the hospital three weeks earlier, she had been peaceful and pleasant. The change was a mystery.

Everyone had thought that her latest stroke would leave her even more miserable than she was before. Instead, there was something magnetic about her. It wasn't her acute medical problems that needed attention. It was definitely something else.

Finally one of the nurses stepped forward. "Dr. Murphy, I don't know if I should tell you this, but some of the other nurses and I have seen some unbelievable things with Mrs. Steiner. The other day she told me she knew who visited me at home. There's no way she should know that." Sure, I thought. This eighty-three-year-old woman at death's door can read minds. What next?

I was next. Two days after the conversation with the nurse, I visited Mrs. Steiner to see if she needed another blood transfusion. Out of nowhere, she asked in her soft, halting voice, "Why . . . did . . . you . . . spank . . . your . . . boy?" I looked at Mrs. Steiner's pale face, then at the nurse who flashed me a "what did I tell you" look. I was baffled and tried to stumble back onto the medical problems at hand. Mrs. Steiner tried to dig me out of the confusion. She continued, "He . . . pressed . . . a . . . button." I was really lost then.

I redirected the conversation to abdominal pain, blood loss, intravenous fluids, and things of that sort. That night I shared this experience with my wife. She was as perplexed as I. We rarely spank our children. What was Mrs. Steiner talking about? Then it hit me.

The day before my visit with Mrs. Steiner our oldest son was teasing our oldest daughter. Shannon pleaded with me, "Daddy, tell Danny to quit poking me in the belly button." I warned Danny. After the fourth poke, I gave him a swat on the fanny.

I had heard about people like Mrs. Steiner but I had never met one. My curiosity was overwhelming. I needed an explanation. I forget my exact words, but I asked Mrs. Steiner what was going on.

"I . . . found . . . God," she said with a serenity that belied her serious illness. I believed her and I told her so. Her granddaughter later told me that Mrs. Steiner had had a religious experience during her latest hospital zation. None of us understood the particulars of this experience, but we knew that Mrs. Steiner was a different woman, a much healthier woman than she had been before the stroke that kept her in the hospital for three weeks.

Mrs. Steiner died two weeks later. And every day before her death, people were drawn to her room.

Some medical experts would undoubtedly find a medical explanation for the change in Mrs. Steiner. For example, they may claim that she had a kind of stroke that left her more pleasant. Perhaps she was no longer depressed because she knew she was going to die. Or whatever. But I don't believe medicine can explain Mrs. Steiner's change.

Faith helps with suffering and dying. The medical profession knows this. That is why many hospitals have such strong chaplain services. What the medical profession needs to recognize is that faith also plays an important part in maintaining health. A senior does not need to be a religious zealot to reap the benefits of faith. Sharing in a faith-filled community (for example, church, synagogue, or group of friends) can make a big difference for many seniors.

Diet

A healthy diet can increase your life expectancy and improve your quality of life. However, the benefits of dieting are not as significant as the media and your doctors would have you believe. Our knowledge about nutrition's role in health is rudimentary at best. This is particularly true for seniors. The vast majority of studies on nutrition and health involve people under sixty-five. We simply don't have much good, reliable information regarding nutrition for seniors. When knowledge is sparse, myths abound.

Some believe "we are what we eat." If this is true, eating is the most important activity that affects health. It is certainly the most frequent activity that affects health, or at least makes us think about health. Health sections of bookstores are replete with books advising us how to improve health and longevity by eating the right foods. Newspaper headlines and magazines frequently warn of dangers associated with certain types of food. One week milk is good for you because it has calcium. The next week it is bad for you because it has cholesterol. What's a milk-lover to do? One year margarine is better than butter for your health. The next year . . . what's this? Butter is now better for you than margarine.

You need to know the potential benefits before you decide to follow a strict diet. A strict diet is one where you follow the letter of the law. For example, if you are on a weight-reduction diet that calls for a maximum of 1,200 calories, you eat 1,200 calories or less. You do not eat 1,300 calories. In contrast, a moderate diet is one where you follow the spirit of the law. You are not preoccupied with measuring every calorie or gram of fat. If the diet calls for a maximum of 1,200 calories, you might eat 1,300 or 1,400 calories.

A moderate diet and a strict diet will both improve your health. However, a strict diet appears no healthier than a moderate diet. However, it may negatively affect your quality of life.

If these benefits (weight loss, lower cholesterol, tighter blood sugar control, etc.) are clinically significant to you, then you should follow a diet. If the benefits are modest, perhaps you shouldn't worry about everything you eat. Strict diets for modest benefits are not worthwhile for most people. They cause unnecessary anxiety and may detract from the quality of life. A patient of mine in a nursing home is an example of someone who didn't weigh the benefits and burdens of a diet the same way her previous doctors had weighed them.

She is an eighty-four-year-old woman whose life is full of discomfort. She has multiple chronic diseases and lives in a nursing home. One of her problems is diabetes, which has damaged the nerves that supply her lower legs. These nerves send painful messages more frequently than anyone should have to endure.

She has psychic as well as physical pain. She is lonely. Her few family members rarely visit, and most of her good friends have died. Her litany of complaints tries the patience of all acquaintances. Caring for her is frustrating. Whenever I approach her room at the end of the hall, I wonder what I can do to make her life a little easier. Most of the time a listening ear is all I have to offer. The nurses and I have tried everything to lessen her pain. Our few successes were fleeting. It's hard for anyone to help her.

One day she caught me by surprise. She leaned forward in bed—no small feat for her—and clasped my hand. With an earnestness I had not seen in her before, she said, "Doctor, there's something you could do that would help me. I know this is a lot to ask, but please hear me. There's nothing I want more than a big scoop of Baskin-Robbins ice cream . . . no, make that two scoops."

My grin told her that she could have all the ice cream she wanted. I assured her that one stroke of a pen would guarantee her two scoops of ice cream each day for the rest of her life. She had not expected me to agree and she beamed when I told her it would be no problem. She found it hard to believe that a doctor would prescribe ice cream for a diabetic. Years before doctors had told her that she could only have "tastes" of ice cream because of her diabetes. She had religiously followed their advice. It was only when she had reached rock bottom that she felt she could ask to indulge.

After she started eating ice cream, the pain in her legs became more tolerable.

How many other people are like her and think that they must resist all temptation in their kitchen or in restaurants? Have doctors gone overboard with warnings about salt, sugar, and cholesterol? These are, after all, some of the ingredients that make meals more pleasurable. Should you feel guilty every time you enjoy a poached egg for breakfast or a chocolate mousse for dessert? For those of you who still quiver at the sight of a salt shaker, juicy steak, or blueberry cobbler, ask yourself if a spartan diet will increase your longevity or improve your quality of life.

In previous chapters, I talked about calcium, salt, cholesterol, and sugar. Now let's take a closer look at vitamins, tobacco, alcohol, and caffeine.

Vitamins

Our society expects a lot from vitamins. Popular publications suggest that vitamins will play an increasing role in preventing and curing the illnesses of mankind. What should you make of these reports?

Mr. Tate came to my office because he wanted to discuss his

medicines. He took two medicines for heart disease, one for hypertension, one for upset stomach, one for depression, and several vitamins. His history and physical suggested that he might not need any of these. He wanted to stop whatever medicines he didn't need. One by one we peeled away his medicines. Mr. Tate did fine. In fact, he was very excited that he didn't need all of these medicines. His enthusiasm told me that I could approach a sacred territory—vitamins.

"You've done so well off the medicines. What about the vitamins you take? Do you think you need all of those?" I reminded him that he had expressed concern about the cost of his vitamins.

"Well, Doc, there's no doubt I need them. I feel a lot better now that I'm taking enough vitamins."

I asked him to explain how he felt better. What symptom did he once have that he has no longer?

"Oh, you know, just better. Got more energy. Besides, I haven't had a cold in two years. It's that vitamin C."

Mr. Tate is lucky. He is more energetic after taking substances that do not have any energy value at all.

A publication from the Department of Health and Human Services, *Some Facts and Myths of Vitamins*,[10] emphasizes that the required amounts are small. "To illustrate the small amounts needed by the human body, let's start with an ounce, which is 28.4 grams. A milligram is $\frac{1}{1000}$ of a gram, and a microgram is $\frac{1}{1000}$ of a milligram. The U.S. Recommended Daily Allowance (U.S. RDA) of vitamin B_{12} for an adult is 6 micrograms a day. Just one ounce of this vitamin could supply the daily needs of 4,724,921 people."

Vitamins are a big business. Dr. Roslyn Alfin-Slater from UCLA explains why people use vitamins not only for pep pills but to treat various ailments. "The unprescribed use of vitamins in large doses to treat chronic and potentially life-threatening diseases continues to increase. This use is partially due to the ready availability of these substances in large quantities; their advertisement by a growing number of vitamin enthusiasts whose motivation is primarily profit-oriented; the lack of information on the distinction between sufficient and excessive vitamin use; and the failure of the scientific community to communicate effectively with the public."[11]

What would Mr. Tate think if he read the rest of the publication from the government? It states the following:

MYTH: Vitamins give you "pep" and "energy."
FACT: Vitamins yield no calories. They, of themselves, provide no extra pep or vitality (beyond the placebo value), nor do they provide unusual levels of well-being.
MYTH: Vitamin C "protects" against the common cold.
FACT: Too bad, but extensive clinical research fails to support this.
MYTH: The more vitamins the better.
FACT: Taking excess vitamins is a complete waste, both in money and effect. In fact, as noted, excess amounts of any of several different vitamins can be harmful.
MYTH: You cannot get enough vitamins from the conventional foods you eat.
FACT: Anyone who eats a reasonably varied diet should normally never need supplemental vitamins.[10]

Mr. Tate may not believe that all he needs is a well-balanced diet or that one multivitamin a day is sufficient. He may be correct in assuming that vitamins help in ways we don't yet understand. For example, recent reports suggest that vitamin E helps prevent heart disease.[12,13] When we know more about vitamin E, he can decide if the individual risk reduction is worth it for him to take vitamin E supplements.

Why should Mr. Tate believe what anyone says about vitamins when he knows that he feels better taking them? I would be a fool to discourage vitamins if he believed they made his life better.

Two reasons explain why he feels better taking vitamins. First, vitamins may have physiologic properties that doctors don't understand. Perhaps fifty years from now a scientist will discover why vitamins make some people feel better. Second, the placebo effect of vitamins, like the placebo effect of many other pills, can be strong. If you believe you will feel better on vitamins, there's a good chance you will.

Tobacco

Why do I even discuss tobacco? It's bad for your health—period. However, if I believe that you—not I—should weigh the benefits and burdens of smoking, then I must try to be open-minded. A 103-year-old patient made this clear to me.

Five days before he died, he leaned back in his rocker and lit up an extraordinary cigar. He must have salvaged it from World War I. He leaned backed a little more and blew five smoke rings. Pneumonia was setting in and had left him with little energy to puff out the perfect ring.

This taunt was benign compared to his antics on his 102nd birthday. On that festive occasion I introduced a medical student to him. I wanted the student to appreciate the fun in geriatrics and I knew my patient would come up with some surprise. He didn't let me down.

The student was diligent. He asked my patient about everything. Reaching the part in the medical history that focuses on habits, the student sheepishly asked, "You don't smoke, do you?"

"Cigarettes?" he responded.

"Yes, cigarettes," the student confirmed.

"No, I quit about twenty years ago. Hasn't Dr. Murphy told you? Cigarettes are bad for your health," he beamed. I knew this was a setup.

Before the student could continue, my patient added, "Now I smoke stogies."

"Do you . . ."

"And you want to know something else?" he interrupted. "I inhale." His grin was wider than the Cheshire cat's. But this mockery of the medical profession didn't deter the student.

"Have you thought of quitting?" the student persisted. At that point a nurse entered the room and saved the medical student from his final blow. I'm not sure what the retort would have been, but it would have been swift and decisive.

This senior inhaled smoke for years and was thriving at 102 years old. Is there a good reason to discourage him from enjoying one of his few remaining pleasures? Not really. What about other seniors who have beaten the odds and continue to smoke in their seventies and eighties?

Smoking cessation helps at any age. Seniors who smoke cigarettes have a risk of death from heart disease that is anywhere from 50 to 200 percent higher than nonsmokers, ex-smokers, or pipe and cigar smokers.[14,15] Therefore, the relative risk reduction of smoking cessation is 50 to 200 percent. Your individual risk reduction, however, is much lower.

One study suggested that if you have moderate heart disease, your individual risk reduction is about 18 percent six years after quitting smoking.[16] In other words, about one in six seniors with moderate heart disease would live longer if they stopped smoking. Your individual risk reduction ranges from 5 to 10 percent if you have either mild or severe heart disease.

Smoking cessation also slows the progression of emphysema.[17] The risk of cancer also decreases with cessation, but the cancer risk reduction is not as great as the risk reduction for heart disease.[15,17]

Many seniors continue to smoke and live as long as they would have if they had quit smoking. Nevertheless, your individual risk reduction is high enough (5 to 20 percent) that you should consider smoking cessation. Your individual risk reduction with smoking cessation is certainly higher than your individual risk reduction from low cholesterol diets (1 to 2 percent).

The new nicotine skin patches may make cessation a realistic goal for many. These patches deliver small doses of nicotine through the skin and therefore diminish the craving for nicotine. The cost of one patch, which lasts one day, is about the cost of a pack of cigarettes.

Alcohol

Alcoholism is a serious problem. Alcohol plays a part in many tragic deaths from motor vehicle accidents, domestic violence, and suicide. Excessive intake often leads to cirrhosis of the liver and death from gastrointestinal bleeding. Although moderate intake of alcohol (one to two drinks a day) may protect against heart disease,[18] the devastating effects of alcohol are too great for doctors to recommend that anyone increase their alcohol consumption.

There are exceptions.

Mrs. Smith is a woman with severe arthritis who requires long-term care. Ever since her husband died thirty years ago, she has watched the evening news while drinking a nightcap. Occasionally, she would drink two when friends were visiting. This moderate amount of alcohol never caused a problem.

When she entered the nursing home, her doctor and nurses overlooked her habit. After weeks of anxiety without her nightcap, Mrs. Smith finally asked a nurse why she couldn't have the drink. Why did her habit have to change now? Was it just because she was so arthritic that she needed nursing care? It didn't make sense to her. And it didn't make sense to the nurse.

At the nurse's prodding, the doctor finally decided that Mrs. Smith's quality of life was more important than the discomfort he felt "prescribing" a nightcap for her. Mrs. Smith resumed her nightcaps and adjusted to nursing-home life much sooner than anyone expected.

Caffeine

Doctors have accused caffeine of causing many problems, including cancer and extra heartbeats. Despite the warnings about caffeine, coffee is a mainstay in many diets.

Recent reviews[19,20] concluded that coffee is not as villainous as some reports suggest. Caffeine is not associated with heart attacks or tumors. The role of caffeine in the production of abnormal heart rhythms or stomach ulcers remains unclear. One expert concluded that moderate ingestion of caffeine does not increase abnormal heart rhythms.[21] Nine or more cups of coffee daily may cause extra heartbeats; five to six cups daily should not.

If you drink four to five cups of coffee a day or less and feel fine, enjoy your coffee. If, on the other hand, you have unexplained symptoms (for example, upset stomach, palpitations, anxiety), try reducing your coffee intake or stopping it altogether. See what happens after a week. You might be pleasantly surprised.

Social Life

Mr. Sutton was one hundred years old and in good health. He lived in a long-term-care facility on the same floor with forty other seniors who shared meals in a dining room. Over the course of two weeks he became withdrawn. At times he was disoriented.

We knew that his vision was getting worse. He, like many of the other residents, had cataracts. We checked several laboratory tests, but all were negative. Out of desperation, we referred him to an ophthalmologist for cataract surgery. We had to do something or Mr. Sutton would fade away. The ophthalmologist did not want to operate. We sent Mr. Sutton back to the ophthalmologist, who eventually agreed that surgery was worth a try.

One day after the operation, Mr. Sutton took the patch off his eye. He exclaimed to everyone in earshot, "I can see! Look at the colors!" When he arrived home two days later, he reminded me of a five-year-old at his own birthday party. His excitement was contagious. Everyone on the floor was happy for him. Dinner that evening was a rare celebration. Seniors who had dined alone in their rooms for months joined the party to welcome Mr. Sutton home.

I greeted Mr. Sutton the next morning. "It must be great to see again, Mr. Sutton." He responded, "Yeah, it is. But let me tell you the best part. I can be with my friends again."

Mr. Sutton might very well have died from social isolation when he couldn't see well enough to join his friends. With his social life intact, who could guess how much longer he would enjoy good health.

Social support can play a role in sustaining good health.[22] Even if social supports don't improve health (i.e., lead to fewer illnesses or a longer life), they usually make seniors *feel* healthier.[23]

A senior's social calendar need not be full. A good friend or two can make all the difference.

Volunteer Work

Mrs. Turner is an eighty-two-year-old woman who used to come into my office every two months. She was tired and thought that I could give her something to make her more energetic. I ran a few tests. They were negative. I wondered if she was depressed. That diagnosis didn't pan out.

I was reluctant to settle on the diagnosis of chronic fatigue (not the chronic fatigue syndrome seen in younger people). It's a common problem in geriatrics. Finally Mrs. Turner helped me sort out the problem.

"You know, Doctor, I used to be full of energy. This just isn't like me. I used to be a foster grandparent. Boy, did I love those kids!"

"That seems like quite a responsibility, Mrs. Turner. That must have made you tired. Did you feel tired then?" I asked.

"Are you kidding? I didn't have time to get tired. Those little ones had me hoppin' up and down the stairs. But I can't do that anymore on account of my knees . . ." She paused in mid-sentence. A light went on and she continued, "You don't suppose I need to do something like that again? What can I do?"

Mrs. Turner had diagnosed her problem. There's no medical code in the diagnostic manual for it, but it's real. Some call it boredom. Mrs. Turner needed to get involved. Her talent was helping children.

A social worker arranged for Mrs. Turner to read to first graders at an elementary school. She didn't have to hop up and down steps. She no longer needed to see the doctor once every two months. And best of all, the first graders loved her.

Mrs. Allen is a seventy-eight-year-old with chronic back pain from severe arthritis. She lives in a nursing home and told me on several occasions that Friday afternoons made life worth living. On Friday afternoons she sings for the Alzheimer's patients. Mrs. Allen lights up when recounting the joy she brings to these people.

"You doctors and nurses can't even get my friends to talk. I get them to sing," she boasts.

A recent study indicated that "giving informal assistance to others appears to bolster feelings of personal control in later life."[24] The study also indicated that people who feel in greater control are less likely to have depression. A dose of volunteer work (or play, depending how you look at it) may be the best prescription for your health.

Sexuality

Mr. Forman, a veteran of World War I, came to the geriatrics clinic at a Veterans Administration hospital because he had abdominal pain. His wife, an attractive seventy-six-year-old who was fourteen years younger than him, accompanied him. He introduced her as his "young bride of fifty-three years."

His history was vague. The exam didn't give us any clues. His x-rays and blood tests were negative. (Are you starting to see a pattern in these medical evaluations?)

I was an intern at the time. My supervising doctor said, "There's something that doesn't fit here. We'll see how he's doing in a couple of weeks."

Two weeks later he returned with his "young bride" and the same vague abdominal pain. Once again, we came up empty-handed.

Two weeks later the story became clearer. We asked Mr. Forman if he was under more stress than usual. Yes, he was. After we asked him what was on his mind, he quietly asked his wife to leave the room. She left, and he told us his problem.

"I don't how to tell you this, but I've been real uneasy lately. I'm worried. My wife and I hardly . . . well, we hardly get together anymore."

I was puzzled. Did Mr. Forman mean that they didn't watch television together? Or maybe they didn't take walks together? Was it grocery shopping? What was he telling us?

My supervising doctor, a much more seasoned clinician than I, read between the lines. "Mr. Forman, are you saying that you and your wife no longer have sexual relations with each other?" the supervising doctor asked.

"Yes, that's it. We hardly get together anymore."

"Just how often do you have sexual relations with your wife?" the supervising doctor continued.

"Oh, about once a week," Mr. Forman said with a straight face. I was waiting for him to follow up with, "Just kidding, Doc. It's actually about once every six months." But he didn't. Instead, he repeated, "Yeah, about once a week."

Finally it dawned on me that Mr. Forman was serious. This ninety-four-year-old man was stressed because he and his wife were having sex only once a week.

Doctors want to feel compassionate. We want to empathize, or at least sympathize, with our patients. This is one time, I must confess, that I couldn't really feel sorry for my patient. I didn't know what to do for him except explain that these problems happen when you get older. That sufficed. His abdominal pain subsided.

Many seniors assume that sexual desire and activity wane with age. But it is the problems associated with aging, not aging itself, that lead to reduced sexual activity. For example, impaired mobility, other illnesses, and lack of a partner can reduce sexual activity in old age.[25] The need for love and sexual intimacy does not diminish with age.[26]

Few seniors can keep up with Mr. Forman. Many would not even want to try if they could. They are content with little or no sexual activity. On the other hand, seniors who have good health and a partner can enjoy sexual intimacy into their seventies, eighties, and maybe nineties.

Intellect

Mrs. Burrows is a ninety-one-year-old with poor vision, memory lapses, and a pacemaker that's on the blink. She says she doesn't want it fixed because she "never wanted it in the first place." Her symptoms would preoccupy most seniors and their doctors. As hard as I'd try to determine what bothered her, she rarely focused on her symptoms. She always wanted to talk about the Russian Revolution, the Industrial Revolution, French satire, and Aristotle.

"I am an intellectual," she proclaimed one day. That much I knew. What fascinated me was how she had gained that status.

Mrs. Burrows was never really a bookworm. At age seventy-four she started attending poetry readings in her life-care community. She thought she could recite poems better than the visiting professor from a local college could. Off she went, devouring poems and learning the history of the authors.

Mrs. Burrows will miss a few questions on a formal mental status test. As long as she's gaining a better understanding of Aristotle, she doesn't really care.

One recent study indicated that increased educational and occupational attainment may reduce the risk of Alzheimer's disease.[27] This is only one study. We don't have other evidence that keeping an active mind will help prevent Alzheimer's disease or other kinds of memory disorders. Nevertheless, it seems that intellectual challenges will ease the burdens of aging for most seniors.

Retirement and Financial Security

The subjects of retirement and financial security are beyond the scope of this book. I mention them for the sake of completeness. They certainly affect health outside the doctor's office. Dr. William McBeath, quoting J. Mitchell, emphasized the importance of these in a recent keynote address to the American Public Health Association.

> *If you*
> *have decent air to breathe,*
> *live in a low-crime neighborhood,*
> *have a meaningful job with adequate pay,*
> *work in a safe environment,*
> *have money to choose good food and time to enjoy*
> *   preparing it,*
> *can afford to take vacations,*
> *have a safe place for your children to play,*
> *enjoy life and look forward to the future;*
> *then (maybe) you can choose health.*[28]

Summary

Health involves much more than the absence of disease. Physical health is only one dimension in your overall health.

The following prescriptions are not the usual prescriptions for health. However, they are probably more effective than any prescription you get inside your doctor's office.

1. Exercise regularly, even if it's moving a leg up and down.
2. Rekindle a lost faith, pray, and reach out to others.
3. Enjoy food.

4. Spend time with friends.
5. Share your talents with someone less fortunate.
6. Rekindle some passion that you thought old age had robbed.
7. Pick up that spy novel that you've been thinking about for years.

Let's remember one other prescription for health outside the doctor's office: Buckle up.

22

You and Your Doctor—
A Relationship Built on Honesty

You now know the benefits and burdens of everday health care. If you and your doctor value these the same way, you will welcome his recommendations. You will work well together to improve your health.

What if you and your doctor don't weigh the benefits and burdens the same way? Will you need a compromise? What can you do to reach that compromise?

In this chapter I will suggest ways to work with your doctor so that he understands how you value health care.

Imagine the following scenarios:

1. You see your doctor for a routine checkup, and he discovers that your cholesterol is 240. He tells you that this is high and he recommends a new medicine to lower your

cholesterol. You're not sure it's worth it, but you're willing to try it for a month or two. At the pharmacy you discover it will cost you seventy dollars a month.

2. Your doctor returns from a continuing medical education course where the instructors emphasized that women over age fifty should have yearly mammograms. He orders a mammogram for you because your last one was fourteen months ago. He doesn't realize you will have to pay one hundred dollars for the mammogram because Medicare won't reimburse for mammograms done within two years of each other.

3. Your doctor says, "You definitely need estrogen. It will protect your bones." You remember the side effects you had last time you tried estrogen.

4. You're convinced the pain in your upper abdomen is from recurrence of ulcers—you had the same pain before when you had ulcers. You tell your doctor about these symptoms, and he says you need to see a gastroenterologist, who will examine your stomach with a scope. Your doctor says, "We have to be sure this is an ulcer and not something else."

5. The pain from your arthritis is more bothersome. Your doctor gives you samples of a new pain medicine. They work a little better than your usual medicine, but they cost twice as much. You don't think the new medicine is worth the extra cost.

In each of these scenarios, you have weighed the burdens and benefits of your doctor's recommendation. You're not sure you want to follow your doctor's advice because the benefits don't outweigh the burdens for you. What do you do?

You have three options (I'm sure there are more, but I will discuss the three that come to mind).

First, you can deceive your doctor, pretending to follow his advice but not really doing what he recommends. This is the approach that Dr. Robert Mendelsohn recommends in his book *Confessions of a Medical Heretic.*[1]

Dr. Mendelsohn began his book with these words: "I do not believe in Modern Medicine. I am a medical heretic. My aim in this book is to persuade you to become a heretic, too." He advocates a doctor-patient relationship that is based on duplicity. He writes, "To fully protect yourself from your doctor, you must learn how to lie to him . . . I advise medical students to learn the fine arts of hypocrisy and duplicity, just as Southern blacks once learned the art of shuffling. Shuffling was the fine art of appearing to be active and obedient when in reality you were nothing of the sort. That's what you have to do with your doctor."

Second, you can obediently follow your doctor's advice and overlook the burdens . . . or quietly bear them. This is what patients do day after day. For many patients, this seems like the best approach.

Third, you can be honest with your doctor and try to work out something that satisfies you both. I recommend that more people consider this approach.

Yes, I know, this may be difficult. It may cause tension. Imagine the following responses that you might make for the scenarios described above:

1. "Doctor, I tried that medicine. I had no side effects, but I'm not going to continue it because it's too expensive. If it decreases my risk of a heart attack by only one or two percent, I don't want to spend seventy dollars a month for it."
2. "I didn't keep my appointment for the mammogram. The chance of it helping me was too small to justify the time and money I'd have to spend for this test."

3. "I don't want to take estrogen because I don't like the bleeding it causes."
4. "Doctor, I don't think endoscopy is necessary because I know my symptoms are from an ulcer. Do you think I could just try antacids for a while and see how I feel?"
5. "The new medicine works all right, but I can't afford to continue using it. I'll just stick with my old medicine."

You might feel comfortable with one or two of these responses. Most of them, however, do not easily roll off the tongue.

If you have reservations about negotiating with your doctor, I can sympathize. I will share two experiences—one as a doctor, one as a patient—to illustrate that I have reservations, too.

When Mrs. Collins told me she was no longer going to take the one sedative that had eased her anxiety, I asked her why. She told me she had changed her mind about the medicine. To emphasize her newfound conviction, she pulled out the book *Worst Pills, Best Pills*[2] and pointed out that her medicine was a "bad pill."

I recall thinking, Oh, brother, I'm supposed to practice medicine when some "expert" who doesn't even know Mrs. Collins is trying to undermine me. How can anyone say that something is either bad or good? Medicine isn't black or white. It depends on the situation, and the authors of that book have no idea about this situation. I can no longer use the one medicine that has helped Mrs. Collins. What if nothing else works as well? I was frustrated.

I appreciate that some of the information in this book may threaten your doctor, especially if you present it to him. However, this should not stop us from being honest with ourselves.

My second experience involved a different perspective. I was the patient.

At 5:00 A.M. I woke with a pain in my right flank. I tried to recall pulling the muscles in my back. No luck. The pain subsided, and I went back to sleep. At 5:30 it returned and was much more intense. I called a friend at the emergency room. "Charlie, I think I'm passing a kidney stone. What should I do?" I accepted his invitation to the emergency room, but felt much better before arriving there.

I was on call that weekend, so I decided to skip the emergency room (I was feeling normal) and see patients. While at the hospital, I ran into a nephrologist (kidney specialist) whom I hadn't seen since medical school. I told him about the pain and asked him what I should do for follow-up. He handed me a specimen cup and asked for a urine specimen. I obliged. Better yet, I delivered the stone. We laughed about the timing. He suggested that I stop by his office to have a few tests. Okay, I thought. He's a great guy and I need a doctor at some point.

Four weeks later I tried to dodge my doctor when I saw him coming down the hall. I hadn't stopped by his office to have the tests and felt embarrassed by not following his recommendation. I had good reasons for not stopping by, but I didn't know how to tell him. How could I tell him:

1. I had read about kidney stones. One article suggested that tests aren't necessary after just one stone.[3] Many people with calcium oxalate stones, which is what I had, don't have a recurrence. Besides, there's no specific therapy. I think it's reasonable to drink more water and see how I do. If I have another stone, I'll stop by to get those tests.
2. I don't have time this month to spend an hour at your office.
3. My health insurance doesn't cover outpatient tests. I'm worried that you'll do a lot of tests that are unlikely to tell us anything and I'll get strapped with a hefty bill.

4. One of my closest patients just died from kidney failure. She had a long history of kidney stones. Granted, she wasn't very conscientious about her health. Nevertheless, I know that kidney stones can lead to bad things. Maybe I need to deny that I have a potentially chronic illness.

I still haven't talked to my own doctor about these concerns. I understand how difficult it may be for you to be honest with your doctor.

Let's explore how we can be honest with our doctors. First, I want to review the modern history of the doctor-patient relationship. This history emphasizes why patients and doctors should be honest with each other.

The History of the Doctor-Patient Relationship

Prior to the 1960s, the doctor-patient relationship was characterized by paternalism. The doctor and patient assumed that the doctor knew what was best for the patient.

Paternalism began to fade in the 1960s for three major reasons. First, it was a time when our society was questioning authority, and medical authorities were no exception. Second, the rapid acceleration in medical research after World War II provided many more diagnostic and therapeutic options than ever before. The expansion of possibilities complicated the doctor-patient relationship. No longer was the decision-making as easy as deciding whether to use an antibiotic or not. The doctor and patient could consider useful options for many problems.

Finally, medical studies revealed that patients with cancer wanted to know their diagnosis and prognosis.[4,5] Before publication of these studies in the 1960s, doctors assumed that such knowledge would harm their patients. Many doctors didn't tell their patients about the diagnosis or prognosis. They protected their patients from the cruel realities of cancer. These studies suggested that patients want involvement with decisions that affect their lives (and their deaths).

During the past thirty to forty years a new model for the doctor-patient relationship emerged. Patient autonomy is the foundation. The patient, not the doctor, decides what is best for the patient.

Although the pendulum may have swung too far in some cases—for example, when patients or families demand unreasonable therapies[6,7]—most doctors and ethicists agree that patient autonomy should be the guiding principle in medical decisions.

Drs. Ezekiel Emanuel and Linda Emanuel summarized three doctor-patient models in addition to the paternalistic model.[8] In the informative model, the doctor presents all the facts to the patient and the patient decides the best alternative. "There is no role for the physician's values, the physician's understanding of the patient's values, or his or her judgment of the worth of the patient's values." The problem with this model is that it "vests the medical decision-making authority with the patient while relegating physicians to technicians" who transmit information and use their skills as the patient directs.

In the interpretive model, the doctor presents all the facts *and* helps the patient interpret these facts based on the patient's values.

In the deliberative model, the doctor presents the facts, helps the patient interpret these facts, *and* "acts as a teacher or friend, engaging the patient in dialogue on what course of action would be best."

Professionals will disagree about the ideal model. No one model is ideal for all doctor-patient meetings. One thing is clear, though. The doctor-patient relationship in the 1990s is different from the relationship in the 1940s because patients today are informed. Doctors share decision-making with patients. They no longer dictate decisions to their patients.

The Future of the Doctor-Patient Relationship

We are beginning to see another revolution in the doctor-patient relationship. In the "golden era" of medicine, doctors didn't have to worry about costs. If a doctor wanted to order a test, he didn't even think about the cost of the test. He just ordered it. If a patient wanted to stay in the hospital another day or so, that was okay. The doctor could accommodate him.

Health care has changed. As Drs. Kevin Grumbach and Thomas Bodenheimer wrote, "Economic realities dictate that the era of absolute clinical autonomy is over. Whether by reins or fences, physicians will have to consider costs when making clinical decisions."[9]

Today doctors have to think about costs at all levels, whether in medical school,[10] at the bedside,[11,12] in societal debates about the fair allocation of resources,[13] or in the boardroom.[14] Most important, doctors need to think about the cost you will incur when they recommend a test or medicine for you.

It's no mystery; the costs of health care are skyrocketing. One way or another we all will pay more out of pocket for health care. Private insurance premiums will rise. Medicare copayments will rise. Taxes will rise. New medicines not covered by insurance will be expensive. Each passing year we feel the burden of health care costs getting heavier.

What will happen in this new revolution? First, society will have to learn how to connect the value of health care with the cost of health care.[15] This subject is beyond the scope of this book. Proposals are abundant in the medical literature and in policy circles.

Second, doctors and patients will have to learn to feel comfortable talking about costs—not just monetary costs, but psychological costs and the cost of time and travel. Doctors are willing to learn and be sensitive to cost concerns.[16–19]

I believe that most doctors want to be sensitive to your burdens. Doctors welcome the trend in medical education that emphasizes humanistic qualities.[20,21] However, incorporating a concern about costs into medical practice will take time. Many doctors don't yet feel comfortable with this role.

How can we help this revolution along? Should we wait for medical schools to teach new approaches? Medical education is certainly a part of the solution, but it is not enough.

We patients need to educate our doctors. In fact, we can do a much better job than the medical schools. Doctors learn much more from their patients than they do from a professor in a classroom.

Consider this example. A new patient asked me about the PSA test. I explained to him what I outlined in chapter 6 about the PSA test. He then asked, "Do you know the cost of this test, Doctor?" He caught me off guard because I really should know the cost of the test and I didn't. "No, not right off hand, but I'll find out for you," I assured him.

I will remember the cost of that test because I learned it to provide care for my patient. We learn best when the knowledge applies to our patients. My patient's question helped me learn the information I need.

More important, I learned something about my patient. I know that he is concerned about costs and that he is willing to discuss this concern. This will help in our future interactions.

You can teach your doctor a lot. Obviously, you are the best one to teach him about your values and expectations. Your questions—particularly the ones he can't answer—will also teach him about medical care in general.

I suggest the following ways to inform your doctor how you weigh the benefits and burdens of his recommendations. Your doctor should be sensitive to your concerns, and you should be sensitive in the way you inform your doctor.

Estimating the Benefit of Tests for You

Estimating the benefit of your doctor's recommendation is the first step. Let's begin with tests. Assume your doctor recommends a test when you have no symptoms (a screening test). As I emphasized in chapters 6 and 7, screening tests must be done for many people so that one person will benefit.

Your question might be, How many screening tests must be done so that one person will benefit? If the answer is one hundred tests—and the test is convenient and painless—then most people would consider this a valuable test. If, on the other hand, the answer is one thousand tests—and the test is inconvenient and uncomfortable—then many people would doubt the value of the test.

Asking questions serves two purposes. First, it encourages your doctor to consider your individual risk reduction, not just the relative risk reduction. Often your doctor will not know the answers. He will have to dig them up, because these answers are not readily available in the medical literature . . . at least not yet.

Second, questions soften your reservations. You express reservations about your doctor's recommendations when you question their value. Try to be sensitive to your doctor's perception that he is recommending the best steps for your health.

If, based on your doctor's response, you don't think the test is valuable enough for you, share your concerns with your doctor. He should get the message without feeling that you are questioning his expertise. He will learn something about you—that not all recommendations by medical experts are valuable to you.

This will encourage your doctor to explore your values the next time he recommends something.

Estimating the Benefit of Medicines for You

Assume you have no symptoms and your doctor recommends a medicine to reduce your risk of heart disease. Consider a similar approach to the one I suggested above. Ask your doctor what the chance is that someone like you will have a heart attack in the next few years. What is the chance that this medicine will actually prevent a heart attack for you?

Questions will soften your reservations and help your doctor consider your individual risk reduction.

If the benefit is not high enough for you, tell your doctor. Nine times out of ten he will respect your values and honesty.

Estimating the Burdens of Tests for You

The burdens of tests include physical discomfort, cost, and inconvenience.

The physical discomforts of tests are usually well known. If the test is a procedure that may have adverse effects, your doctor will discuss these effects with you before doing the procedure.

Cost is a different matter. Your doctor is unlikely to discuss the cost of the test he recommends. If you believe the test may be expensive, make sure you know what your out-of-pocket costs will be. Ask how much Medicare will cover and how much you will have to pay. If your doctor doesn't know the answer, ask him if someone in his office can help you. Usually a member of the office staff can answer these questions for you.

Inconvenient tests are those that require more time (time for travel and time for the test) than you have open on your calendar. If you don't have enough time for a test at the moment, ask your doctor if there's any problem with postponing it.

Estimating the Burdens of Medicines for You

The burdens of medicines include side effects, inconvenience, and costs.

When your doctor recommends a medicine, ask him about the common side effects. Asking about all side effects is unhelpful, because many medicines can theoretically cause almost any side effect you can imagine.

If taking a medicine three or four times a day is inconvenient for you, tell your doctor. Long-acting preparations are available for many medicines, and your doctor should be willing to try these. Realize, however, that they may cost more.

Finally, ask your doctor about the cost of the medicine. Ask if a less expensive medicine would work just as well.

Your doctor should get the message. He realizes that if he ignores your concern about cost, you may not take the medicine at all. If he does ignore your concerns about cost—or makes you feel uncomfortable expressing this concern—remember that there are many other doctors who would be more sensitive.

Weigh the benefits and burdens of your doctor's recommendations. If you have reservations about your doctor's recommendations, be honest with him. Try to be as sensitive with your doctor as you expect him to be with you.

Epilogue

Health care is entering a new era. No matter what happens in the debate on health-care reform, one thing is certain: the delivery of health care will change significantly in the coming decade. One of our greatest challenges will be to preserve, and perhaps improve, the doctor-patient relationship.

What are some of the changes we can expect? First, the population of seniors will continue to grow. America is graying. The fastest growing segment of the population consists of seniors over age eighty. No one predicts a reversal of this trend. Our society will need much better information about health care that is effective and desirable for seniors. Although we've made great strides in medical research, we have a long way to go before answering many questions for this growing population. Consider a recent report on inappropriate drug use for seniors. The authors suggest that at least one in four seniors in the United States is taking a prescription drug that experts would consider inappropriate. That's big news, yet most newspapers that covered the story buried it in the middle of the paper. We can expect seniors to spend more time on center stage in the future. And when this research does reach the front page, we should look at it with a critical eye.

Second, we will continue to discover new technologies that will lead to better diagnostic tests and better treatments. Though we will gain most of our knowledge in incremental steps, a few quantum leaps in knowledge may be closer than people think. For example, breakthroughs in genetic research could revolutionize the prevention of and treatments for chronic disease. Imagine a medicine that could alter the genetic code of a fifty-year-old who runs a high risk of getting Alzheimer's disease by the age of seventy. Imagine similar medicines that would help prevent coronary artery disease, diabetes, and osteoarthritis. Medicine may look very different after the genetic revolution comes to fruition.

Third, our society must decide if it is serious about controlling the rising cost of health care. Currently we spend 14 percent of our gross national product on health care; some experts predict that after the turn of the century that figure will rise to 20 percent. No doubt, many people's lives will improve because of this commitment. But let's not forget the trade-offs. The more our society spends on health care, the less it spends on the many other services that make communities healthier, such as housing, transportation, recreation, and education. At what point do we say that our focus on medical care has caused too many sacrifices in other areas? The debate on health-care reform is encouraging us to think about these trade-offs. If we are truly serious about cost control, we will have to do a better job of linking the value and the cost of health care. The health-care reform debates of 1994 are just warm-ups for the coming debates on cost control.

These three forces (the aging population, technological advances, and rising health-care costs) appear to be on a collision course. Can we accommodate our growing population of seniors and control medical costs? Can we accomplish these goals *and* improve the quality of health care, including improving the doctor-patient relationship? I believe we can and that one of the answers is honest medicine.

Honest medicine means that we are honest with ourselves, with our doctors, and with our policy makers. Before we can be honest, we need a critical eye. We must realize that the medical establishment and the media will be inclined to portray medical progress in the most dramatic light. They may suggest that something statistically significant is also clinically significant. You, not just your doctors and the medical profession, should decide if something is clinically significant.

The profession and the media will probably continue to advertise relative risk reductions. You should ask about your individual risk reduction. Once you know the benefits and burdens for you, you can decide if it is worth pursuing.

We will all need to be more involved in the debate about the value and costs of health care. As health-care reform proceeds, individuals will have to make tough choices about the value and cost of their health care. Not everyone will get everything they want. Those who want more than most of their peers will probably have to pay more; those who want less will probably pay less.

Honesty will promote the most productive research, the most cost-effective tests and therapies, and the most fair insurance plans. It will also foster the best medical care at the bedside.

A doctor-patient relationship built on honesty has been and will continue to be the foundation of good health care. A relationship built on mutual trust should be enjoyable and healthy. Honesty will help you and your doctor learn all you can about the most important part of health care, your health.

Acknowledgments

Many people contributed to this book. I am particularly grateful to the following.

Seniors at the Denver Veterans Administration Hospital, Hebrew Rehabilitation Centre for Aged in Boston, Jewish Memorial Hospital in Boston, Thomas House in Washington, D.C., and Presbyterian/St. Luke's Senior Citizen's Health Center in Denver shared their stories with me. They gave me the ideas for this book.

Dr. Jeff Hoeg, a friend and colleague, encouraged me to write this book when the ideas were in their infancy.

Patrick Peyton, a friend from earlier years in Denver, was acting CEO for Grove Press when my idea was reaching the toddler stage. I told him about it but felt that writing a book would be too complicated and risky for me at the time. He said nonsense. Go for it.

Jim Moser is executive editor at Grove/Atlantic. He got me started and let me work at my own pace. I've learned a great deal from his keen eye for detail and his view of the big picture. His guidance and good humor were invaluable during the many revisions of the manuscript.

Amy Ryan, the copy editor, added the finishing touches.

Dean Winstanley, my brother-in-law, who wrote *The Colorado Guide,* helped me plan a schedule.

His parents, Stan and Marion Winstanley, read every word of the manuscript with a critical eye. Their encouragement and suggestions kept me going in the early stages.

One of my patients, Zaidee Reed, was thumbing through a magazine one day while waiting to see me. "How would you like to read a whole book?" I asked. She agreed to review the manuscript, and her candor has made a big difference.

Two of my sisters, Sheila Winstanley and Mary Ann Hogsett, and my father, Joseph Murphy, M.D., reviewed the manuscript. Their comments led to changes in both tone and format.

The staff at the Senior Citizen's Health Center was very supportive during the time I needed to complete this book.

Mary DeMund and Dorothy Struble, librarians at Presbyterian/St. Luke's Medical Center, retrieved articles faster than I could recite the titles.

Brad Brouillette, the pharmacist for the Senior Citizen's Health Center, determined the wholesale prices for the medicines I list in this book.

Beth Barbour, the office manager at the Senior Citizen's Health Center, helped prepare the manuscript.

My children have been very patient. Often they asked if I could play and then spared me the anguish of declining. They let me off the hook with, "That's okay, Dad, we can play after you finish your book."

Finally, my wife, Susan, has been my major support from beginning to end. She planted the seed, helped me form the idea, and told me to nurture it. She has kept the household running while I've been glued to the word processor. She had the wisdom to say, "Don, I'd be happy to review the manuscript, but don't you think you ought to ask someone else?" I attribute our healthy marriage to her advice.

References

A list of journal titles and their abbreviations can be found at the end of the reference section.

Chapter 1
1. Skrabanek P, McCormick J. *Follies and Fallacies in Medicine*. Buffalo, N.Y.: Prometheus Books, 1990.
2. Stolley PD, Lasky T. Johannes Fibiger and his Nobel Prize for the hypothesis that a worm causes stomach cancer. *Ann Intern Med* 1992; 116:765–769.
3. Payer L. *Medicine and Culture*. New York: Penguin Books, 1989.

Chapter 2
1. Moore M. Beware the bracken fern, in Moore M (ed): *Health Risks and the Press*. Washington, D.C.: The Media Institute, 1989:1–18.
2. Mandel JS, Bond MPH, Church TR, et al. Reducing mortality from colorectal cancer by screening for fecal occult blood. *N Engl J Med* 1993; 328:1365–1371.

Chapter 3

1. Angell M. The interpretation of epidemiologic studies. *N Engl J Med* 1990; 323:823–825.
2. Easterbrook PJ, Berlin JA, Gopalan R, et al. Publication bias in clinical research. *Lancet* 1991; 337:867–872.
3. Dickersin K, Min Y, Meinert CL. Factors influencing publication of research results: Follow-up of applications submitted to two institutional review boards. *JAMA* 1992; 267:374–378.
4. Cohn V. Reporters as gatekeepers, in Moore M (ed): *Health Risks and the Press.* Washington, D.C.: The Media Institute, 1989:35–51.
5. Schwitzer G. The magical medical media tour. *JAMA* 1992; 267:1969–1971.

Chapter 4

1. Huycke LI, Huycke MM. Characteristics of potential plaintiffs in malpractice litigation. *Ann Intern Med* 1994; 120:792–798.
2. Skrabanek P, McCormick J. *Follies and Fallacies in Medicine.* Buffalo, N.Y.: Prometheus Books, 1990.
3. Murphy DJ, Burrows D, Santilli S, et al. The influence of the probability of survival on patients' preferences regarding cardiopulmonary resuscitation. *N Engl J Med* 1994; 330:545–549.
4. Murphy DJ, Santilli S, Shubinski R, et al. Seniors' preferences for screening and prophylaxis based on absolute risk reduction. Abstracts at the American Geriatric Society meeting, May 1994.

Chapter 5

1. Bruhn JG. The doctor's touch: tactile communication in the doctor-patient relationship. *South Med J* 1978; 71:1469–1473.
2. Colburn D. The annual physical: Who needs it? *Washington Post,* September 17, 1991:10–13.
3. Joint National Committee on Detection, Evaluation, and Treatment of High Blood Pressure. The fifth report of the Joint National Committee on Detection, Evaluation, and Treatment of High Blood Pressure (JNC V). *Arch Intern Med* 1993; 153:154–183.
4. Lipsitz LA, Storch HA, Minaker KL, et al. Intra-individual variability in postural blood pressure in the elderly. *Clin Sci* 1985; 69:337–341.

5. Oboler SK, LaForce FM. The periodic physical examination in asymptomatic adults. *Ann Intern Med* 1989; 110:214–226.

6. Stone DH, Shannon DJ. Screening for impaired visual acuity in middle age in general practice. *Br Med J* 1978; 2:859–861.

7. Woolf SH, Kamerow DB, Lawrence RS, et al. The periodic health examination of older adults: The recommendations of the U.S. Preventive Services Task Force. Part II: Screening tests. *J Am Geriatr Soc* 1990; 38:933–942.

8. Mulrow CD, Aguilar C, Endicott JE, et al. Quality-of-life changes and hearing impairment: A randomized trial. *Ann Intern Med* 1990; 113:188–194.

9. Heyman A, Wilkinson WE, Heyden S, et al. Risk of stroke in asymptomatic persons with cervical arterial bruits: A population study in Evans County, Georgia. *N Engl J Med* 1980; 302:838–841.

10. Meissner I, Wiebers DO, Whisnant JP, et al. The natural history of asymptomatic carotid artery occlusive lesions. *JAMA* 1987; 258:-2704–2707.

11. Chambers BR, Norris JW. The case against surgery for asymptomatic carotid stenosis. *Stroke* 1984; 15:964–967.

12. Hobson RW, Weiss DG, Fields WS, et al. Efficacy of carotid endarterectomy for asymptomatic carotid stenosis. *N Engl J Med* 1993; 328:221–227.

13. Barnett HJM, Haines SJ. Carotid endarterectomy for asymptomatic carotid stenosis. *N Engl J Med* 1993; 328:276–278.

14. Rojeski MT, Gharib H. Nodular thyroid disease: evaluation and management. *N Engl J Med* 1985; 313:428–436.

15. U.S. Preventive Services Task Force. Screening for breast cancer, in *Guide to Clinical Preventive Services*. Baltimore: Williams and Wilkins, 1982.

16. Canadian Task Force on the Periodic Health Examination. The periodic health examination: 2. 1985 update. *Can Med Assoc J* 1986; 134:724–727.

17. O'Malley MS, Fletcher SW. Screening for breast cancer with breast self-examination: A critical review. *JAMA* 1987; 257:2197–2203.

18. Sutton MA, Gibbons RP, Correa RJ. Is deleting the digital rectal examination a good idea? *West J Med* 1991; 155:43–46.

19. Canadian Task Force on the Periodic Health Examination. The Peri-

odic health examination, 1991 update: 3. Secondary prevention of prostate cancer. *Can Med Assoc J* 1991; 145:413–428.

20. Selby JV. How should we screen for colorectal cancer? *JAMA* 1993; 269:1294–1295.

21. Ahlquist DA, Wieand HS, Moertel CG, et al. Accuracy of fecal occult blood screening for colorectal neoplasis: A prospective study using Hemoccult and HemoQuant tests. *JAMA* 1993; 269:1262–1267.

22. Allison JE, Feldman R, Tekawa IS. Hemoccult screening in detecting colorectal neoplasm: Sensitivity, specificity, and predictive value. Long-term follow-up in a large group practice setting. *Ann Intern Med* 1990; 112:328–333.

23. Knight KK, Fielding JE, Battista RN. Occult blood screening for colorectal cancer. *JAMA* 1989; 261:587–594.

24. Mandel JS, Bond MPH, Church TR, et al. Reducing mortality from colorectal cancer by screening for fecal occult blood. *N Engl J Med* 1993; 328:1365–1371.

25. Lang CA, Ransohoff DF. Fecal occult blood screening for colorectal cancer: Is mortality reduced by chance selection for screening colonoscopy? *JAMA* 1994; 271:1011–1013.

26. Eddy DM. Screening for cervical cancer. *Ann Intern Med* 1990; 113:-214–226.

27. Miller AB, Anderson G, Brisson J, et al. Report of a national workshop on screening for cancer of the cervix. *Can Med Assoc J* 1991; 145:-1301–1318.

28. Van Wijngaarden WJ, Duncan ID. Rationale for stopping cervical screening in women over 50. *BMJ* 1993; 306:967–971.

Chapter 6

1. The Swedish Council on Technology Assessment in Health Care. Preoperative routines. *Int J Technol Assess Health Care* 1991; 7:95–100.

2. Narr BJ, Hansen TR, Warner MA. Preoperative laboratory screening in healthy Mayo patients: Cost-effective elimination of tests and unchanged outcomes. *Mayo Clin Proc* 1991; 66:155–159.

3. Hubbell FA, Frye EB, Akin BV, et al. Routine admission laboratory testing for general medical patients. *Med Care* 1988; 26:619–630.

4. Domoto K, Ben R, Wei JY, et al. Yield of routine annual laboratory screening in the institutionalized elderly. *Am J Public Health* 1985; 75:243–245.

5. Joseph C, Lyles Y. Routine laboratory assessment of nursing home patients. *J Am Geriatr Soc* 1992; 40:98–100.

6. Woolf SH, Kamerow DB, Lawrence RS, et al. The periodic health examination of older adults: The recommendations of the U.S. Preventive Services Task Force. Part II. Screening tests. *J Am Geriatr Soc* 1990; 38:933–942.

7. Ruttimann S, Clemencon D, Dubach UC. Usefulness of complete blood counts as a case-finding tool in medical outpatients. *Ann Intern Med* 1992; 116:44–50.

8. Singer DE, Samet JH, Coley CM, et al. Screening for diabetes mellitus. *Ann Intern Med* 1988; 109:639–649.

9. Cebul RD, Beck JR. Biochemical profiles: Applications in ambulatory screening and preadmission testing of adults. *Ann Intern Med* 1987; 106:403–413.

10. Pearson TA. Guidelines for the detection and treatment of elevated serum cholesterol: Which is the baby and which is the bathwater? *Ann Intern Med* 1991; 115:324–326.

11. Manolio TA, Furberg CD, Wahl PW, et al. Eligibility for cholesterol referral in community-dwelling older adults: The Cardiovascular Health Study. *Ann Intern Med* 1992; 116:641–649.

12. Eisenberg JM. Should the elderly be screened for hypercholesterolemia? *Arch Intern Med* 1991; 151:1063–1065.

13. Denke MA, Grundy SM. Hypercholesterolemia in elderly persons: Resolving the treatment dilemma. *Ann Intern Med* 1990; 112:780–792.

14. Garber AM, Wagner JL. Practice guidelines and cholesterol policy. *Health Aff* 1991; summer:52–66.

15. Garber AM, Littenberg B, Sox HC, et al. Costs and health consequences of cholesterol screening for asymptomatic older Americans. *Arch Intern Med* 1991; 151:1089–1095.

16. Garber AM, Sox HC, Littenberg B. Screening asymptomatic adults for cardiac risk factors: The serum cholesterol level. *Ann Intern Med* 1989; 110:622–639.

17. Hetland ML, Haarbo J, Christiansen C. One measurement of serum total cholesterol is enough to predict future levels in healthy post-menopausal women. *Am J Med* 1992; 92:25–28.

18. Mogadam M, Ahmed SW, Mensch AH, et al. Within-person fluctuations of serum cholesterol and lipoproteins. *Arch Intern Med* 1990; 150:1645–1648.

19. Bookstein L, Gidding SS, Donovan M, et al. Day-to-day variability of serum cholesterol, triglyceride, and high-density lipoprotein cholesterol levels: Impact on the assessment of risk according to the National Cholesterol Education Program Guidelines. *Arch Intern Med* 1990; 150:1653–1657.

20. Cooper GR, Myers GL, Smith J, et al. Blood lipid measurements: Variations and practical utility. *JAMA* 1992; 267:1652–1660.

21. Fischer PM, Guinan KH, Burke JJ, et al. Impact of a public cholesterol screening program. *Arch Intern Med* 1990; 150:2567–2572.

22. Krahn M, Naylor D, Basinski AS, et al. Comparison of an aggressive (U.S.) and a less aggressive (Canadian) policy for cholesterol screening and treatment. *Ann Intern Med* 1991; 115:248–255.

23. Catalona WJ, Smith DS, Ratliff TL, et al. Measurement of prostate-specific antigen in serum as a screening test for prostate cancer. *N Engl J Med* 1991; 324:1156–1161.

24. Coney R. Measurement of prostate-specific antigen as a screening test for prostate cancer. *N Engl J Med* 1991; 325:964.

25. Crawford ED, Schutz MJ, Clejan S, et al. The effect of digital rectal examination on prostate-specific antigen levels. *JAMA* 1992; 267:-2227–2228.

26. Catalona WJ, Smith DS, Ratliff TL, et al. Detection of organ-confined prostate cancer is increased through prostate-specific antigen-based screening. *JAMA* 1993; 270:948–954.

27. Carter HB, Pearson JD, Metter J, et al. Longitudinal evaluation of prostate-specific antigen levels in men with and without prostate disease. *JAMA* 1992; 267:2215–2220.

28. Jewett HJ, Bridge RW, Gray GF, et al. The palpable nodule of prostatic cancer: Results 15 years after radical excision. *JAMA* 1968; 203:4036–4068.

29. Johansson J, Adami H, Andersson S, et al. High 10-year survival rate in

patients with early, untreated prostatic cancer. *JAMA* 1992; 267:-2191–2196.

30. Oesterling JE. Prostate-specific antigen: Improving its ability to diagnose early prostate cancer. *JAMA* 1992; 267:2236–2238.

31. Abrutyn E, Mossey J, Berline JA, et al. Does asymptomatic bacteriuria predict mortality and does antimicrobial treatment reduce mortality in elderly ambulatory women? *Ann Intern Med* 1994; 120:827–833.

32. Tape TG, Mushlin AI. The utility of routine chest radiographs. *Ann Intern Med* 1986; 104:663–670.

33. Hubbell FA, Greenfield S, Tyler JL, et al. The impact of routine admission chest x-ray films on patient care. *N Engl J Med* 1985; 312:209–213.

34. Rucker L, Frye EB, Staten MA. Usefulness of screening chest roentgenograms in preoperative patients. *JAMA* 1983; 250:3209–3211.

35. O'Rourke MA, Feussner JR, Feigl P, et al. Age trends of lung cancer stage at diagnosis: Implications for lung cancer screening in the elderly. *JAMA* 1987; 258:921–926.

36. Moorman JR, Hlatky MA, Eddy DM, et al. The yield of routine admission electrocardiogram: A study in a general medical service. *Ann Intern Med* 1985; 103:590–595.

37. Gold BS, Young ML, Kinman JL, et al. The utility of preoperative electrocardiograms in the ambulatory surgical patient. *Arch Intern Med* 1992; 152:301–305.

38. Ziemba SE, Hubbell FA, Fine MJ, et al. Resting electrocardiograms as baseline tests: Impact on the management of elderly patients. *Am J Med* 1991; 91:576–583.

39. Sox HC. The baseline electrocardiogram. *Am J Med* 1991; 91:573–575.

40. Woolf SH, Kamerow DB. Testing for uncommon conditions: The heroic search for positive test results. *Arch Intern Med* 1990; 150:-2451–2458.

41. Larson EB. Medical technologies: Restraint or discretion? *J Gen Intern Med* 1990; 5:178–179.

42. Deyo RA, Diehl AK, Rosenthal M. Reducing roentgenography use. Can patient expectations be altered? *Arch Intern Med* 1987; 147:-141–145.

43. Marton KI, Sox HC, Alexander J, et al. Attitudes of patients toward diagnostic tests: The case of the upper gastrointestinal series roentgenogram. *Med Decis Making* 1982; 2:439–448.

44. Woo B, Cook EF, Weisberg M, et al. Screening procedures in the asymptomatic adult: Comparison of physicians' recommendations, patients' desires, published guidelines, and actual practice. *JAMA* 1985; 254:1480–1484.

45. Kassirer JP. Our stubborn quest for diagnostic certainty: A cause of excessive testing. *N Engl J Med* 1989; 320:1489–1491.

46. Robin ED. Of hydras, lemmings, and diagnostic tests. *Arch Intern Med* 1987; 147:1704–1705.

47. Schroeder SA, Showstack JA. Financial incentives to perform medical procedures and laboratory tests: Illustrative models of office practice. *Med Care* 1978; 16:289–298.

48. Epstein AM, Begg CB, McNeil BJ. The use of ambulatory testing in prepaid and fee-for-service group practices: Relation to perceived profitability. *N Engl J Med* 1986; 314:1089–1094.

49. Hillman BJ, Joseph CA, Mabry MR, et al. Frequency and costs of diagnostic imaging in office practice—a comparison of self-referring and radiologist-referring physicians. *N Engl J Med* 1990; 323:1604–1608.

50. Iglehart JK. Congress moves to regulate self-referral and physicians' ownership of clinical laboratories. *N Engl J Med* 1990; 322:1682–1687.

51. Epstein AM, McNeil BJ. Physician characteristics and organizational factors influencing use of ambulatory tests. *Med Decis Making* 1985; 5:401–413.

52. Bock RS. The pressure to keep prices high at a walk-in clinic: A personal experience. *N Engl J Med* 1981; 319:785–787.

53. Moran DW, Wolfe PR. Can managed care control costs? *Health Aff* 1991; winter:120–128.

54. Chassin MR, Brook RH, Park RE, et al. Variations in the use of medical and surgical services by the Medicare population. *N Engl J Med* 1986; 314:285–290.

55. Weisman CS, Morlock LL, Teitelbaum MA, et al. Practice changes in response to the malpractice litigation climate. Results of a Maryland physician survey. *Med Care* 1989; 27:16–24.

Chapter 7

1. Vrazo F. Misdiagnosing breast cancer: One of the most active—and costliest—areas of malpractice. *Washington Post,* October 23, 1990.
2. American Academy of Family Physicians. *Positions on the Clinical Aspects of Medical Practice.* Kansas City, MO.: American Academy of Family Physicians, 1991.
3. American College of Radiology. *Guidelines for Mammography.* Reston, VA.: American College of Radiology, 1982.
4. Hayward RSA, Steinberg EP, Ford DE, et al. Preventive care guidelines: 1991. *Ann Intern Med* 1991; 114:758–783.
5. Wallis C. A puzzling plague. *Time,* January 14, 1991:48–52.
6. Feig SA. Decreased breast cancer mortality through mammographic screening: Results of clinical trials. *Radiology* 1988; 167:659–665.
7. Klemi PJ, Joensuu H, Toikkanen S, et al. Aggressiveness of breast cancers found with and without screening. *BMJ* 1992; 304:467–469.
8. Mandelblatt JS, Wheat ME, Monane M, et al. Breast cancer screening for elderly women with and without comorbid conditions: A decision analysis model. *Ann Intern Med* 1992; 116:722–730.
9. Skrabanek P, McCormick J. *Follies and Fallacies in Medicine.* Buffalo, N.Y.: Prometheus Books, 1990.
10. Skrabanek P. Mass mammography: The time for reappraisal. *Int J Technol Assess Health Care* 1989; 5:423–430.
11. Schmidt JG. The epidemiology of mass breast cancer screening—a plea for a valid measure of benefit. *J Clin Epidemiol* 1990; 43:215–225.
12. Gram IT, Slenker SE. Cancer anxiety and attitudes toward mammography among screening attenders, nonattenders, and women never invited. *Am J Public Health* 1992; 82:249–251.
13. Lerman C, Trock B, Rimer BK. Psychological and behavioral implications of abnormal mammograms. *Ann Intern Med* 1991; 114:657–661.
14. Brown ML, Kessler LG, Rueter FG. Is the supply of mammography machines outstripping need and demand? An economic analysis. *Ann Intern Med* 1990; 113:547–552.
15. Roberts MM. Breast screening: Time for a rethink. *BMJ* 1989; 299:-1153–1155.
16. Miller AB, Baines CJ, To T, et al. Canadian National Breast Screening

Study: 1. Breast cancer detection and death rates among women aged 40 to 49 years. *Can Med Assoc J* 1992; 147:1459.

17. McGill DB. The president and the power of the colonoscope. *Mayo Clin Proc* 1985; 60:886–889.

18. Eddy DM. Screening for colorectal cancer. *Ann Intern Med* 1990; 113:373–384.

19. Selby JV, Friedman GD, Quesenberry CP, et all. A case-control study of screening sigmoidoscopy and mortality from colorectal cancer. *N Engl J Med* 1992; 326:653–657.

20. Ransohoff DF, Lang CA. Sigmoidoscopic screening in the 1990s. *JAMA* 1993; 269:1278–1281.

21. Cutler JL, Ramcharan S, Feldman R, et al. Multiphasic checkup evaluation study: I. Methods and population. *Prev Med* 1973; 2:197–206.

22. Selby JV, Friedman GD. Sigmoidoscopy in the periodic health examination of asymptomatic adults. *JAMA* 1989; 261:595–601.

23. Neugut AI, Pita S. Role of sigmoidoscopy in screening for colorectal cancer: A critical review. *Gastroenterology* 1988; 95:492–499.

24. Lieberman DA. Colon cancer screening: The dilemma of positive screening tests. *Arch Intern Med* 1990; 150:740–744.

25. Provenzale D, Garrett JW, Condon SE, et al. Risk for colon adenomas in patients with rectosigmoid hyperplastic polyps. *Ann Intern Med* 1990; 113:760–763.

26. Lieberman DA, Smith FW. Screening for colon malignancy with colonoscopy. *Am J Gastroenterol* 1991; 86:946–951.

27. Atkin WS, Morson BC, Cuzick J. Long-term risk of colorectal cancer after excision of rectosigmoid adenomas. *N Engl J Med* 1992; 326:-658–662.

28. Ransohoff DF, Lang CA. Screening for colorectal cancer. *N Engl J Med* 1991; 325:37–41.

29. Ransohoff DF, Lang CA, Kuo HS. Colonoscopic surveillance after polypectomy: Considerations of cost effectiveness. *Ann Intern Med* 1991; 114:177–182.

30. Winawer SJ, Zauber AG, O'Brien MJ, et al. Randomized comparison of surveillance intervals after colonoscopic removal of newly diagnosed adenomatous polyps. *N Engl J Med* 1993; 328:901–906.

31. Bond JH. Polyp guideline: Diagnosis, treatment, and surveillance for patients with nonfamilial colorectal polyps. *Ann Intern Med* 1993; 119:836–843.

32. Van Ness MM, Chobanian SJ, Winters C, et al. A study of patient acceptance of double-contrast barium enema and colonoscopy: Which procedure is preferred by patients? *Arch Intern Med* 1987; 147:2175–2176.

33. MacCarty RL. Colorectal cancer: The case for barium enema. *Mayo Clin Proc* 1992; 67:253–257.

34. Gittes RF. Carcinoma of the prostate. *N Engl J Med* 1991; 324:236–244.

35. Canadian Task Force on the Periodic Health Examination. Periodic health examination, 1991 update: 3. Secondary prevention of prostate cancer. *Can Med Assoc J* 1991; 145:413–428.

36. Jacobs I, Davies AP, Bridges J, et al. Prevalence screening for ovarian cancer in postmenopausal women by CA 125 measurement and ultrasonography. *BMJ* 1993; 306:1030–1034.

37. Schapira MM, Matchar DB, Young MJ. The effectiveness of ovarian cancer screening: A decision analysis model. *Ann Intern Med* 1993; 118:838–843.

38. Webb MJ. Screening for ovarian cancer: Still a long way to go. *BMJ* 1993; 306:1015–1016.

39. Granai CO. Ovarian cancer—unrealistic expectations. *N Engl J Med* 1992; 327:197–200.

40. Giagnoni E, Secchi MB, Wu SC, et al. Prognostic value of exercise testing in asymptomatic normotensive subjects: A prospective matched study. *N Engl J Med* 1983; 309:1085–1089.

41. Detrano R, Froelicher V. A logical approach to screening for coronary artery disease. *Ann Intern Med* 1987; 106:846–852.

42. Bodenheimer MM. Risk stratification in coronary disease: A contrary viewpoint. *Ann Intern Med* 1992; 116:927–936.

43. Sox HC, Littenberg B, Garber AM. The role of exercise testing in screening for coronary artery disease. *Ann Intern Med* 1989; 110:-456–469.

44. Cohn PF. Silent myocardial ischemia. *Ann Intern Med* 1988; 109:-312–317.

45. Epstein SE, Quyyumi AA, Bonow RO. Myocardial ischemia—silent or symptomatic. *N Engl J Med* 1988; 318:1038–1042.
46. Freedman S, Raffin TA, Rothkopf MH, et al. The value of a stage prop: Screening for chronic obstructive pulmonary disease. *Chest* 1984; 85:406–408.
47. Nevitt MP, Ballard DJ, Hallett JW. Prognosis of abdominal aortic aneurysms: A population-based study. *N Engl J Med* 1989; 321:-1009–1014.
48. Crawford ES, Hess KR. Abdominal aortic aneurysm. *N Engl J Med* 1989; 321:1040–1042.
49. Bluth EI. Ultrasound of the abdominal aorta. *Arch Intern Med* 1984; 144:377–380.
50. Canadian Task Force on the Periodic Health Examination. Periodic health examination, 1991 update: 5. Screening for abdominal aortic aneurysm. *Can Med Assoc J* 1991; 145:783–789.
51. Santiago F. Screening for abdominal aortic aneurysms: The U-boat in the belly. *JAMA* 1987; 258:1732.
52. Collin J, Araujo L, Walton J, et al. Oxford screening programme for abdominal aortic aneurysm in men aged 65 to 74 years. *Lancet* 1988; ii:613–615.
53. Collin J. Screening for abdominal aortic aneurysms. *Br J Surg* 1985; 72:851–852.
54. Webster MW, et al. Ultrasound screening of first-degree relatives of patients with an abdominal aortic aneurysm. *J Vasc Surg* 1991; 13:9–14.
55. Johansen K, Koepsell T. Familial tendency for abdominal aortic aneurysms. *JAMA* 1986; 256:1934–1936.
56. Chrischilles EA, Butler CD, Davis CS, et al. A model of lifetime osteoporosis impact. *Arch Intern Med* 1991; 151:2026–2032.
57. Need AG, Nordin BEC, Horowitz M, et al. Osteoporosis: New insights from bone densitometry. *J Am Geriatr Soc* 1990; 38:1153–1158.
58. Johnston CC, Slemenda CW, Melton LJ. Clinical use of bone densitometry. *N Engl J Med* 1991; 324:1105–1109.
59. Ross PD, Davis JW, Epstein RS, et al. Pre-existing fractures and bone mass predict vertebral fracture incidence in women. *Ann Intern Med* 1991; 114:919–923.

60. Hui SL, Slemenda CW, Johnston CC. Baseline measurement of bone mass predicts fracture in white women. *Ann Intern Med* 1989; 111:-355–361.
61. Cummings SR, Black DM, Nevitt MC, et al. Appendicular bone density and age predict hip fracture in women. *JAMA* 1990; 263:665–668.
62. Hansen MA, Overgaard K, Riis BJ, et al. Role of peak bone mass and bone loss in postmenopausal osteoporosis: 12 year study. *BMJ* 1991; 303:961–964.
63. Clinical Efficacy Assessment Subcommittee and Health and Public Policy Committee, American College of Physicians. Bone mineral density. *Ann Intern Med* 1988; 15:846.
64. Hall FM, Davis MA, Baran DT. Bone mineral screening for osteoporosis. *N Engl J Med* 1987; 316:212–214.
65. Melton LJ, Eddy DM, Johnston CC. Screening for osteoporosis. *Ann Intern Med* 1990; 112:516–528.
66. Rubin SM, Cummings SR. Results of bone densitometry affect women's decisions about taking measures to prevent fractures. *Ann Intern Med* 1992; 116:990–995.

Chapter 8

1. Forrow L, Taylor WC, Arnold RM. Absolutely relative: How research results are summarized can affect treatment decisions. *Am J Med* 1992; 92:121–124.
2. Everitt DE, Avorn J. Drug prescribing for the elderly. *Arch Intern Med* 1986; 146:2393–2396.
3. Ouslander JG. Drug therapy in the elderly. *Ann Intern Med* 1981; 95:-711–722.
4. Law R, Chalmers C. Medicines and elderly people: A general practice survey. *BMJ* 1976; 1:565–568.
5. Cohn V. Over 60? Some pills aren't for you. *Washington Post,* October 25, 1988:18.
6. Wolfe S, Health Research Group. *Worst Pills, Best Pills: The Older Adult's Guide to Avoiding Drug-Induced Death or Illness.* Washington, D.C.: Pantheon, 1990.
7. Graedon T, Graedon J. *50+: The Graedons' Peoples' Pharmacy for Older Adults.* New York: Pantheon, 1990.

8. *AARP Pharmacy Service Prescription Drug Handbook.* Washington, D.C.: AARP, 1994.
9. Gurwitz JH, Avorn J. The ambiguous relation between aging and adverse drug reactions. *Ann Intern Med* 1991; 114:956–966.
10. Klein LE, German PS, Levine DM, et al. Medication problems among outpatients: A study with emphasis on the elderly. *Arch Intern Med* 1984; 144:1185–1188.
11. *Physicians' Desk Reference,* ed 48. Montvale, N.J.: Medical Economics Data, 1994.

Chapter 9

1. Mills JA. Aspirin, the ageless remedy? *N Engl J Med* 1991; 325:1303–1304.
2. Steering Committee of the Physicians' Health Study Research Group. Final report on the aspirin component of the ongoing Physicians' Health Study. *N Engl J Med* 1989; 321:129–135.
3. Peto R, Gray R, Collins R, et al. Randomised trial of prophylactic daily aspirin in British male doctors. *BMJ* 1988; 296:313–316.
4. Manson JE, Stampfer MJ, Colditz GA, et al. A prospective study of aspirin use and primary prevention of cardiovascular disease in women. *JAMA* 1993; 266:521–527.
5. Kaplan RM. Physicians' Health Study: Aspirin and primary prevention of coronary heart disease. *N Engl J Med* 1989; 321:1826–1827.
6. Canadian Task Force on the Periodic Health Examination. Periodic health examination, 1991 update: 6. Acetylsalicylic acid and the primary prevention of cardiovascular disease. *Can Med Assoc J* 1991; 145:1091–1095.
7. Dalen JE. An apple a day or an aspirin a day? *Arch Intern Med* 1991; 151:1066–1068.
8. Paganini-Hill A, Chao A, Ross RK, et al. Aspirin use and chronic disease: A cohort study of the elderly. *BMJ* 1989; 229:1247–1250.
9. Thun MJ, Namboodiri MM, Heath CW. Aspirin use and reduced risk of fatal colon cancer. *N Engl J Med* 1991; 325:1593–1596.

Chapter 10

1. Dawson-Hughes B, et al. A controlled trial of the effect of calcium supplementation on bone density in postmenopausal women. *N Engl J Med* 1990; 323:878–883.

2. Cauley JA, et al. Endogenous estrogen levels and calcium intakes in postmenopausal women: Relationships with cortical bone measures. *JAMA* 1988; 260:3150–3155.

3. Prince RL, Smith M, Dick IM, et al. Prevention of postmenopausal osteoporosis: A comparative study of exercise, calcium supplementation, and hormone-replacement therapy. *N Engl J Med* 1991; 325:-1189–1195.

4. Aloia JF, Vaswani A, Yeh JK, et al. Calcium supplementation with and without hormone replacement therapy to prevent postmenopausal bone loss. *Ann Intern Med* 1994; 120:97–103.

5. Riggs BL. A new option for treating osteoporosis. *N Engl J Med* 1990; 323:124–125.

6. Resnick NM, Greenspan SL. "Senile" osteoporosis reconsidered. *JAMA* 1989; 261:1025–1029.

7. Orwoll ES, et al. The rate of bone mineral loss in normal men and the effects of calcium and cholecalciferol supplementation. *Ann Intern Med* 1990; 112:29–34.

8. Nilas L, et al. Calcium supplementation and postmenopausal bone loss. *Br Med J* 1984; 27:1103–1106.

9. Riis B, et al. Does calcium supplementation prevent postmenopausal bone loss? A double-blind, controlled clinical study. *N Engl J Med* 1987; 316:173–177.

10. Kanis JA, Johnell O, Gullberg B, et al. Evidence for efficacy of drugs affecting bone metabolism in preventing hip fracture. *BMJ* 1992; 305:1124–1128.

11. Chapuy MC, Arlot ME, Duboeuf F, et al. Vitamin D_3 and calcium to prevent hip fractures in elderly women. *N Engl J Med* 1992; 327:-1637–1642.

12. Emphasis on calcium, exercise prophylaxis challenged. *Int Med News* 1986; 19:69.

13. Ettinger B, et al. Postmenopausal bone loss is prevented by treatment

with low-dosage estrogen with calcium. *Ann Intern Med* 1987; 106:40–45.

14. Nachtigall LE, et al. Estrogen replacement therapy I: A 10-year prospective study in relationship to osteoporosis. *Obstet Gynecol* 1979; 53:277–281.

15. Richelson LS, et al. Relative contribution of aging and estrogen deficiency to postmenopausal bone loss. *N Engl J Med* 1984; 311:1273–1275.

16. Horsman A, et al. The effect of estrogen dose on postmenopausal bone loss. *N Engl J Med* 1983; 309:1405–1407.

17. Lindsay R, et al. Prevention of spinal osteoporosis in oophorectomized women. *Lancet* 1980; ii:1151–1153.

18. Harris ST, Genant HK, Baylink DJ, et al. The effects of estrone (Ogen) on spinal bone density of postmenopausal women. *Arch Intern Med* 1991; 151:1980–1984.

19. Felson DT, Zhang Y, Hannan MT, et al. The effect of postmenopausal estrogen therapy on bone density in elderly women. *N Engl J Med* 1993; 329:1141–1146.

20. Kiel DP, et al. Hip fracture and the use of estrogens in postmenopausal women. The Framingham Study. *N Engl J Med* 1987; 317:1169–1174.

21. Weiss NS, et al. Decreased risk of fractures of the hip and lower forearm with postmenopausal use of estrogen. *N Engl J Med* 1980; 303:-1195–1198.

22. Ettinger B, et al. Long-term estrogen replacement therapy prevents bone loss and fractures. *Ann Intern Med* 1985; 102:319–324.

23. Paganini-Hill A, et al. Menopausal estrogen therapy and hip fractures. *Ann Intern Med* 1981; 95:28–31.

24. Naessen T, Persson I, Adami H, et al. Hormone replacement therapy and the risk for first hip fracture: A prospective, population-based cohort study. *Ann Intern Med* 1990; 113:95–103.

25. Cummings SR, et al. Lifetime risks of hip, colles', or vertebral fracture and coronary heart disease among white postmenopausal women. *Arch Intern Med* 1989; 149:2445–2448.

26. Stampfer MJ, Colditz GA, Willett WC, et al. Postmenopausal estrogen therapy and cardiovascular disease: Ten-year follow-up from the Nurses' Health Study. *N Engl J Med* 1991; 756:762.

27. Henderson BE, et al. Decreased mortality in users of estrogen replacement therapy. *Arch Intern Med* 1991; 151:75–78.
28. Barrett-Connor E, Bush TL. Estrogen and coronary heart disease in women. *JAMA* 1991; 265:1861–1867.
29. Goldman L, Tosteson ANA. Uncertainty about postmenopausal estrogen: Time for action, not debate. *N Engl J Med* 1991; 325:-800–802.
30. Finucane FF, Madans JH, Bush TL, et al. Decreased risk of stroke among postmenopausal hormone users: Results from a national cohort. *Arch Intern Med* 1993; 153:73–79.
31. Falkeborn M, Persson I, Terent A, et al. Hormone replacement therapy and the risk of stroke: Follow-up up a population-based cohort in Sweden. *Arch Intern Med* 1993; 153:1201–1209.
32. Grady D, Rubin SM, Petitti DB, et al. Hormone therapy to prevent disease and prolong life in postmenopausal women. *Ann Intern Med* 1992; 117:1016–1037.
33. Shapiro S, Kelly JP, Rosenberg L, et al. Risk of localized widespread endometrial cancer in relation to recent and discontinued use of conjugated estrogens. *N Engl J Med* 1985; 313:969–972.
34. Colditz GA, et al. Prospective study of estrogen replacement therapy and risk of breast cancer in postmenopausal women. *JAMA* 1990; 264:2648–2653.
35. Steinberg KK, et al. A meta-analysis of the effects of estrogen replacement therapy on the risk of breast cancer. *JAMA* 1991; 265:1985–1990.
36. Bergkvist L, et al. The risk of breast cancer after estrogen and estrogen-progestin replacement. *N Engl J Med* 1989; 321:293–297.
37. Kaufman DW, Palmer JR, Mouzon J, et al. Estrogen replacement therapy and the risk of breast cancer: Results from the case-control surveillance study. *Am J Epidemiol* 1991; 134:1375–1385.
38. Dupont WD, Page DL. Menopausal estrogen replacement therapy and breast cancer. *Arch Intern Med* 1991; 151:67–72.
39. Devor M, Barrett-Connor E, Renvall M, et al. Estrogen replacement therapy and the risk of venous thrombosis. *Am J Med* 1992; 92:275–282.
40. Watts NB, et al. Intermittent cyclical etidronate treatment of postmenopausal osteoporosis. *N Engl J Med* 1990; 323:73–79.

41. Storm T, et al. Effect of intermittent cyclical etidronate therapy on bone mass and fracture rate in women with postmenopausal osteoporosis. *N Engl J Med* 1990; 322:1265–1271.

42. Harris ST, Watts NB, Jackson RD, et al. Four-year study of intermittent cyclic etidronate treatment of postmenopausal osteoporosis: Three years of blinded therapy followed by one year of open therapy. *Am J Med* 1993; 95:557–567.

43. Marcus R. Cyclic etidronate: Has the rose lost its bloom? *Am J Med* 1993; 95:555–556.

44. Gallagher JC, Goldgar D. Treatment of postmenopausal osteoporosis with high doses of synthetic calcitriol: A randomized controlled study. *Ann Intern Med* 1990; 113:649–655.

45. Dawson-Hughes B, Dallal GE, Krall EA, et al. Effect of vitamin D supplementation on wintertime and overall bone loss in healthy postmenopausal women. *Ann Intern Med* 1991; 115:505–512.

46. Aloia JF, et al. Calcitriol in the treatment of postmenopausal osteoporosis. *Am J Med* 1988; 84:401–408.

47. Ott SM, Chesnut CH. Calcitriol treatment is not effective in postmenopausal osteoporosis. *Ann Intern Med* 1989; 110:267–274.

48. Tilyard MW, Spears GFS, Thomson J, et al. Treatment of postmenopausal osteoporosis with calcitriol or calcium. *N Engl J Med* 1992; 326:357–362.

49. Riggs BL, et al. Effect of fluoride treatment on the fracture rate in postmenopausal women with osteoporosis. *N Engl J Med* 1990; 322:802–809.

50. Gruber HE, et al. Long-term calcitonin therapy in postmenopausal osteoporosis. *Metabolism* 1984; 33:295–303.

51. Reginster JY, Denis D, Albert A, et al. One-year controlled randomised trial of prevention of early postmenopausal bone loss by intranasal calcitonin. *Lancet* 1987; ii:1481–1484.

Chapter 11

1. Kaplan NM. The appropriate goals of antihypertensive therapy: Neither too much nor too little. *Ann Intern Med* 1992; 116:686–690.

2. Kawachi I, Wilson N. The evolution of antihypertensive therapy. *Soc Sci Med* 1990; 31:1239–1243.

3. Medical Research Council Working Party. MRC trial of treatment of mild hypertension: Principal results. *Br Med J* 1985; 291:97–104.
4. Joint National Committee on Detection, Evaluation, and Treatment of High Blood Pressure. The fifth report of the Joint National Committee on Detection, Evaluation, and Treatment of High Blood Pressure (JNC V). *Arch Intern Med* 1993; 153:154–183.
5. National High Blood Pressure Education Program Working Group. National High Blood Pressure Education Program working group report on primary prevention of hypertension. *Arch Intern Med* 1993; 153:186–208.
6. Neaton JD, Grimm RH, Prineas RJ, et al. Treatment of mild hypertension study: Final results. *JAMA* 1993; 270:713–724.
7. Forrow L, Wartman SA, Brock DW. Science, ethics, and the making of clinical decisions: Implications for risk factor intervention. *JAMA* 1988; 259:3161–3167.
8. MacMahon S, Peto R, Cutler J, et al. Blood pressure, stroke, and coronary heart disease. Part 1. Prolonged differences in blood pressure: Prospective observational studies corrected for the regression dilution bias. *Lancet* 1990; 335:765–774.
9. SHEP Cooperative Research Group. Prevention of stroke by antihypertensive drug treatment in older persons with isolated systolic hypertension: Final results of the Systolic Hypertension in the Elderly Program (SHEP). *JAMA* 1991; 265:3255–3264.
10. Amery A, Birkenhager W, Brixko P, et al. Mortality and morbidity results from the European Working Party on High Blood Pressure in the Elderly trial. *Lancet* 1985; 1:1349–1354.
11. Dahlof B, Lindholm LH, Hansson L, et al. Morbidity and mortality in the Swedish Trial in Old Patients with Hypertension (STOP-Hypertension). *Lancet* 1991; 338:1281–1285.
12. MRC Working Party. Medical Research Council trial of treatment of hypertension in older adults: Principal results. *BMJ* 1992; 304:405–412.
13. Whitcomb B, Byyny RL. Perspective on hypertension in the elderly. *West J Med* 1990; 152:392–400.
14. Applegate WB, Phillips HL, Schnaper H, et al. A randomized controlled trial of the effects of three antihypertensive agents on blood

pressure control and quality of life in older women. *Arch Intern Med* 1991; 151:1817–1823.

15. Tjoa HI, Kaplan NM. Treatment of hypertension in the elderly. *JAMA* 1990; 264:1015–1018.

16. Materson BJ, Reda DJ, Cushman WC, et al. Single-drug therapy for hypertension in men: A comparison of six antihypertensive agents with placebo. *N Engl J Med* 1993; 328:914–921.

17. Magarian GJ. Reserpin: A relic from the past or a neglected drug of the present for achieving cost containment in treating hypertension? *J Gen Intern Med* 1991; 6:561–572.

18. Lederle FA, Applegate WA, Grimm RH. Reserpine and the medical marketplace. *Arch Intern Med* 1993; 153:705–706.

19. Payne TH, Goodson JD, Morgan MM, et al. Do resident and staff physicians differ in the types and costs of antihypertensive drugs they select? *J Gen Intern Med* 1991; 6:439–444.

20. Messerli FH. Antihypertensive therapy—going to the heart of the matter. *Circulation* 1990; 81:1128–1135.

21. Mattila K, Haavisto M, Rajala S, et al. Blood pressure and five year survival in the very old. *BMJ* 1988; 296:887–889.

22. Langer RD, Ganiats TG, Barrett-Connor E. Factors associated with paradoxical survival at higher blood pressures in the very old. *Am J Epidemiol* 1991; 134:29–38.

23. Taylor JO, Cornoni-Huntley J, Curb D, et al. Blood pressure and mortality risk in the elderly. *Am J Epidemiol* 1991; 134:489–501.

24. McCloskey LW, Psaty BM, Koepsell TD, et al. Level of blood pressure and risk of myocardial infarction among treated hypertensive patients. *Arch Intern Med* 1992; 152:513–520.

25. Schoenberger JA, Testa M, Ross AD, et al. Efficacy, safety, and quality-of-life assessment of captopril antihypertensive therapy in clinical practice. *Arch Intern Med* 1990; 150:301–306.

26. Croog SH, Levine S, Testa MA, et al. The effects of antihypertensive therapy on the quality of life. *N Engl J Med* 1986; 314:1657–1664.

27. Dimsdale JE. Reflections on the impact of antihypertensive medications on mood, sedation, and neuropsychologic functioning. *Arch Intern Med* 1992; 152:35–39.

28. The Treatment of Mild Hypertension Research Group. The Treat-

ment of Mild Hypertension Study: A randomized, placebo-controlled trial of a nutritional-hygienic regimen along with various drug monotherapies. *Arch Intern Med* 1991; 151:1413–1423.

29. Davidson RA, Caranasos GJ. Should the elderly hypertensive be treated? Evidence from clinical trials. *Arch Intern Med* 1987; 147:-1933–1937.

30. Steiner JF, Fihn SD, Blair B, et al. Appropriate reductions in compliance among well-controlled hypertensive patients. *J Clin Epidemiol* 1991; 44:1361–1371.

31. Freis ED. Rationale against the drug treatment of marginal diastolic systemic hypertension. *Am J Cardiol* 1990; 66:368–371.

32. World Hypertension League. Physical exercise in the management of hypertension: A consensus statement by the World Hypertension League. *J Hypertens* 1991; 9:283–287.

33. Schotte DE, Stunkard AJ. The effects of weight reduction on blood pressure in 301 obese patients. *Arch Intern Med* 1990; 150:1701–1704.

34. Parker M, Puddey IB, Beilin LJ, et al. Two-way factorial study of alcohol and salt restriction in treated hypertensive men. *Hypertension* 1990; 16:398–406.

35. Moore TJ. Overkill. *The Washingtonian*, August 1990: 64–67, 194–204.

36. Law MR, Frost CD, Wald NJ. By how much does dietary salt reduction lower blood pressure? I: Analysis of observational data among populations. *Br Med J* 1991; 302:811–815.

37. Law MR, Frost CD, Wald NJ. By how much does dietary salt reduction lower blood pressure? III: Analysis of data from trials of salt reduction. *Br Med J* 1991; 302:819–824.

Chapter 12

1. Brown G, Albers JJ, Fisher LD, et al. Regression of coronary artery disease as a result of intensive lipid-lowering therapy in men with high levels of apolipoprotein B. *N Engl J Med* 1990; 323:1289–1298.

2. Blankenhorn DH, Azen SP, Kramsch DM, et al. Coronary angiographic changes with lovastatin therapy: The Monitored Atherosclerosis Regression Study (MARS). *Ann Intern Med* 1993; 119:969–976.

3. Expert Panel on Detection, Evaluation, and Treatment of High Blood Cholesterol in Adults. Summary of the second report of the National Cholesterol Education Program (NCEP) Expert Panel on Detection, Evaluation, and Treatment of High Blood Cholesterol in Adults (Adult Treatment Panel II). *JAMA* 1993; 269:3015–3023.

4. Smith R. *The Cholesterol Conspiracy.* St. Louis: Little, Brown, 1991.

5. Vaughan DE. "*The Cholesterol Conspiracy.*" Review in *N Engl J Med* 1991; 325:1257.

6. Thompson WG. Cholesterol: Myth or reality? *South Med J* 1990; 83:-435–440.

7. Castelli WP, Wilson PWF, Levy D, et al. Cardiovascular risk factors in the elderly. *Am J Cardiol* 1989; 63:12H–19H.

8. Benfante R, Reed D. Is elevated serum cholesterol level a risk factor for coronary heart disease in the elderly? *JAMA* 1990; 263:393–396.

9. Rubin SM, Sidney S, Black DM. High blood cholesterol in elderly men and the excess risk for coronary heart disease. *Ann Intern Med* 1990; 113:916–920.

10. Pekkanen J, Linn S, Heiss G, et al. Ten-year mortality from cardiovascular disease in relation to cholesterol level among men with and without preexisting cardiovascular disease. *N Engl J Med* 1990; 322:-1700–1707.

11. Malenka DJ, Baron JA. Cholesterol and coronary heart disease. The importance of patient-specific attributable risk. *Arch Intern Med* 1988; 148:2247–2252.

12. Smith GD, Shipley MJ, Marmot MG, et al. Plasma cholesterol concentration and mortality: The Whitehall Study. *JAMA* 1992; 267:70–76.

13. Forette B, Tortrat D, Wolmark Y. Cholesterol as risk factor for mortality in elderly women. *Lancet* 1989; i:868–870.

14. Brett AS. Treating hypercholesterolemia: How should practicing physicians interpret the published data for patients? *N Engl J Med* 1989; 321:676–680.

15. Lipid Research Clinics Program. The Lipid Research Clinics Coronary Primary Prevention Trial results: I. Reduction in incidence of coronary heart disease. *JAMA* 1984; 251:351–364.

16. Frick MH, Elo O, Haapa K, et al. Helsinki Heart Study: Primary-prevention trial with gemfibrozil in middle-aged men with dyslipidemia.

Safety of treatment, changes in risk factors, and incidence of coronary heart disease. *N Engl J Med* 1987; 317:1237–1245.

17. LaRosa JC, Applegate W, Crouse JR, et al. Cholesterol lowering in the elderly: Results of the Cholesterol Reduction in Seniors Program (CRISP) pilot study. *Arch Intern Med* 1994; 154:529–539.

18. Muldoon MF, Manuck SB, Matthews KA. Lowering cholesterol concentrations and mortality: A quantitative review of primary prevention trials. *Br Med J* 1990; 301:309–314.

19. Holme I. An analysis of randomized trials evaluating the effect of cholesterol reduction on total mortality and coronary heart disease incidence. *Circulation* 1990; 82:1916–1924.

20. The Toronto Working Group on Cholesterol Policy. Asymptomatic hypercholesterolemia: A clinical policy review. *J Clin Epidemiol* 1990; 43:1021–1121.

21. Criqui MH. Cholesterol, primary and secondary prevention, and all-cause mortality. *Ann Intern Med* 1991; 115:973–976.

22. Goldman L, Weinstein MC, Goldman PA, et al. Cost-effectiveness of HMG-CoA reductase inhibition for primary and secondary prevention of coronary heart disease. *JAMA* 1991; 265:1145–1151.

23. Grover SA, Abrahamowicz M, Joseph L, et al. The benefits of treating hyperlipidemia to prevent coronary heart disease: Estimating changes in life expectancy and morbidity. *JAMA* 1992; 267:816–822.

24. Leaf A, Ryan TJ. Prevention of coronary artery disease: A medical imperative. *N Engl J Med* 1990; 323:1416–1419.

25. Cummings P, Psaty BM. The association between cholesterol and death from injury. *Ann Intern Med* 1994; 120:848–855.

26. Law MR, Thompson SG, Wald NJ. Assessing possible hazards of reducing serum cholesterol. *BMJ* 1994; 308:373–379.

27. Smith GD, Pekkanen J. Should there be a moratorium on the use of cholesterol lowering drugs? *Br Med J* 1992; 304:431–434.

28. Smith GD, Song F, Sheldon TA. Cholesterol lowering and mortality: The importance of considering initial level of risk. *BMJ* 1993; 306:-1367–1373.

29. Canner PL, Berge KG, Wenger NK, et al. Fifteen year mortality in Coronary Drug Project patients: Long-term benefit with niacin. *J Am Coll Cardiol* 1986; 8:1245–1255.

30. Strandberg TE, Salomaa VV, Naukkarinen VA, et al. Long-term mor-

tality after 5-year multifactorial primary prevention of cardiovascular diseases in middle-aged men. *JAMA* 1991; 266:1225–1229.

31. Miettinen TA, Huttunen JK, Naukkarinen VA, et al. Multifactorial primary prevention of cardiovascular diseases in middle-aged men. *JAMA* 1985; 254:2097–2102.

32. Wilhelmson L, Berglund G, Elmfeldt D, et al. The multifactorial primary prevention trial in Göteborg, Sweden. *Eur Heart J* 1986; 7:279–288.

33. The Multiple Risk Factor Intervention Trial Research Group. Mortality rates after 10.5 years for participants in the Multiple Risk Factor Intervention Trial: Findings related to a priori hypotheses of the trial. *JAMA* 1990; 263:1795–1801.

34. Multiple Risk Factor Intervention Trial Research Group. Multiple Risk Factor Intervention Trial: Risk factor changes and mortality results. *JAMA* 1982; 248:1465–1477.

35. Oliver MF. Doubts about preventing coronary heart disease. *Br Med J* 1992; 304:1003–1004.

36. Bradford RH, Shear CL, Chremos AN, et al. Expanded clinical evaluation of lovastatin (EXCEL) study: Design and patient characteristics of a double-blind, placebo-controlled study in patients with moderate hypercholesterolemia. *Am J Cardiol* 1990; 66:44B–55B.

37. Hoeg JM, Brewer B. 3-hydroxy-3-methylglutaryl-coenzyme A reductase inhibitors in the treatment of hypercholesterolemia. *JAMA* 1987; 258:3532–3536.

38. Schulman KA, Kinosian B, Jacobson TA, et al. Reducing high blood cholesterol level with drugs: Cost-effectiveness of pharmacologic management. *JAMA* 1990; 264:3025–3033.

39. Fihn SD. A prudent approach to control of cholesterol levels. *JAMA* 1987; 258:2416–2418.

40. Watts GF, Lewis B, Brunt JNH, et al. Effects on coronary artery disease of lipid-lowering diet, or diet plus cholestyramine, in the St. Thomas' Atherosclerosis Regression Study (STARS). *Lancet* 1992; 339:563–569.

41. National Heart, Lung, and Blood Institute, National Cholesterol Education Program. Report of the Expert Panel on Population Strategies for Blood Cholesterol Reduction: Executive summary. *Arch Intern Med* 1991; 151:1071–1084.

42. Taylor WC, Pass TM, Shepard DS, et al. Cholesterol reduction and life expectancy: A model incorporating multiple risk factors. *Ann Intern Med* 1987; 106:605–614.

43. Browner WS, Westenhouse J, Tice JA. What if Americans ate less fat? A quantitative estimate of the effect on mortality. *JAMA* 1991; 265:-3285–3291.

44. Ramsay LE, Yeo WW, Jackson PR. Dietary reduction of serum cholesterol concentration: Time to think again. *Br Med J* 1991; 303:953–957.

45. Ulbricht TLV, Southgate DAT. Coronary heart disease: Seven dietary factors. *Lancet* 1991; 338:985–992.

Chapter 13

1. Coplen SE, Antman EM, Berlin JA, et al. Efficacy and safety of quinidine therapy for maintenance of sinus rhythm after cardioversion: A meta-analysis of randomized control trials. *Circulation* 1990; 82:-1106–1116.

2. Falk RH. Proarrhythmia in patients treated for atrial fibrillation or flutter. *Ann Intern Med* 1992; 117:141–150.

3. Falk RH, Leavitt JI. Digoxin for atrial fibrillation: A drug whose time has gone? *Ann Intern Med* 1991; 114:573–575.

4. Disch DL, Greenberg ML, Holzberger PT, et al. Managing chronic atrial fibrillation: A Markov decision analysis comparing warfarin, quinidine, and low-dose amiodarone. *Ann Intern Med* 1994; 120:-449–457.

5. Kopecky SL, Gersh BJ, McGoon MD, et al. The natural history of lone atrial fibrillation: A population-based study over three decades. *N Engl J Med* 1987; 317:669–674.

6. Flegel KM, Shipley MJ, Rose G. Risk of stroke in non-rheumatic atrial fibrillation. *Lancet* 1987; i:526–529.

7. Wolf PA, Dawber TR, Thomas HE, et al. Epidemiologic assessment of chronic atrial fibrillation and risk of stroke: The Framingham Study. *Neurology* 1978; 28:973–977.

8. The Stroke Prevention in Atrial Fibrillation Investigators. Predictors of thromboembolism in atrial fibrillation: I. Clinical features of patients at risk. *Ann Intern Med* 1992; 116:1–5.

9. Petersen P, Kastrup J, Helweg-Larsen S, et al. Risk factors for thrombo-

embolic complications in chronic atrial fibrillation: The Copenhagen AFASAK Study. *Arch Intern Med* 1990; 150:819–821.

10. Cairns JA, Connolly SJ. Nonrheumatic atrial fibrillation: Risk of stroke and role of antithrombotic therapy. *Circulation* 1991; 84:469–481.

11. Albers GW, et al. Stroke prevention in nonvalvular atrial fibrillation. *Ann Intern Med* 1991; 115:727–736.

12. Stroke Prevention in Atrial Fibrillation Investigators. Stroke Prevention in Atrial Fibrillation Study: Final results. *Circulation* 1991; 84:-527–539.

13. Connolly SJ, Laupacis A, Gent M, et al. Canadian Atrial Fibrillation Anticoagulation (CAFA) Study. *J Am Coll Cardiol* 1991; 18:349–355.

14. The Boston Area Anticoagulation Trial for Atrial Fibrillation Investigators. The effect of low-dose warfarin on the risk of stroke in patients with nonrheumatic atrial fibrillation. *N Engl J Med* 1990; 323:1505–1511.

15. Petersen P, Boysen G, Godtfredsen J, et al. Placebo-controlled, randomised trial of warfarin and aspirin for prevention of thromboembolic complications in chronic atrial fibrillation: The Copenhagen AFASAK Study. *Lancet* 1989; i:175–179.

16. Stroke Prevention in Atrial Fibrillation Study Group Investigators. Preliminary report of the Stroke Prevention in Atrial Fibrillation Study. *N Engl J Med* 1990; 322:863–868.

17. Cairns JA. Stroke Prevention in Atrial Fibrillation Trial. *Circulation* 1991; 84:933–935.

18. Lancaster TR, Singer DE, Sheehan MA, et al. The impact of long-term warfarin therapy on quality of life: Evidence from a randomized trial. *Arch Intern Med* 1991; 151:1944–1949.

19. Kennedy HL, Whitlock JA, Sprague MK, et al. Long-term follow-up of asymptomatic healthy subjects with frequent and complex ventricular ectopy. *N Engl J Med* 1985; 312:193–197.

20. The Cardiac Arrhythmia Suppression Trial (CAST) Investigators. Preliminary report: Effect of encainide and flecainide on mortality in a randomized trial of arrhythmia suppression after myocardial infarction. *N Engl J Med* 1989; 321:406–412.

21. Ruskin JN. The Cardiac Arrhythmia Suppression Trial (CAST). *N Engl J Med* 1989; 321:386–388.

22. Powell AC, Gold MR, Brooks R, et al. Electrophysiologic response to moricizine in patients with sustained ventricular arrhythmias. *Ann Intern Med* 1992; 116:382–387.

23. Damle R, Levine J, Matos J, et al. Efficacy and risks of moricizine in inducible sustained ventricular tachycardia. *Ann Intern Med* 1992; 116:375–381.

24. Aronow WS, Mercando AD, Epstein S, et al. Effect of quinidine or procainamide versus no antiarrhythmic on sudden cardiac death, total cardiac death, and total death in elderly patients with heart disease and complex ventricular arrhythmias. *Am J Cardiol* 1990; 66:423–428.

25. Pratt CM, Delclos G, Wierman AM, et al. The changing base line of complex ventricular arrhythmias: A new consideration in assessing long-term antiarrhythmic drug therapy. *N Engl J Med* 1985; 313:1444–1449.

26. Josephson ME. Antiarrhythmic agents and the danger of proarrhythmic events. *Ann Intern Med* 1989; 111:101–103.

27. Nygaard TW, Sellers D, Cook TS, et al. Adverse reactions to antiarrhythmic drugs during therapy for ventricular arrhythmias. *JAMA* 1986; 256:55–57.

Chapter 14

1. Kabadi UM. Self-monitoring of blood glucose in elderly diabetics: An unaffordable exercise in futility? *J Am Geriatr Soc* 1991; 39:731–732.

2. Singer DE, Coley CM, Samet JH, et al. Tests of glycemia in diabetes mellitus: Their use in establishing a diagnosis and in treatment. *Ann Intern Med* 1989; 110:125–137.

3. Morley JE, Mooradian AD, Rosenthal MJ, et al. Diabetes mellitus in elderly patients: Is it different? *Am J Med* 1987; 83:533–544.

4. Lipson LG. Diabetes in the elderly: Diagnosis, pathogenesis, and therapy. *Am J Med* 1986; 80(suppl 5A):10–21.

5. Brownlee M, Vlassara H, Cerami A. Nonenzymatic glycosylation and the pathogenesis of diabetic complications. *Ann Intern Med* 1984; 101:527–537.

6. Cogan DG, Kinoshita JH, Kador PF, et al. Aldose reductase and complications of diabetes. *Ann Intern Med* 1984; 101:82–91.

7. Friedman EA. Diabetic nephropathy: Strategies in prevention and management. *Kidney Int* 1982; 21:780–791.
8. Stern MP, Haffner SM. Prospective assessment of metabolic control in diabetes mellitus: The complications question. *JAMA* 1988; 260:-2896–2897.
9. The Diabetes Control and Complications Trial Research Group. The effect of intensive treatment of diabetes on the development and progression of long-term complications in insulin-dependent diabetes mellitus. *N Engl J Med* 1993; 329:977–986.
10. Nathan DM, Singer DE, Hurxthal K, et al. The clinical information value of the glycosylated hemoglobin assay. *N Engl J Med* 1984; 310:341–346.
11. Larsen ML, Horder M, Mogensen EF. Effect of long-term monitoring of glycosylated hemoglobin levels in insulin-dependent diabetes mellitus. *N Engl J Med* 1990; 323:1021–1025.
12. Nathan DM. Hemoglobin A_{1C}—infatuation or the real thing? *N Engl J Med* 1990; 323:1062–1064.
13. The Kroc Collaborative Study Group. Diabetic retinopathy after two years of intensified insulin treatment: Follow-up of the Kroc Collaborative Study. *JAMA* 1988; 260:37–41.
14. Brinchmann-Hansen O, Dahl-Jorgensen K, Sandvik L, et al. Blood glucose concentrations and progression of diabetic retinopathy: The seven year results of the Oslo Study. *BMJ* 1992; 304:19–22.
15. Reichard P, Berglund B, Britz A, et al. Intensified conventional insulin treatment retards the microvascular complications of insulin-dependent diabetes mellitus (IDDM): The Stockholm Diabetes Intervention Study (SDIS) after 5 years. *J Intern Med* 1991; 230:-101–108.
16. Nathan DM. Long-term complications of diabetes mellitus. *N Engl J Med* 1993; 328:1676–1685.
17. Morisaki N, Watanabe S, Kobayashi J, et al. Diabetic control and progression of retinopathy in elderly patients: Five-year follow-up study. *J Am Geriatr Soc* 1994; 42:142–145.
18. Nathan DM, Singer DE, Godine JE, et al. Retinopathy in older Type II diabetics: Association with glucose control. *Diabetes Care* 1986; 35:797–801.

19. Singer DE, Nathan DM, Fogel HA, et al. Screening for diabetic retinopathy. *Ann Intern Med* 1992; 116:660–671.
20. Harati Y. Diabetic peripheral neuropathies. *Ann Intern Med* 1987; 107:546–559.
21. Judzewitsch RG, Jaspan JB, Polonsky KS, et al. Aldose reductase inhibition improves nerve conduction velocity in diabetic patients. *N Engl J Med* 1983; 308:119–125.
22. Parving H, Andersen AR, Smidt UM, et al. Early aggressive antihypertensive treatment reduces rate of decline in kidney function in diabetic nephropathy. *Lancet* 1983; i:1175–1178.
23. Reichard P, Rosenqvist U. Nephropathy is delayed by intensified insulin treatment in patients with insulin-dependent diabetes mellitus and retinopathy. *J Intern Med* 1989; 226:81–87.
24. Feldt-Rasmussen B, Mathiesen ER, Deckert T. Effect of two years of strict metabolic control on progression of incipient nephropathy in insulin-dependent diabetes. *Lancet* 1986; 2:1300–1304.
25. Rocher L. Diabetic nephropathy: The internist's role. *Arch Intern Med* 1990; 150:26–28.
26. Lewis EJ, Hunsicker LG, Bain RP, et al. The effect of angiotensin-converting-enzyme inhibition on diabetic nephropathy. *N Engl J Med* 1993; 329:1456–1462.
27. Viberti G, Mogensen CE, Groop LC, et al. Effect of captopril on progression to clinical proteinuria in patients with insulin-dependent diabetes mellitus and microalbuminuria. *JAMA* 1994; 271:275–279.
28. Raskin P, Rosenstock J. Blood glucose control and diabetic complications. *Ann Intern Med* 1986; 105:254–263.
29. Widom B, Simonson DC. Glycemic control and neuropsychologic function during hypoglycemia in patients with insulin-dependent diabetes mellitus. *Ann Intern Med* 1990; 112:904–912.
30. Tayback M, Kumanyika S, Chee E. Body weight as a risk factor in the elderly. *Arch Intern Med* 1990; 150:1065–1072.
31. Wood FC, Bierman EL. Is diet the cornerstone in management of diabetes? *N Engl J Med* 1986; 315:1224–1226.
32. Bantle JP. Clinical aspects of sucrose and fructose metabolism. *Diabetes Care* 1989; 12:56–61.
33. Hollenbeck CB, Coulston AM, Reaven GM. Effects of sucrose on car-

bohydrate and lipid metabolism in NIDDM patients. *Diabetes Care* 1989; 12:62–66.

Chapter 15

1. Oldridge NB, Guyatt GH, Fischer ME, et al. Cardiac rehabilitation after myocardial infarction: Combined experience of randomized clinical trials. *JAMA* 1988; 260:945–950.
2. Greenland P, Chu JS. Efficacy of cardiac rehabilitation services: With emphasis on patients after myocardial infarction. *Ann Intern Med* 1988; 109:650–663.
3. Winslow EBJ. Cardiac rehabilitation. *JAMA* 1987; 258:1937–1938.
4. Edmunds LH, Stephenson LW, Edie RN, et al. Open-heart surgery in octogenarians. *N Engl J Med* 1988; 319:131–136.
5. Freeman WK, Schaff HV, O'Brien PC, et al. Cardiac surgery in the octogenarian: Perioperative outcome and clinical follow-up. *J Am Coll Cardiol* 1991; 18:29–35.
6. Mick MJ, Simpfendorfer C, Arnold AZ, et al. Early and late results of coronary angioplasty and bypass in octogenarians. *Am J Cardiol* 1991; 68:1316–1320.
7. Jeroudi MO, Kleinman NS, Minor ST, et al. Percutaneous transluminal coronary angioplasty in octogenarians. *Ann Intern Med* 1990; 113:423–428.
8. Bedotto JB, Rutherford BD, McConahay DR, et al. Results of multivessel percutaneous transluminal coronary angioplasty in persons aged 65 years and older. *Am J Cardiol* 1991; 1951:1055.
9. Thompson RC, Holmes DR, Gersh BJ, et al. Percutaneous transluminal coronary angioplasty in the elderly: Early and long-term results. *J Am Coll Cardiol* 1991; 17:1245–1250.
10. Gold S, Wong WF, Schatz IJ, et al. Invasive treatment for coronary artery disease in the elderly. *Arch Intern Med* 1991; 151:1085–1088.
11. Iskandrian AS, Segal BL. Should cardiac surgery be performed in octogenarians? *J Am Coll Cardiol* 1991; 18:36–37.
12. Goldenberg IF, Cohn JN. New inotropic drugs for heart failure. *JAMA* 1987; 258:493–496.
13. Braunwald E. ACE inhibitors—a cornerstone of the treatment of heart failure. *N Engl J Med* 1991; 325:351–353.

14. Schocken DD, Robinson BE, Krug-Fite J, et al. Digitalis use in a retirement community. *J Am Geriatr Soc* 1986; 34:504–506.
15. Smith TW. Digitalis: Mechanisms of action and clinical use. *N Engl J Med* 1988; 318:358–365.
16. Forman DE, Coletta D, Kenny D, et al. Clinical issues related to discontinuing digoxin therapy in elderly nursing home patients. *Arch Intern Med* 1991; 151:2194–2198.
17. Gheoghiade M, Beller GA. Effects of discontinuing maintenance digoxin therapy in patients with ischemic heart disease and congestive heart failure in sinus rhythm. *Am J Cardiol* 1983; 51:1243–1250.
18. Aronow WS, Starling L, Etienne F. Lack of efficacy of digoxin in treatment of compensated congestive heart failure with third heart sound and sinus rhythm in elderly patients receiving diuretic therapy. *Am J Cardiol* 1986; 58:168–169.
19. Fleg JL, Gottlieb SH, Lakatta EG. Is digoxin really important in treatment of compensated heart failure? A placebo-controlled crossover study in patients with sinus rhythm. *Am J Med* 1982; 73:244–250.
20. Sueta CA, Carey TS, Burnett CK. Reassessment of indications for digoxin: Are patients being withdrawn? *Arch Intern Med* 1989; 149:609–612.
21. Boman K, Allgulander S, Skoglund M. Is maintenance digoxin necessary in geriatric patients? *Acta Med Scand* 1981; 493:495.
22. Mulrow CD, Feussner JR, Velez R. Reevaluation of digitalis efficacy: New light on an old leaf. *Ann Intern Med* 1984; 101:113–117.
23. Packer M, Gheorghiade M, Young JB, et al. Withdrawal of digoxin from patients with chronic heart failure treated with angiotensin-converting-enzyme inhibitors. *N Engl J Med* 1993; 329:1–7.
24. Uretsky BF, Young JB, Shahidi FE, et al. Randomized study assessing the effect of digoxin withdrawal in patients with mild to moderate chronic congestive heart failure: Results of the PROVED trial. *J Am Coll Cardiol* 1993; 22:955–962.
25. The Captopril-Digoxin Multicenter Research Group. Comparative effects of therapy with captopril and digoxin in patients with mild to moderate heart failure. *JAMA* 1988; 259:539–544.
26. The SOLVD Investigators. Effect of enalapril on survival in patients

with reduced left ventricular ejection fractions and congestive heart failure. *N Engl J Med* 1991; 325:293–302.

27. CONSENSUS Trial Study Group. Effects of enalapril on mortality in severe congestive heart failure. Results of the Cooperative North Scandinavian Enalapril Survival Study (CONSENSUS). *N Engl J Med* 1987; 316:1429–1435.

28. Culliford AT, Galloway AC, Colvin SB, et al. Aortic valve replacement for aortic stenosis in persons aged 80 years and over. *Am J Cardiol* 1991; 67:1256–1260.

29. Sherman W, Hershman R, Lazzam C, et al. Balloon valvuloplasty in adult aortic stenosis: Determinants of clinical outcome. *Ann Intern Med* 1989; 110:421–425.

30. Cheitlin MD. Severe aortic stenosis in the sick octogenarian: A clear indicator for balloon valvuloplasty as the initial procedure. *Circulation* 1989; 80:1906–1908.

31. Jackson G, Thomas S, Monaghan M, et al. Inoperable aortic stenosis in the elderly: Benefit from percutaneous transluminal valvuloplasty. *BMJ* 1987; 294:83–86.

32. Brady ST, Davis CA, Kussmaul WG, et al. Percutaneous aortic balloon valvuloplasty in octogenarians: Morbidity and mortality. *Ann Intern Med* 1989; 110:761–766.

Chapter 16

1. Burrows B, Barbee RA, Cline MG, et al. Characteristics of asthma among elderly adults in a sample of the general population. *Chest* 1991; 100:935–942.

2. Braman SS, Kaemmerlen JT, Davis SM. Asthma in the elderly: A comparison between patients with recently acquired and long-standing disease. *Am Rev Respir Dis* 1991; 143:336–340.

3. Owens MW, Kinasewitz GT, Lambert RS, et al. Influence of spirometry and chest roentgenography on the management of pulmonary outpatients. *Arch Intern Med* 1987; 147:1966–1969.

4. Casanova JE, Kaufman J. Utility of pulmonary function testing in the management of chronic obstructive pulmonary disease. *J Gen Intern Med* 1993; 8:448–450.

5. Sherman S, Skoney JA, Ravikrishan KP. Routine chest radiographs in

exacerbations of chronic obstructive pulmonary disease: Diagnostic value. *Arch Intern Med* 1989; 149:2493–2496.

6. Nett LM. The physician's role in smoking cessation: A present and future agenda. *Chest* 1990; 97(suppl):28S–32S.

7. Casaburi R, Wasserman K. Exercise training in pulmonary rehabilitation. *N Engl J Med* 1986; 314:1509–1511.

8. Opolade CO, Beck KC, Viggiano RW, et al. Exercise limitation and pulmonary rehabilitation in chronic obstructive pulmonary disease. *Mayo Clin Proc* 1992; 67:144–157.

9. Smith K, Cook D, Guyatt GH, et al. Respiratory muscle training in chronic airflow limitation: A meta-analysis. *Am Rev Respir Dis* 1992; 145:533–539.

10. Hill NS. The use of theophylline in "irreversible" chronic obstructive pulmonary disease: An update. *Arch Intern Med* 1988; 148:2579–2584.

11. Rossing TH. Methylxanthines in 1989. *Ann Intern Med* 1989; 110:-502–504.

12. Littenberg B. Aminophylline treatment in severe, acute asthma: A meta-analysis. *JAMA* 1988; 259:1678–1684.

13. McFadden ER. Methylxanthines in the treatment of asthma: The rise, the fall, and the possible rise again. *Ann Intern Med* 1991; 115:323–324.

14. Aubier M, De Troyer A, Sampson M, et al. Aminophylline improves diaphragmatic contractility. *N Engl J Med* 1981; 305:249–252.

15. Murciano D, Aubier M, Lecocguic Y, et al. Effects of theophylline on diaphragmatic strength and fatigue in patients with chronic obstructive pulmonary disease. *N Engl J Med* 1984; 311:349–353.

16. Rice KL, Leatherman JW, Duane PG, et al. Aminophylline for acute exacerbations of chronic obstructive pulmonary disease: A controlled trial. *Ann Intern Med* 1987; 107:305–309.

17. Shannon M, Lovejoy FH. The influence of age vs peak serum concentration on life-threatening events after chronic theophylline intoxication. *Arch Intern Med* 1990; 150:2045–2048.

18. Spitzer WO, Suissa S, Ernst R, et al. The use of B-agonists and the risk of death and near death from asthma. *N Engl J Med* 1992; 326:501–506.

19. Morgan EJ, Petty TL. Summary of the National Mucolytic Study. *Chest* 1990; 97(suppl):24S–27S.
20. Murata GH, Gorby MS, Chick TW, et al. Intravenous and oral corticosteroids for the prevention of relapse after treatment of decompensated COPD: Effect on patients with a history of multiple relapses. *Chest* 1990; 98:845–849.
21. Callahan CM, Dittus RS, Katz BP. Oral corticosteroid therapy for patients with stable chronic obstructive pulmonary disease: A meta-analysis. *Ann Intern Med* 1991; 114:216–223.
22. Anthonisen NR, Manfreda J, Warren CPW, et al. Antibiotic therapy in exacerbations of chronic obstructive pulmonary disease. *Ann Intern Med* 1987; 106:196–204.
23. Nicotra MB, Rivera M, Awe RJ. Antibiotic therapy of acute exacerbations of chronic bronchitis: A controlled study using tetracycline. *Ann Intern Med* 1982; 97:18–21.

Chapter 17

1. Felson DT, et al. The prevalence of knee osteoarthritis in the elderly: The Framingham Osteoarthritis Study. *Arthritis Rheum* 1987; 30:-914–918.
2. Wilson MG, Michet CJ, Ilstrup DM, et al. Idiopathic symptomatic osteoarthritis of the hip and knee: A population-based incidence study. *Mayo Clin Proc* 1990; 65:1214–1221.
3. Kovar PA, Allegrante JP, MacKenzie R, et al. Supervised fitness walking in patients with osteoarthritis of the knee: A randomized, controlled trial. *Ann Intern Med* 1992; 116:529–534.
4. Felson DT, Zhang Y, Anthony JM, et al. Weight loss reduces the risk for symptomatic knee osteoarthritis in women: The Framingham Study. *Ann Intern Med* 1992; 116:535–539.
5. Liang MH, Fortin P. Management of osteoarthritis of the hip and knee. *N Engl J Med* 1991; 325:125–127.
6. Fisher NM, Pendergast DR, Gresham GE, et al. Muscle rehabilitation: Its effect on muscular and functional performance of patients with knee osteoarthritis. *Arch Phys Med Rehabil* 1991; 72:367–374.
7. Loeb DS, Ahlquist DA, Talley NJ. Management of gastroduodenopathy associated with use of nonsteroidal anti-inflammatory drugs. *Mayo Clin Proc* 1992; 67:354–364.

8. Gabriel SE, Jaakkimainen L, Bombardier C. Risk for serious gastrointestinal complications related to use of nonsteroidal anti-inflammatory drugs: A meta-analysis. *Ann Intern Med* 1991; 115:787–796.
9. Brooks PM, Day RO. Nonsteroidal anti-inflammatory drugs—differences and similarities. *N Engl J Med* 1991; 324:1716–1724.
10. Bradley JD, Brandt KD, Katz BP, et al. Comparison of an anti-inflammatory dose of ibuprofen, an analgesic dose of ibuprofen, and acetaminophen in the treatment of patients with osteoarthritis of the knee. *N Engl J Med* 1991; 325:87–91.
11. Harris WH, Sledge CB. Total hip and total knee replacement (first of two parts). *N Engl J Med* 1990; 323:56–57.

Chapter 18

1. Talley NJ, Phillips SF. Non-ulcer dyspepsia: Potential causes and pathophysiology. *Ann Intern Med* 1988; 108:865–879.
2. Graham DY, Lew GM, Klein PD, et al. Effect of treatment of *Helicobacter pylori* infection on the long-term recurrence of gastric or duodenal ulcer: A randomized, controlled study. *Ann Intern Med* 1992; 116:705–708.
3. Graham DY, Lew GM, Evans DG, et al. Effect of triple therapy (antibiotics plus bismuth) on duodenal ulcer healing: A randomized clinical trial. *Ann Intern Med* 1991; 115:2666–2691.
4. Katz KD. Practical pharmacology and cost-effective management of peptic ulcer disease. *Am J Surg* 1992; 163:349–359.
5. Hixson LJ, Kelley CL, Jones WN, et al. Current trends in the pharmacotherapy for gastroesophageal reflux disease. *Arch Intern Med* 1992; 152:717–723.
6. Hixson LJ, Kelley CL, Jones WN, et al. Current trends in the pharmacotherapy for peptic ulcer disease. *Arch Intern Med* 1992; 152:726–732.
7. Cantu TG, Korek JS. Central nervous system reactions to histamine-2 receptor blockers. *Ann Intern Med* 1991; 114:1027–1034.
8. Strum WB. Prevention of duodenal ulcer recurrence. *Ann Intern Med* 1986; 105:757–761.
9. Van Deventer GM, Elashoff JD, Reedy TJ, et al. A randomized study of maintenance therapy with ranitidine to prevent the recurrence of duodenal ulcer. *N Engel J Med* 1989; 320:1113–1119.

10. Hui WM, Lam SK, Lok ASF, et al. Maintenance therapy for duodenal ulcer: A randomized controlled comparison of seven forms of treatment. *Am J Med* 1992; 92:265–274.

11. Spechler SJ, Department of Veterans Affairs Gastroesophageal Reflux Disease Study Group. Comparison of medical and surgical therapy for complicated gastroesophageal reflux disease in veterans. *N Engl J Med* 1992; 326:786–792.

Chapter 19

1. Resnick NM, Yalla SV. Management of urinary incontinence in the elderly. *N Engl J Med* 1985; 313:800–805.

2. Ouslander JG. Urinary incontinence: Out of the closet. *JAMA* 1989; 261:2695–2696.

3. National Institutes of Health Consensus Development Conference. Urinary incontinence in adults. *J Am Geriatr Soc* 1990; 38:265–272.

4. Burgio KL, Whitehead WE, Engel BT. Urinary incontinence in the elderly: Bladder-sphincter biofeedback and toileting skills training. *Ann Intern Med* 1985; 104:507–515.

5. Fantl JA, Wyman JF, McClish DK, et al. Efficacy of bladder training in older women with urinary incontinence. *JAMA* 1991; 265:609–613.

6. Wells TJ, Brink CA, Diokno AC, et al. Pelvic muscle exercise for stress urinary incontinence in elderly women. *J Am Geriatr Soc* 1991; 39:-785–791.

7. Hu T, Igou JF, Kaltreider DL, et al. A clinical trial of a behavioral therapy to reduce urinary incontinence in nursing homes: Outcome and implications. *JAMA* 1989; 261:2656–2662.

8. Hadley EC. Bladder training and related therapies for urinary incontinence in older people. *JAMA* 1986; 256:372–379.

9. O'Brien J, Austin M, Sethi P, et al. Urinary incontinence: Prevalence, need for treatment, and effectiveness of intervention by nurse. *BMJ* 1991; 303:1308–1312.

10. Blaivas JG, Olsson CA. Stress incontinence: Classification and surgical approach. *J Urol* 1988; 139:727–731.

Chapter 20

1. Aronson MK, Ooi WL, Geva DL, et al. Dementia: Age-dependent incidence, prevalence, and mortality in the old. *Arch Intern Med* 1991; 151:989–992.

2. Evans DA, Funkenstein HH, Albert MS, et al. Prevalence of Alzheimer's disease in a community population of older persons. *JAMA* 1989; 262:2551–2556.

3. Skoog I, Nilsson L, Palmertz B, et al. A population-based study of dementia in 85-year-olds. *N Engl J Med* 1993; 328:153–158.

4. Larson EB, Reifler BV, Sumi SM, et al. Features of potentially reversible dementia in elderly outpatients. *West J Med* 1986; 145:488–492.

5. Friedland RP. "Normal"-pressure hydrocephalus and the saga of the treatable dementias. *JAMA* 1989; 262:2577–2581.

6. Summers WK, Majovski LV, Marsh GM, et al. Oral tetrahydroaminoacridine in long-term treatment of senile dementia, Alzheimer type. *N Engl J Med* 1986; 315:1241–1245.

7. Waldholz M. A psychiatrist's work leads to a U.S. study of Alzheimer's drug. *Wall Street Journal*, August 4, 1987:16.

8. Division of Neuropharmacological Drug Products, Office of New Drug Evaluation (I), Center for Drug Evaluation and Review. Tacrine as a treatment for Alzheimer's dementia: An interim report from the FDA. *N Engl J Med* 1991; 324:349–352.

9. White H, Davis PB. Cognitive screening tests: An aid in the care of elderly outpatients. *J Gen Intern Med* 1990; 5:438–445.

10. Kokmen E, Naessens JM, Offord KP. A short test of mental status: Description and preliminary results. *Mayo Clin Proc* 1987; 62:281–288.

11. Larson EB, Reifler BV, Featherstone HJ, et al. Dementia in elderly outpatients: A prospective study. *Ann Intern Med* 1984; 100:417–423.

12. Gordon M, Freedman M. Evaluating dementia: What price testing? *Can Med Assoc J* 1990; 142:1367–1370.

13. Barry PP, Moskowitz MA. The diagnosis of reversible dementia in the elderly: A critical review. *Arch Intern Med* 1988; 148:1914–1918.

14. Siu AL. Screening for dementia and investigating its causes. *Ann Intern Med* 1991; 115:122–132.

15. Organizing Committee, Canadian Consensus Conference on the Assessment of Dementia. Assessing dementia: The Canadian consensus. *Can Med Assoc J* 1991; 144:851–853.

16. Consensus Conference. Differential diagnosis of dementing diseases. *JAMA* 1987; 258:3411–3416.

17. Winograd CH, Jarvik LF. Physician management of the demented patient. *J Am Geriatr Soc* 1986; 34:295–308.

18. Howell T, Watts DT. Behavioral complications of dementia: A clinical approach for the general internist. *J Gen Intern Med* 1990; 5:431–437.

19. O'Connor DW, Pollitt PA, Brook CPB, et al. Does early intervention reduce the number of elderly people with dementia admitted to institutions for long term care? *BMJ* 1991; 302:871–875.

20. Cook P, James I. Cerebral vasodilators (first of two parts). *N Engl J Med* 1981; 305:1508–1512.

21. Hollister LE, Yesavage J. Ergoloid mesylates for senile dementias: Unanswered questions. *Ann Intern Med* 1984; 100:894–898.

22. Cholinergic treatment in Alzheimer's disease: Encouraging results. *Lancet 1987; i:139–141.*

23. Eagger SA, Levy R, Sahakian BJ. Tacrine in Alzheimer's disease. *Lancet* 1991; 337:989–992.

24. Farlow M, Garcon SI, Hershey LA, et al. A controlled trial of tacrine in Alzheimer's disease. *JAMA* 1993; 268:2523–2529.

25. Davis KL, Thal LJ, Gamzu ER, et al. A double-blind, placebo-controlled multicenter study of tacrine for Alzheimer's disease. *N Engl J Med* 1992; 327:1253–1259.

26. Knapp MJ, Knopman DS, Solomon PR, et al. A 30-week randomized controlled trial of high-dose tacrine in patients with Alzheimer's disease. *JAMA* 1994; 271:985–991.

27. Gauthier S, Bouchard R, Lamontagne A, et al. Tetrahydroaminoacridine-lecithin combination treatment in patients with intermediate-stage Alzheimer's disease: Results of a Canadian double-blind, crossover, multicenter study. *N Engl J Med* 1990; 322:1272–1276.

28. Chatellier G, Lacomblez L, et al. Tacrine (tetrahydroaminoacridine; THA) and lecithin in senile dementia of the Alzheimer type: a multicentre trial. *BMJ* 1990; 300:495–499.

29. Skolnick AA. Brain researchers bullish on prospects for preserving mental functioning in elderly. *JAMA* 1992; 267:2154–2158.
30. Cooper JK. Drug treatment of Alzheimer's disease. *Arch Intern Med* 1991; 151:245–249.
31. Schneider LS, Pollock VE, Lyness SA. A meta-analysis of controlled trials of neuroleptic treatment in dementia. *J Am Geriatr Soc* 1990; 38:553–563.

Chapter 21
1. Mason M. Up to speed at 91. *Washington Post,* 1990.
2. Fiatarone MA, Marks EC, Ryan ND, et al. High-intensity strength training in nonagenarians: Effects on skeletal muscle. *JAMA* 1990; 263:3029–3034.
3. King AC, Haskell WL, Taylor B, et al. Group- vs home-based exercise training in healthy older men and women: A community-based clinical trial. *JAMA* 1991; 266:1535–1542.
4. Wheat ME. Exercise in the elderly. *West J Med* 1987; 147:477–480.
5. Institute of Medicine. Physical inactivity, in Berg RL, Cassells JS (eds). *The Second 50 Years: Promoting Health and Preventing Disability.* Washington, D.C.: National Academy Press, 1990:224–242.
6. Epstein AM, Hall JA, Besdine R, et al. The emergence of geriatric assessment units: The "new technology of geriatrics." *Ann Intern Med* 1987; 106:299–303.
7. Larson DB, Larson SS. Religious commitment and health: Valuing the relationship. *Second Opinion* 1991; July:27–40.
8. Koenig HG, Moberg DO, Kvale JN. Religious activities and attitudes of older adults in a geriatric assessment clinic. *J Am Geriatr Soc* 1988; 36:362–374.
9. Pressman P, Lyons JS, Larson DB, et al. Religious belief, depression, and ambulation status in elderly women with broken hips. *Am J Psychiatry* 1990; 147:758–760.
10. U.S. Department of Health and Human Services. Some facts and myths of vitamins. *FDA Consumer* 1988: HHS Publication No. (FDA) 88–2117.
11. Morley JE, Mooradian AD, Silver AJ, et al. Nutrition in the elderly. *Ann Intern Med* 1988; 109:890–904.

12. Rimm EB, Stampfer MJ, Ascherio A, et al. Vitamin E consumption and the risk of coronary heart disease in men. *N Eng J Med* 1993; 328:-1450–1456.
13. Stampfer MJ, Hennekens CH, Manson JE, et al. Vitamin E consumption and the risk of coronary disease in women. *N Engl J Med* 1993; 328:1444–1449.
14. Jajich CL, Ostfeld AM, Freeman DH. Smoking and coronary heart disease mortality in the elderly. *JAMA* 1984; 252:2831–2834.
15. LaCroix AZ, Lang J, Scherr P, et al. Smoking and mortality among older men and women in three communities. *N Engl J Med* 1991; 324:1619–1625.
16. Hermanson B, Omenn GS, Kronmal RA, et al. Beneficial six-year outcome of smoking cessation in older men and women with coronary artery disease: Results from the CASS registry. *N Engl J Med* 1988; 319:1365–1369.
17. Institute of Medicine. Cigarette smoking in Berg RL, Cassells JS (eds). *The Second 50 Years: Promoting Health and Preventing Disability.* Washington, D.C.: National Academy Press, 1990:193–201.
18. Steinberg D, Pearson TA, Kuller LH. Alcohol and atherosclerosis. *Ann Intern Med* 1991; 114:967–976.
19. Curatolo PW, Robertson D. The health consequences of caffeine. *Ann Intern Med* 1983; 98:641–653.
20. Chou T. Wake up and smell the coffee: Caffeine, coffee, and the medical consequences. *West J Med* 1992; 157:544–553.
21. Myers MG. Caffeine and cardiac arrhythmias. *Ann Intern Med* 1991; 114:147–150.
22. Institute of Medicine. Social isolation among older individuals: The relationship to mortality and morbidity, in Berg RL, Cassells JS (eds). *The Second 50 Years: Promoting Health and Preventing Disability.* Washington, D.C.: National Academy Press, 1990:243–262.
23. Clarke M, Clarke SJ, Jagger C. Social intervention and the elderly: A randomized controlled trial. *Am J Epidemiol* 1993; 136:1517–1523.
24. Krause N, Herzog AR, Baker E. Providing support to others and well-being in later life. *J Gerontol* 1992; 47:P300–P311.
25. Diokno AC, Brown MB, Herzog R. Sexual function in the elderly. *Arch Intern Med* 1990; 150:197–200.

26. Mooradian AD, Greiff V. Sexuality in older women. *Arch Intern Med* 1990; 150:1033–1038.
27. Stern Y, Gurland B, Tatemichi TK, et al. Influence of education and occupation on the incidence of Alzheimer's disease. *JAMA* 1994; 271:1004–1010.
28. McBeath WH. Health for all: A public health vision. *Am J Public Health* 1991; 81:1560–1565.

Chapter 22

1. Mendelsohn RS. *Confessions of a Medical Heretic.* Chicago: Contemporary Books, 1979.
2. Wolfe S, Health Research Group. *Worst Pills, Best Pills: The Older Adult's Guide to Avoiding Drug-Induced Death or Illness.* Washington, D.C.: Pantheon, 1990.
3. Uribarri J, Oh MS, Carroll HJ. The first kidney stone. *Ann Intern Med* 1989; 111:1006–1009.
4. Holland JC. Now we tell—but how well? *J Clin Oncol* 1989; 7:557–559.
5. Fletcher J. On truth telling. *Pharos* 1988; spring:37.
6. Brett AS, McCullough LB. When patients request specific interventions: Defining the limits of the physician's obligation. *N Engl J Med* 1986; 315:1347–1351.
7. Yarborough M. Continued treatment of the fatally ill for the benefit of others. *J Am Geriatr Soc* 1988; 36:63–67.
8. Emanuel EJ, Emanuel LL. Four models of the physician-patient relationship. *JAMA* 1992; 267:2221–2226.
9. Grumbach K, Bodenheimer T. Reins or fences: A physician's view of cost containment. *Health Aff* 1990; winter:120–126.
10. Karpf M, Levey GS. Training primary care physicians. *Ann Intern Med* 1992; 116:514–515.
11. Eddy DM. What do we do about costs? *JAMA* 1990; 264:1161–1170.
12. Morreim EH. Fiscal scarcity and the inevitability of bedside budget balancing. *Arch Intern Med* 1989; 149:1012–1015.
13. Angell M. Cost containment and the physician. *JAMA* 1985; 254:-1203–1207.

14. Lowes R. Hospital Ethics Committees. *Medical World News* January 1994; 24–37.

15. Eddy DM. Connecting value and costs: Whom do we ask, and what do we ask them? *JAMA* 1990; 264:1737–1739.

16. Tierney WM, Miller ME, McDonald CJ. The effect on test ordering of informing physicians of the charges for outpatient diagnostic tests. *N Engl J Med* 1990; 322:1499–1504.

17. Davidoff F, Goodspeed R, Clive J. Changing test ordering behavior: A randomized controlled trial comparing probabilistic reasoning with cost-containment education. *Med Care* 1989; 27:45–58.

18. Pugh JA, Frazier LM, DeLong E, et al. Effect of daily charge feedback on inpatient charges and physician knowledge and behavior. *Arch Intern Med* 1989; 149:426–429.

19. Frazier LM, Brown JT, Divine GW, et al. Can physician education lower the cost of prescription drugs? A prospective, controlled trial. *Ann Intern Med* 1991; 115:116–121.

20. Branch WT, Arky RA, Woo B, et al. Teaching medicine as a human experience: A patient-doctor relationship course for faculty and first-year medical students. *Ann Intern Med* 1991; 114:482–489.

21. Arnold RM, Povar GJ, Howell JD. The humanities, humanistic behavior, and the humane physician: A cautionary note. *Ann Intern Med* 1987; 106:313–318.

Journal Abbreviations

Acta Med Scand—Acta Med Scandinavica
Am J Cardiol—American Journal of Cardiology
Am J Epidemiol—American Journal of Epidemiology
Am J Gastroenterol—American Journal of Gastroenterology
Am J Med—American Journal of Medicine
Am J Psychiatry—American Journal of Psychiatry
Am J Public Health—American Journal of Public Health
Am J Surg—American Journal of Surgery
Am Rev Respir Dis—American Review of Respiratory Disease
Ann Intern Med—Annals of Internal Medicine
Arch Phys Med Rehabil—Archives of Physical Medicine and Rehabilitation
Arthritis Rheum—Arthritis and Rheumatism

BMJ—BMJ
Br J Surg—British Journal of Surgery
Br Med J—British Medical Journal
Can Med Assoc J—Canadian Medical Association Journal
Chest—Chest
Circulation—Circulation
Clin Sci—Clinical Science
Diabetes Care—Diabetes Care
Eur Heart J—European Heart Journal
FDA Consumer—FDA Consumer
Gastroenterology—Gastroenterology
Health Aff—Health Affairs
Hypertension—Hypertension
Int J Technol Assess Health Care—International Journal of Technology
    Assessment in Health Care
Int Med News—International Medical News
JAMA—Journal of the American Medical Association
J Am Coll Cardiol—Journal of the American College of Cardiology
J Am Geriatr Soc—Journal of the American Geriatrics Society
J Chronic Dis—Journal of Chronic Disease
J Clin Epidemiol—Journal of Clinical Epidemiology
J Clin Oncol—Journal of Clinical Oncology
J Gen Intern Med—Journal of General Internal Medicine
J Gerontol—Journal of Gerontology
J Hypertens—Journal of Hypertension
J Intern Med—Journal of Internal Medicine
J Urol—Journal of Urology
J Vasc Surg—Journal of Vascular Surgery
Kidney Int—Kidney International
Lancet—Lancet
Mayo Clin Proc—Mayo Clinic Proceedings
Med Care—Medical Care
Med Decis Making—Medical Decision Making
Metabolism—Metabolism
N Engl J Med—New England Journal of Medicine
Neurology—Neurology

Obstet Gynecol—Obstetrics and Gynecology
Pharos—Pharos of Alpha Omega Alpha Honor Medical Society
Prev Med—Preventive Medicine
Radiology—Radiology
Second Opinion—Second Opinion
Soc Sci Med—Social Science and Medicine
South Med J—Southern Medical Journal
Stroke—Stroke
West J Med—Western Journal of Medicine

Index